Just The

Textbook Key Facts

Textbook Outlines, Highlights, and Practice Quizzes

Economics

by Campbell McConnell, 20th Edition

All "Just the Facts101" Material Written or Prepared by Cram101 Textbook Reviews

Title Page

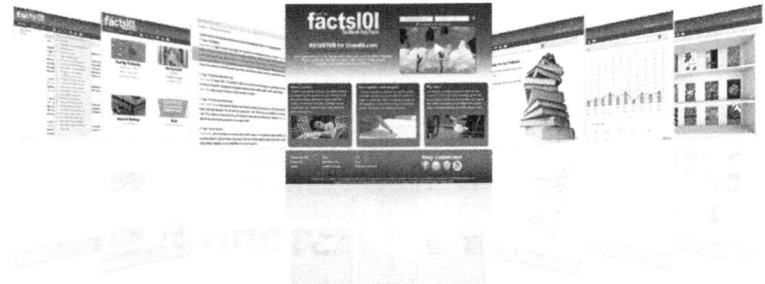

LEARNING SYSTEM

"Just the Facts101" is a Content Technologies publication and tool designed to give you all the facts from your textbooks. Visit JustTheFacts101.com for the full practice test for each of your chapters for virtually any of your textbooks.

Facts101 has built custom study tools specific to your textbook. We provide all of the factual testable information and unlike traditional study guides, we will never send you back to your textbook for more information.

YOU WILL NEVER HAVE TO HIGHLIGHT A BOOK AGAIN!

Facts101 StudyGuides

All of the information in this StudyGuide is written specifically for your textbook. We include the key terms, places, people, and concepts... the information you can expect on your next exam!

Want to take a practice test?

Throughout each chapter of this StudyGuide you will find links to JustTheFacts101.com where you can select specific chapters to take a complete test on, or you can subscribe and get practice tests for up to 12 of your textbooks, along with other exclusive Jtf101.com tools like problem solving labs and reference libraries.

JustTheFacts101.com

Only Jtf101.com gives you the outlines, highlights, and PRACTICE TESTS specific to your textbook. JustTheFacts101.com is an online application where you'll discover study tools designed to make the most of your limited study time.

By purchasing this book, you get 50% off the normal monthly subscription fee!. Just enter the promotional code **'DK73DW24335'** on the Jtf101.com registration screen.

www.JustTheFacts101.com

Economics
Campbell McConnell, 20th

CONTENTS

Economics
Campbell McConnell, 20th

CONTENTS (continued)

1. Limits, Alternatives, and Choices

CHAPTER OUTLINE: KEY TERMS, PEOPLE, PLACES, CONCEPTS

_____ Federal Reserve Bank

_____ Great Recession

_____ Leverage

_____ Product market

_____ Recession

_____ State bank

_____ Income

_____ Lottery

_____ Marginal cost

_____ National income

_____ Product

_____ Full employment

_____ Marginal utility

_____ Opportunity cost

_____ Scarcity

_____ Utility

_____ Perspective

_____ Ceteris paribus

_____ Economic law

_____ Scientific method

_____ Economic policy

1. Limits, Alternatives, and Choices
CHAPTER OUTLINE: KEY TERMS, PEOPLE, PLACES, CONCEPTS

	Macroeconomics
	Microeconomics
	Normative economics
	Phillips curve
	Positive economics
	Public good
	Aggregate supply
	Supply shock
	Commercial bank
	Lump-sum tax
	Federal funds
	Trade-off
	Capital
	Economic growth
	Freedom
	Market system
	Capital good
	Factors of production
	Production
	Pollution
	Great Depression

CHAPTER OUTLINE: KEY TERMS, PEOPLE, PLACES, CONCEPTS

	Average fixed cost
	International trade
	Stock exchange
	Causation
	Expression
	Variable cost

CHAPTER HIGHLIGHTS & NOTES: KEY TERMS, PEOPLE, PLACES, CONCEPTS

Federal Reserve Bank | A Federal Reserve Bank is a regional bank of the Federal Reserve System, the central banking system of the United States. There are twelve in total, one for each of the twelve Federal Reserve Districts that were created by the Federal Reserve Act of 1913. The banks are jointly responsible for implementing the monetary policy set forth by the Federal Open Market Committee, and are divided as follows:

Some banks also possess branches, with the whole system being headquartered at the Eccles Building in Washington, D.C.

Great Recession | The Great Recession was a global economic decline in the late 2000s. According to aggregated national data, a worldwide recession began in Q3-2008 and ended in Q1-2009.

It is related to a liquidity crisis, commonly being dated to have started when several central banks had to step in with liquidity lending to the interbank lending market on 9 August 2007. This was a response to a situation where BNP Paribas temporarily had to block money withdrawals from three hedge funds--citing a 'complete evaporation of liquidity'.

Leverage | In finance, leverage is a general term for any technique to multiply gains and losses. Most often this involves buying more of an asset by using borrowed funds. The belief is that the income from the asset will be more than the pay for the cost of borrowing.

Product market | Product market is where goods and services produced by businesses are sold to households. The households use the income they receive from the sale of resources to purchase the products.

1. Limits, Alternatives, and Choices

Recession	In economics, a recession is a business cycle contraction. It is a general slowdown in economic activity. Macroeconomic indicators such as GDP (gross domestic product), investment spending, capacity utilization, household income, business profits, and inflation fall, while bankruptcies and the unemployment rate rise.
State bank	A state bank is generally a financial institution that is chartered by a state. It differs from a reserve bank in that it does not necessarily control monetary policy (indeed, the state in question may have no legal capacity to create monetary policy), but instead usually offers only retail and commercial services. A state bank that has been in operation for five years or less is called a de novo bank.
Income	Income is the consumption and savings opportunity gained by an entity within a specified timeframe, which is generally expressed in monetary terms. However, for households and individuals, 'income is the sum of all the wages, salaries, profits, interests payments, rents and other forms of earnings received... in a given period of time.' In the field of public economics, the term may refer to the accumulation of both monetary and non-monetary consumption ability, with the former (monetary) being used as a proxy for total income.
Lottery	In expected utility theory, a lottery is a discrete distribution of probability on a set of states of nature. The elements of a lottery correspond to the probability that a certain outcome arises from a given state of nature. In economics, individuals are assumed to rank lotteries according to a rational system of preferences, although it is now accepted that people make irrational choices systematically.
Marginal cost	In economics and finance, marginal cost is the change in the total cost that arises when the quantity produced has an increment by unit. That is, it is the cost of producing one more unit of a good. In general terms, marginal cost at each level of production includes any additional costs required to produce the next unit.
National income	A variety of measures of national income and output are used in economics to estimate total economic activity in a country or region, including gross domestic product, gross national product (GNP), net national income and adjusted national income. All are specially concerned with counting the total amount of goods and services produced within some 'boundary'. The boundary is usually defined by geography or citizenship, and may also restrict the goods and services that are counted.
Product	In marketing, a product is anything that can be offered to a market that might satisfy a want or need. In retailing, products are called merchandise. In manufacturing, products are bought as raw materials and sold as finished goods.

1. Limits, Alternatives, and Choices

Full employment	Full employment, in macroeconomics, is the level of employment rates where there is no cyclical or deficient-demand unemployment. It is defined by the majority of mainstream economists as being an acceptable level of unemployment somewhere above 0%. The discrepancy from 0% arises due to non-cyclical types of unemployment.
Marginal utility	In economics, the marginal utility of a good or service is the gain from an increase or loss from a decrease in the consumption of that good or service. Economists sometimes speak of a law of diminishing marginal utility, meaning that the first unit of consumption of a good or service yields more utility than the second and subsequent units, with a continuing reduction for greater amounts. The marginal decision rule states that a good or service should be consumed at a quantity at which the marginal utility is equal to the marginal cost.
Opportunity cost	In microeconomic theory, the opportunity cost of a choice is the value of the best alternative forgone, in a situation in which a choice needs to be made between several mutually exclusive alternatives given limited resources. Assuming the best choice is made, it is the 'cost' incurred by not enjoying the benefit that would be had by taking the second best choice available. The New Oxford American Dictionary defines it as 'the loss of potential gain from other alternatives when one alternative is chosen'.
Scarcity	Scarcity is the fundamental economic problem of having seemingly unlimited human wants in a world of limited resources. It states that society has insufficient productive resources to fulfill all human wants and needs. A common misconception on sacarcity is that an item has to be important for it to be scarce.
Utility	Utility, or usefulness, is the ability of something to satisfy needs or wants. Utility is an important concept in economics and game theory, because it represents satisfaction experienced by the consumer of a good. Not coincidentally, a good is something that satisfies human wants and provides utility, for example, to a consumer making a purchase.
Perspective	Perspective in pharmacoeconomics refers to the economic vantage point of a pharmacoeconomic analysis, such as a cost-effectiveness analysis or cost-utility analysis. This affects the types of costs (resource expenditures) and benefits that are relevant to the analysis. Five general perspectives are often cited in pharmacoeconomics, including institutional, third party, patient, governmental and societal.
Ceteris paribus	Ceteris paribus or caeteris paribus is a Latin phrase meaning 'with other things the same' or 'all other things being equal or held constant.' As an ablative absolute, it is commonly posed to mean 'all other things being equal.' A prediction or a statement about causal, empirical, or logical relation between two states of affairs is ceteris paribus via acknowledgement that the prediction can fail or the relation can be abolished by intervening factors.

1. Limits, Alternatives, and Choices

	A ceteris paribus assumption is often key to scientific inquiry, as scientists seek to screen out factors that perturb a relation of interest. Thus, epidemiologists seek to control independent variables as factors that may influence dependent variables--the outcomes or effects of interest.
Economic law	In the legal system of the Soviet Union, economic law was the legal theory and system under which economic relations were a legal discipline independent of criminal law and civil law. In the Law of the United States and some other legal systems this approximately corresponds to the commercial law (business law).
Scientific method	The scientific method is a body of techniques for investigating phenomena, acquiring new knowledge, or correcting and integrating previous knowledge. To be termed scientific, a method of inquiry must be based on empirical and measurable evidence subject to specific principles of reasoning. The Oxford English Dictionary defines the scientific method as: 'a method or procedure that has characterized natural science since the 17th century, consisting in systematic observation, measurement, and experiment, and the formulation, testing, and modification of hypotheses.'
	The chief characteristic which distinguishes the scientific method from other methods of acquiring knowledge is that scientists seek to let reality speak for itself, supporting a theory when a theory's predictions are confirmed and challenging a theory when its predictions prove false.
Economic policy	Economic policy refers to the actions that governments take in the economic field. It covers the systems for setting interest rates and government budget as well as the labor market, national ownership, and many other areas of government interventions into the economy.
	Such policies are often influenced by international institutions like the International Monetary Fund or World Bank as well as political beliefs and the consequent policies of parties.
Macroeconomics	Macroeconomics is the study of the macroeconomy. It is a branch of economics dealing with the performance, structure, behavior, and decision-making of an economy as a whole, rather than individual markets. This includes national, regional, and global economies.
Microeconomics	Microeconomics is a branch of economics that studies the behavior of individuals and small impacting players in making decisions on the allocation of limited resources . Typically, it applies to markets where goods or services are bought and sold. Microeconomics examines how these decisions and behaviors affect the supply and demand for goods and services, which determines prices, and how prices, in turn, determine the quantity supplied and quantity demanded of goods and services.
Normative economics	Normative economics is a part of economics that expresses value or normative judgments about economic fairness, or what the outcome of the economy or goals of public policy ought to be.

	Economists commonly prefer to distinguish normative economics from positive economics ('what is'). Many normative (value) judgments, however, are held conditionally, to be given up if facts or knowledge of facts changes, so that a change of values may be purely scientific.
Phillips curve	In economics, the Phillips curve is a historical inverse relationship between rates of unemployment and corresponding rates of inflation that result in an economy. Stated simply, decreased unemployment, (i.e., increased levels of employment) in an economy will correlate with higher rates of inflation. While there is a short run tradeoff between unemployment and inflation, it has not been observed in the long run.
Positive economics	Positive economics is the branch of economics that concerns the description and explanation of economic phenomena. It focuses on facts and cause-and-effect behavioral relationships and includes the development and testing of economics theories. Earlier terms were value-free economics and its German counterpart wertfrei economics.
Public good	In economics, a public good is a good that is both non-excludable and non-rivalrous in that individuals cannot be effectively excluded from use and where use by one individual does not reduce availability to others. Examples of public goods include fresh air, knowledge, lighthouses, national defense, flood control systems and street lighting. Public goods that are available everywhere are sometimes referred to as global public goods.
Aggregate supply	In economics, aggregate supply is the total supply of goods and services that firms in a national economy plan on selling during a specific time period. It is the total amount of goods and services that firms are willing to sell at a given price level in an economy.
Supply shock	A supply shock is an event that suddenly changes the price of a commodity or service. It may be caused by a sudden increase or decrease in the supply of a particular good. This sudden change affects the equilibrium price.
Commercial bank	A commercial bank is a type of bank that provides services such as accepting deposits, making business loans, and offering basic investment products. Commercial bank can also refer to a bank or a division of a bank that mostly deals with deposits and loans from corporations or large businesses, as opposed to individual members of the public . In the US the term commercial bank was often used to distinguish it from an investment bank due to differences in bank regulation.

1. Limits, Alternatives, and Choices

Lump-sum tax	A lump-sum tax is a tax that is a fixed amount, no matter the change in circumstance of the taxed entity. (A lump-sum subsidy or lump-sum redistribution is defined similarly). It is one of the various modes used for taxation: income, things owned (property taxes), money spent (sales taxes), miscellaneous (excise taxes).
Federal funds	In the United States, federal funds are overnight borrowings between banks and other entities to maintain their bank reserves at the Federal Reserve. Banks keep reserves at Federal Reserve Banks to meet their reserve requirements and to clear financial transactions. Transactions in the federal funds market enable depository institutions with reserve balances in excess of reserve requirements to lend reserves to institutions with reserve deficiencies.
Trade-off	A trade-off is a situation that involves losing one quality or aspect of something in return for gaining another quality or aspect. More colloquially, if one thing increases, some other thing must decrease. Trade-offs can occur for many reasons, including simple physics (into a given amount of space, you can fit many small objects or fewer large objects).
Capital	In economics, capital goods, real capital, or capital assets are already-produced durable goods or any non-financial asset that is used in production of goods or services. Capital goods are not significantly consumed in the production process though they may depreciate. How a capital good or is maintained or returned to its pre-production state varies with the type of capital involved.
Economic growth	Economic growth is the increase in the market value of the goods and services produced by an economy over time. It is conventionally measured as the percent rate of increase in real gross domestic product, or real GDP. Of more importance is the growth of the ratio of GDP to population (GDP per capita), which is also called per capita income. An increase in per capita income is referred to as intensive growth.
Freedom	Freedom is a London-based anarchist newspaper published monthly by Freedom Press ceasing print publication in 2014. The paper was started in 1886 by volunteers including Peter Kropotkin and Charlotte Wilson and continues to 2014 as an unpaid project. Originally, the subtitle was 'A Journal of Anarchist Socialism.' The title was changed to 'A Journal of Anarchist Communism' in June 1889. Today it is unlabelled.
Market system	A market system is any systematic process enabling many market players to bid and ask: helping bidders and sellers interact and make deals. It is not just the price mechanism but the entire system of regulation, qualification, credentials, reputations and clearing that surrounds that mechanism and makes it operate in a social context.

1. Limits, Alternatives, and Choices

Capital good	A capital good is a durable good that is used in the production of goods or services. Capital goods are one of the three types of producer goods, the other two being land and labor, which are also known collectively as primary factors of production. This classification originated during the classical economic period and has remained the dominant method for classification.
Factors of production	In economics, factors of production are the inputs to the production process. Finished goods are the output. Input determines the quantity of output i.e. output depends upon input.
Production	Production is a process of combining various material inputs and immaterial inputs in order to make something for consumption (the output). It is the act of creating output, a good or service which has value and contributes to the utility of individuals. Economic well-being is created in a production process, meaning all economic activities that aim directly or indirectly to satisfy human needs.
Pollution	Pollution is the introduction of contaminants into the natural environment that cause adverse change. Pollution can take the form of chemical substances or energy, such as noise, heat or light. Pollutants, the components of pollution, can be either foreign substances/energies or naturally occurring contaminants.
Great Depression	The Great Depression was a severe worldwide economic depression in the decade preceding World War II. The timing of the Great Depression varied across nations, but in most countries it started in 1930 and lasted until the late 1930s or middle 1940s. It was the longest, deepest, and most widespread depression of the 20th century. In the 21st century, the Great Depression is commonly used as an example of how far the world's economy can decline.
Average fixed cost	In economics, average fixed cost is the fixed costs of production (FC) divided by the quantity (Q) of output produced. Fixed costs are those costs that must be incurred in fixed quantity regardless of the level of output produced. $$AFC = \frac{FC}{Q}.$$ Average fixed cost is a per-unit-of-output measure of fixed costs.
International trade	International trade is the exchange of capital, goods, and services across international borders or territories. In most countries, such trade represents a significant share of gross domestic product (GDP). While international trade has been present throughout much of history, its economic, social, and political importance has been on the rise in recent centuries.
Stock exchange	A stock exchange is a form of exchange which provides services for stock brokers and traders to trade stocks, bonds, and other securities.

1. Limits, Alternatives, and Choices

Stock exchanges also provide facilities for issue and redemption of securities and other financial instruments, and capital events including the payment of income and dividends. Securities traded on a stock exchange include stock issued by companies, unit trusts, derivatives, pooled investment products and bonds.

Causation

Causation is a belief that events occur in predictable ways and that one event leads to another. If the relationship between the variables is non-spurious (there is not a third variable causing the effect), the temporal order is in line (cause before effect), and the study is longitudinal, it may be deduced that it is a causal relationship.

Expression

In mathematics, an expression is a finite combination of symbols that is well-formed according to rules that depend on the context. Symbols can designate numbers (constants), variables, operations, functions, and other mathematical symbols, as well as punctuation, symbols of grouping, and other syntactic symbols. The use of expressions can range from the simple: $0 + 0$

to the complex:

$$f(a) + \sum_{k=1}^{n} \frac{1}{k!} \frac{d^k}{dt^k} \bigg|_{t=0} f(u(t)) + \int_0^1 \frac{(1-t)^n}{n!} \frac{d^{n+1}}{dt^{n+1}} f(u(t))\, dt.$$

We can think of algebraic expressions as generalizations of common arithmetic operations that are formed by combining numbers, variables, and mathematical operations.

Variable cost

Variable costs are costs that change in proportion to the good or service that a business produces. Variable costs are also the sum of marginal costs over all units produced. They can also be considered normal costs.

1. Limits, Alternatives, and Choices

1. A _____ is a regional bank of the Federal Reserve System, the central banking system of the United States. There are twelve in total, one for each of the twelve Federal Reserve Districts that were created by the Federal Reserve Act of 1913. The banks are jointly responsible for implementing the monetary policy set forth by the Federal Open Market Committee, and are divided as follows:

   Some banks also possess branches, with the whole system being headquartered at the Eccles Building in Washington, D.C.

   a. Beige Book
   b. Federal Reserve Bank
   c. Credit channel
   d. Depository Institutions Deregulation and Monetary Control Act

2. _____ is the increase in the market value of the goods and services produced by an economy over time. It is conventionally measured as the percent rate of increase in real gross domestic product, or real GDP. Of more importance is the growth of the ratio of GDP to population (GDP per capita), which is also called per capita income. An increase in per capita income is referred to as intensive growth.

   a. Baker cube
   b. Bereavement benefit
   c. Biological standard of living
   d. Economic growth

3. In economics, _____ is the total supply of goods and services that firms in a national economy plan on selling during a specific time period. It is the total amount of goods and services that firms are willing to sell at a given price level in an economy.

   a. Fuel protests in the United Kingdom
   b. Battle of Annaberg
   c. Aggregate supply
   d. Freikorps Oberland

4. In microeconomic theory, the _____ of a choice is the value of the best alternative forgone, in a situation in which a choice needs to be made between several mutually exclusive alternatives given limited resources. Assuming the best choice is made, it is the 'cost' incurred by not enjoying the benefit that would be had by taking the second best choice available. The New Oxford American Dictionary defines it as 'the loss of potential gain from other alternatives when one alternative is chosen'.

   a. Benefit principle
   b. Bliss point
   c. Club good
   d. Opportunity cost

1. Limits, Alternatives, and Choices

5. _____ is the consumption and savings opportunity gained by an entity within a specified timeframe, which is generally expressed in monetary terms. However, for households and individuals, '_____ is the sum of all the wages, salaries, profits, interests payments, rents and other forms of earnings received... in a given period of time.'

In the field of public economics, the term may refer to the accumulation of both monetary and non-monetary consumption ability, with the former (monetary) being used as a proxy for total _____.

a. Fuel protests in the United Kingdom
b. Income
c. Freikorps Lichtschlag
d. Freikorps Oberland

Determinants of Supply

R - Resource Prices/Cost
O - other goods/(prices) services
T - technology
T - taxes/subsidies
E - expectations (sellers)
N - Number of Sellers

Determinants of Demand

T - tastes + wants
R - related goods - price of other goods
I - income
B - buyers (population)
E - expectations (buyer) / future

buy them together
Compliments - pb + jelly. Price pb goes down, demand goes up for jelly

Substitutes - coke + pepsi. Price coke goes up, you'll buy pepsi instead

PPF

Opportunity Cost -
MB - MC
Marginal Benefit - Marg Cost

increase demand
decrease in supply

ANSWER KEY
1. Limits, Alternatives, and Choices

---

1. b
2. d
3. c
4. d
5. b

You can take the complete Chapter Practice Test

for 1. Limits, Alternatives, and Choices
on all key terms, persons, places, and concepts.

Online 99 Cents

http://www.JustTheFacts101.com

Use www.JustTheFacts101.com for all your study needs

including Facts101's online interactive problem solving labs in

chemistry, statistics, mathematics, and more.

2. The Market System and the Circular Flow

	Economic system
	Capitalism
	Great Recession
	Market system
	Private property
	Recession
	Commercial bank
	Freedom
	Index of Economic Freedom
	Capital good
	Income
	National income
	Product
	Specialization
	Barter
	Coincidence of wants
	Medium of exchange
	Market failure
	Total cost
	Total revenue
	Revenue

2. The Market System and the Circular Flow
CHAPTER OUTLINE: KEY TERMS, PEOPLE, PLACES, CONCEPTS

_____ Consumer sovereignty

_____ Interest rate

_____ Capital

_____ Capital accumulation

_____ Creative destruction

_____ Market economy

_____ Coordination failure

_____ State bank

_____ Lottery

_____ Expression

_____ Partnership

_____ Product market

_____ Economic growth

2. The Market System and the Circular Flow

CHAPTER HIGHLIGHTS & NOTES: KEY TERMS, PEOPLE, PLACES, CONCEPTS

Economic system	An economic system is a system of production and distribution of goods and services as well as allocation of resources in a society. It includes the combination of the various institutions, agencies, entities (or even sectors as described by some authors) and consumers that comprise the economic structure of a given community. A related concept is the mode of production.
Capitalism	Capitalism is an economic system in which trade, industry, and the means of production are controlled by private owners with the goal of making profits in a market economy. Central characteristics of capitalism include capital accumulation, competitive markets and wage labor. In a capitalist economy, the parties to a transaction typically determine the prices at which assets, goods, and services are exchanged.
Great Recession	The Great Recession was a global economic decline in the late 2000s. According to aggregated national data, a worldwide recession began in Q3-2008 and ended in Q1-2009. It is related to a liquidity crisis, commonly being dated to have started when several central banks had to step in with liquidity lending to the interbank lending market on 9 August 2007. This was a response to a situation where BNP Paribas temporarily had to block money withdrawals from three hedge funds--citing a 'complete evaporation of liquidity'.
Market system	A market system is any systematic process enabling many market players to bid and ask: helping bidders and sellers interact and make deals. It is not just the price mechanism but the entire system of regulation, qualification, credentials, reputations and clearing that surrounds that mechanism and makes it operate in a social context. Because a market system relies on the assumption that players are constantly involved and unequally enabled, a market system is distinguished specifically from a voting system where candidates seek the support of voters on a less regular basis.
Private property	Private property is a legal designation of the ownership of property by non-governmental legal entities. Private property is distinguishable from public property, which is owned by a state entity; and collective property, which is owned by a group of non-governmental entities. Private property is further distinguished from personal property, which refers to property for personal use and consumption.
Recession	In economics, a recession is a business cycle contraction. It is a general slowdown in economic activity. Macroeconomic indicators such as GDP (gross domestic product), investment spending, capacity utilization, household income, business profits, and inflation fall, while bankruptcies and the unemployment rate rise.
Commercial bank	A commercial bank is a type of bank that provides services such as accepting deposits, making business loans, and offering basic investment products.

2. The Market System and the Circular Flow

Commercial bank can also refer to a bank or a division of a bank that mostly deals with deposits and loans from corporations or large businesses, as opposed to individual members of the public .

In the US the term commercial bank was often used to distinguish it from an investment bank due to differences in bank regulation.

Freedom

Freedom is a London-based anarchist newspaper published monthly by Freedom Press ceasing print publication in 2014.

The paper was started in 1886 by volunteers including Peter Kropotkin and Charlotte Wilson and continues to 2014 as an unpaid project. Originally, the subtitle was 'A Journal of Anarchist Socialism.' The title was changed to 'A Journal of Anarchist Communism' in June 1889. Today it is unlabelled.

Index of Economic Freedom

The Index of Economic Freedom is an annual index and ranking created by The Heritage Foundation and The Wall Street Journal in 1995 to measure the degree of economic freedom in the world's nations. The creators of the index took an approach similar to Adam Smith's in The Wealth of Nations, that 'basic institutions that protect the liberty of individuals to pursue their own economic interests result in greater prosperity for the larger society'.

Capital good

A capital good is a durable good that is used in the production of goods or services. Capital goods are one of the three types of producer goods, the other two being land and labor, which are also known collectively as primary factors of production. This classification originated during the classical economic period and has remained the dominant method for classification.

Income

Income is the consumption and savings opportunity gained by an entity within a specified timeframe, which is generally expressed in monetary terms. However, for households and individuals, 'income is the sum of all the wages, salaries, profits, interests payments, rents and other forms of earnings received... in a given period of time.'

In the field of public economics, the term may refer to the accumulation of both monetary and non-monetary consumption ability, with the former (monetary) being used as a proxy for total income.

National income

A variety of measures of national income and output are used in economics to estimate total economic activity in a country or region, including gross domestic product, gross national product (GNP), net national income and adjusted national income. All are specially concerned with counting the total amount of goods and services produced within some 'boundary'. The boundary is usually defined by geography or citizenship, and may also restrict the goods and services that are counted.

Product

In marketing, a product is anything that can be offered to a market that might satisfy a want or need. In retailing, products are called merchandise.

Specialization	Specialization is the separation of tasks within a system. In a multicellular creature, cells are specialized for functions such as bone construction or oxygen transport. In capitalist societies, individual workers specialize for functions such as building construction or gasoline transport.
Barter	Barter is a system of exchange by which goods or services are directly exchanged for other goods or services without using a medium of exchange, such as money. It is distinguishable from gift economies in that the reciprocal exchange is immediate and not delayed in time. It is usually bilateral, but may be multilateral (i.e., mediated through barter organizations) and usually exists parallel to monetary systems in most developed countries, though to a very limited extent.
Coincidence of wants	The coincidence of wants problem (often 'double coincidence of wants') is an important category of transaction costs that impose severe limitations on economies lacking money and thus dominated by barter or other in-kind transactions. The problem is caused by the improbability of the wants, needs or events that cause or motivate a transaction occurring at the same time and the same place. One example is the bar musician who is 'paid' with liquor or food, items which his landlord will not accept as rent payment, when the musician would rather have a month's shelter.
Medium of exchange	A medium of exchange is an intermediary used in trade to avoid the inconveniences of a pure barter system.
	By contrast, as William Stanley Jevons argued, in a barter system there must be a coincidence of wants before two people can trade - one must want exactly what the other has to offer, when and where it is offered, so that the exchange can occur. A medium of exchange permits the value of goods to be assessed and rendered in terms of the intermediary, most often, a form of money widely accepted to buy any other good.
Market failure	Market failure is a concept within economic theory describing when the allocation of goods and services by a free market is not efficient. That is, there exists another conceivable outcome where a market participant may be made better-off without making someone else worse-off. (The outcome is not Pareto optimal).
Total cost	In economics, and cost accounting, total cost describes the total economic cost of production and is made up of variable costs, which vary according to the quantity of a good produced and include inputs such as labor and raw materials, plus fixed costs, which are independent of the quantity of a good produced and include inputs (capital) that cannot be varied in the short term, such as buildings and machinery. Total cost in economics includes the total opportunity cost of each factor of production as part of its fixed or variable costs.
	The rate at which total cost changes as the amount produced changes is called marginal cost.
Total revenue	Total revenue is the total receipts of a firm from the sale of any given quantity of a product.

2. The Market System and the Circular Flow

	It can be calculated as the selling price of the firm's product times the quantity sold, i.e. total revenue = price × quantity, or letting TR be the total revenue function: $$TR(Q) = P(Q) \times Q$$ where Q is the quantity of output sold, and P(Q) is the inverse demand function (the demand function solved out for price in terms of quantity demanded).
Revenue	In business, revenue or turnover is income that a company receives from its normal business activities, usually from the sale of goods and services to customers. In many countries, revenue is referred to as turnover. Some companies receive revenue from interest, royalties, or other fees.
Consumer sovereignty	In economics, consumer sovereignty is the assertion that consumer preferences determine the production of goods and services. The term was coined by William Harold Hutt in his book Economists and the Public (1936).
Interest rate	An interest rate is the rate at which interest is paid by a borrower for the use of money that they borrow from a lender (creditor). Specifically, the interest rate is a percent of principal (P) paid a certain amount of times (m) per period (usually quoted per annum). For example, a small company borrows capital from a bank to buy new assets for its business, and in return the lender receives interest at a predetermined interest rate for deferring the use of funds and instead lending it to the borrower.
Capital	In economics, capital goods, real capital, or capital assets are already-produced durable goods or any non-financial asset that is used in production of goods or services. Capital goods are not significantly consumed in the production process though they may depreciate. How a capital good or is maintained or returned to its pre-production state varies with the type of capital involved.
Capital accumulation	The accumulation of capital refers to the accumulation of capital, where capital is defined as money or a financial asset invested for the purpose of making more money . This activity forms the basis of the economic system of capitalism, where economic activity is structured around the accumulation of capital (investment in order to realize a financial profit). In a more broad sense, capital accumulation may refer to the gathering or amassing of any objects of value as judged by one's perceived reproductive interest group.
Creative destruction	Creative destruction, sometimes known as Schumpeter's gale, is a term in economics which has since the 1950s become most readily identified with the Austrian American economist Joseph Schumpeter's theory of economic innovation and business cycle.

Creative destruction describes the 'process of industrial mutation that incessantly revolutionizes the economic structure from within, incessantly destroying the old one, incessantly creating a new one.'

The German Marxist sociologist Werner Sombart who has been credited with the first use of these terms in his work Krieg und Kapitalismus ('War and Capitalism', 1913). In the earlier work of Marx, however, the idea of creative destruction or annihilation (German: Vernichtung) implies not only that capitalism destroys and reconfigures previous economic orders, but also that it must ceaselessly devalue existing wealth (whether through war, dereliction, or regular and periodic economic crises) in order to clear the ground for the creation of new wealth.

Market economy	A Market economy is an economy in which decisions regarding investment, production and distribution are based on supply and demand, and prices of goods and services are determined in a free price system. The major defining characteristic of a market economy is that decisions on investment and the allocation of producer goods are mainly made through markets. This is contrasted with a planned economy, where investment and production decisions are embodied in a plan of production.
Coordination failure	In economics, coordination failure is a concept that can explain recessions through the failure of firms and other price setters to coordinate. In an economic system with multiple equilibria, coordination failure occurs when a group of firms could achieve a more desirable equilibrium but fail to because they do not coordinate their decision making. Coordination failure can result in a self-fulfilling prophecy.
State bank	A state bank is generally a financial institution that is chartered by a state. It differs from a reserve bank in that it does not necessarily control monetary policy (indeed, the state in question may have no legal capacity to create monetary policy), but instead usually offers only retail and commercial services. A state bank that has been in operation for five years or less is called a de novo bank.
Lottery	In expected utility theory, a lottery is a discrete distribution of probability on a set of states of nature. The elements of a lottery correspond to the probability that a certain outcome arises from a given state of nature. In economics, individuals are assumed to rank lotteries according to a rational system of preferences, although it is now accepted that people make irrational choices systematically.
Expression	In mathematics, an expression is a finite combination of symbols that is well-formed according to rules that depend on the context. Symbols can designate numbers (constants), variables, operations, functions, and other mathematical symbols, as well as punctuation, symbols of grouping, and other syntactic symbols. The use of expressions can range from the simple: $0 + 0$

2. The Market System and the Circular Flow

to the complex:
$$f(a) + \sum_{k=1}^{n} \frac{1}{k!} \frac{d^k}{dt^k}\bigg|_{t=0} f(u(t)) + \int_0^1 \frac{(1-t)^n}{n!} \frac{d^{n+1}}{dt^{n+1}} f(u(t))\, dt.$$

We can think of algebraic expressions as generalizations of common arithmetic operations that are formed by combining numbers, variables, and mathematical operations.

Partnership	A partnership in the People's Republic of China is a business entity governed by the Partnership Enterprise Law passed by order of the President of the People's Republic of China to authorize and govern partnership enterprises. A partnership is a type of business entity in which partners share with each other the profits or losses of the business undertaking in which all have invested.
Product market	Product market is where goods and services produced by businesses are sold to households. The households use the income they receive from the sale of resources to purchase the products. The money they spend is returned to the businesses as revenue.
Economic growth	Economic growth is the increase in the market value of the goods and services produced by an economy over time. It is conventionally measured as the percent rate of increase in real gross domestic product, or real GDP. Of more importance is the growth of the ratio of GDP to population (GDP per capita), which is also called per capita income. An increase in per capita income is referred to as intensive growth.

1. In economics, a _____ is a business cycle contraction. It is a general slowdown in economic activity. Macroeconomic indicators such as GDP (gross domestic product), investment spending, capacity utilization, household income, business profits, and inflation fall, while bankruptcies and the unemployment rate rise.

    a. Depression
    b. General glut
    c. Global recession
    d. Recession

2. . In business, _____ or turnover is income that a company receives from its normal business activities, usually from the sale of goods and services to customers. In many countries, _____ is referred to as turnover. Some companies receive _____ from interest, royalties, or other fees.

    a. Benefit principle
    b. Revenue

c. Club good

d. Conjectural variation

3. An _____ is a system of production and distribution of goods and services as well as allocation of resources in a society. It includes the combination of the various institutions, agencies, entities (or even sectors as described by some authors) and consumers that comprise the economic structure of a given community. A related concept is the mode of production.

a. Fuel protests in the United Kingdom

b. Battle of Annaberg

c. Freikorps Lichtschlag

d. Economic system

4. _____ is the consumption and savings opportunity gained by an entity within a specified timeframe, which is generally expressed in monetary terms. However, for households and individuals, '_____ is the sum of all the wages, salaries, profits, interests payments, rents and other forms of earnings received... in a given period of time.'

In the field of public economics, the term may refer to the accumulation of both monetary and non-monetary consumption ability, with the former (monetary) being used as a proxy for total _____.

a. Fuel protests in the United Kingdom

b. Battle of Annaberg

c. Freikorps Lichtschlag

d. Income

5. _____ is an economic system in which trade, industry, and the means of production are controlled by private owners with the goal of making profits in a market economy. Central characteristics of _____ include capital accumulation, competitive markets and wage labor. In a capitalist economy, the parties to a transaction typically determine the prices at which assets, goods, and services are exchanged.

a. Fuel protests in the United Kingdom

b. Battle of Annaberg

c. Freikorps Lichtschlag

d. Capitalism

1. d
2. b
3. d
4. d
5. d

You can take the complete Chapter Practice Test

for 2. The Market System and the Circular Flow
on all key terms, persons, places, and concepts.

Online 99 Cents

http://www.JustTheFacts101.com

Use www.JustTheFacts101.com for all your study needs

including Facts101's online interactive problem solving labs in

chemistry, statistics, mathematics, and more.

3. Demand, Supply, and Market Equilibrium

CHAPTER OUTLINE: KEY TERMS, PEOPLE, PLACES, CONCEPTS

Stock exchange

Demand curve

Expression

Income

Law of demand

Marginal utility

National income

Product

Quantitative easing

Relative price

Complementary good

Independent goods

Inferior good

Normal good

Product market

Substitute good

Monopoly

Law of supply

Price level

Allocative efficiency

Market system

3. Demand, Supply, and Market Equilibrium

CHAPTER OUTLINE: KEY TERMS, PEOPLE, PLACES, CONCEPTS

	Productive efficiency
	Interest rate
	Rationing
	Full employment
	Market price
	International trade
	Rent control
	Black market
	Price floor
	Primary market
	Secondary market
	Misery index

CHAPTER HIGHLIGHTS & NOTES: KEY TERMS, PEOPLE, PLACES, CONCEPTS

Stock exchange	A stock exchange is a form of exchange which provides services for stock brokers and traders to trade stocks, bonds, and other securities. Stock exchanges also provide facilities for issue and redemption of securities and other financial instruments, and capital events including the payment of income and dividends. Securities traded on a stock exchange include stock issued by companies, unit trusts, derivatives, pooled investment products and bonds.
Demand curve	In economics, the demand curve is the graph depicting the relationship between the price of a certain commodity and the amount of it that consumers are willing and able to purchase at that given price. It is a graphic representation of a demand schedule.

3. Demand, Supply, and Market Equilibrium

Expression	In mathematics, an expression is a finite combination of symbols that is well-formed according to rules that depend on the context. Symbols can designate numbers (constants), variables, operations, functions, and other mathematical symbols, as well as punctuation, symbols of grouping, and other syntactic symbols. The use of expressions can range from the simple: $0 + 0$

to the complex:

$$f(a) + \sum_{k=1}^{n} \frac{1}{k!} \frac{d^k}{dt^k} \bigg|_{t=0} f(u(t)) + \int_0^1 \frac{(1-t)^n}{n!} \frac{d^{n+1}}{dt^{n+1}} f(u(t)) \, dt.$$

We can think of algebraic expressions as generalizations of common arithmetic operations that are formed by combining numbers, variables, and mathematical operations.

Income	Income is the consumption and savings opportunity gained by an entity within a specified timeframe, which is generally expressed in monetary terms. However, for households and individuals, 'income is the sum of all the wages, salaries, profits, interests payments, rents and other forms of earnings received... in a given period of time.' In the field of public economics, the term may refer to the accumulation of both monetary and non-monetary consumption ability, with the former (monetary) being used as a proxy for total income.
Law of demand	In economics, the law states that, all else being equal, as the price of a product increases, quantity demanded falls; likewise, as the price of a product decreases, quantity demanded increases. In other words, the law of demand states that the quantity demanded and the price of a commodity are inversely related, other things remaining constant. If the income of the consumer, prices of the related goods, and preferences of the consumer remain unchanged, then the change in quantity of good demanded by the consumer will be negatively correlated to the change in the price of the good.
Marginal utility	In economics, the marginal utility of a good or service is the gain from an increase or loss from a decrease in the consumption of that good or service. Economists sometimes speak of a law of diminishing marginal utility, meaning that the first unit of consumption of a good or service yields more utility than the second and subsequent units, with a continuing reduction for greater amounts. The marginal decision rule states that a good or service should be consumed at a quantity at which the marginal utility is equal to the marginal cost.
National income	A variety of measures of national income and output are used in economics to estimate total economic activity in a country or region, including gross domestic product, gross national product (GNP), net national income and adjusted national income. All are specially concerned with counting the total amount of goods and services produced within some 'boundary'.

Product	In marketing, a product is anything that can be offered to a market that might satisfy a want or need. In retailing, products are called merchandise. In manufacturing, products are bought as raw materials and sold as finished goods.
Quantitative easing	Quantitative easing is an unconventional monetary policy used by central banks to stimulate the economy when standard monetary policy has become ineffective. A central bank implements quantitative easing by buying specified amounts of financial assets from commercial banks and other private institutions, thus raising the prices of those financial assets and lowering their yield, while simultaneously increasing the monetary base. This is distinguished from the more usual policy of buying or selling short term government bonds in order to keep interbank interest rates at a specified target value.
Relative price	A relative price is the price of a commodity such as a good or service in terms of another; i.e., the ratio of two prices. A relative price may be expressed in terms of a ratio between any two prices or the ratio between the price of one particular good and a weighted average of all other goods available in the market. A relative price is an opportunity cost.
Complementary good	In economics, a complementary good is a good with a negative cross elasticity of demand, in contrast to a substitute good. This means a good's demand is increased when the price of another good is decreased. Conversely, the demand for a good is decreased when the price of another good is increased.
Independent goods	Independent goods are goods that have a zero cross elasticity of demand. Changes in the price of one good will have no effect on the demand of an independent good. For example, a person's demand for nails is independent of his or her demand for bread, since they are two unrelated types of goods.
Inferior good	In economics, an inferior good is a good that decreases in demand when consumer income rises, unlike normal goods, for which the opposite is observed. Normal goods are those for which consumers' demand increases when their income increases. This would be the opposite of a superior good, one that is often associated with wealth and the wealthy, whereas an inferior good is often associated with lower socio-economic groups.
Normal good	In economics, normal goods are any goods for which demand increases when income increases, and falls when income decreases but price remains constant, i.e. with a positive income elasticity of demand. The term does not necessarily refer to the quality of the good, but an abnormal good would clearly not be in demand, except for possibly lower socioeconomic groups. In particular, when the price of a normal good is zero, the demand is infinite.
Product market	Product market is where goods and services produced by businesses are sold to households. The households use the income they receive from the sale of resources to purchase the products.

3. Demand, Supply, and Market Equilibrium

Substitute good	In economics, one way that two or more goods can be classified is by examining the relationship of the demand schedules when the price of one good changes. This relationship between demand schedules leads to classification of goods as either substitutes or complements. Substitute goods are goods which, as a result of changed conditions, may replace each other in use (or consumption).
Monopoly	A monopoly (from Greek monos μ???? + polein p??e?? (to sell)) exists when a specific person or enterprise is the only supplier of a particular commodity (this contrasts with a monopsony which relates to a single entity's control of a market to purchase a good or service, and with oligopoly which consists of a few entities dominating an industry). Monopolies are thus characterized by a lack of economic competition to produce the good or service and a lack of viable substitute goods. The verb 'monopolize' refers to the process by which a company gains the ability to raise prices or exclude competitors.
Law of supply	The law of supply is a fundamental principle of economic theory which states that, all else equal, an increase in price results in an increase in quantity supplied. In other words, there is a direct relationship between price and quantity: quantities respond in the same direction as price changes. This means that producers are willing to offer more products for sale on the market at higher prices by increasing production as a way of increasing profits.
Price level	The general price level is a hypothetical measure of overall prices for some set of goods and services, in a given region during a given interval, normalized relative to some base set. Typically, a price level is approximated with a price index.
Allocative efficiency	Allocative efficiency is a type of economic efficiency in which economy/producers produce only those types of goods and services that are more desirable in the society and also in high demand. According to the formula the point of allocative efficiency is a point where price is equal to marginal cost (P=MC)or (MC=MR). At this point the social surplus is maximized with no deadweight loss, or the value society puts on that level of output produced minus the value of resources used to achieve that level, yet can be applied to other things such as level of pollution.
Market system	A market system is any systematic process enabling many market players to bid and ask: helping bidders and sellers interact and make deals. It is not just the price mechanism but the entire system of regulation, qualification, credentials, reputations and clearing that surrounds that mechanism and makes it operate in a social context.
	Because a market system relies on the assumption that players are constantly involved and unequally enabled, a market system is distinguished specifically from a voting system where candidates seek the support of voters on a less regular basis.
Productive efficiency	Productive efficiency occurs when the economy is using all of its resources efficiently.

	The concept is illustrated on a production possibility frontier (PPF) where all points on the curve are points of maximum productive efficiency. An equilibrium may be productively efficient without being allocatively efficient-- i.e. it may result in a distribution of goods where social welfare is not maximized.
Interest rate	An interest rate is the rate at which interest is paid by a borrower for the use of money that they borrow from a lender (creditor). Specifically, the interest rate is a percent of principal (P) paid a certain amount of times (m) per period (usually quoted per annum). For example, a small company borrows capital from a bank to buy new assets for its business, and in return the lender receives interest at a predetermined interest rate for deferring the use of funds and instead lending it to the borrower.
Rationing	Rationing is the controlled distribution of scarce resources, goods, or services. Rationing controls the size of the ration, one's allotted portion of the resources being distributed on a particular day or at a particular time.
Full employment	Full employment, in macroeconomics, is the level of employment rates where there is no cyclical or deficient-demand unemployment. It is defined by the majority of mainstream economists as being an acceptable level of unemployment somewhere above 0%. The discrepancy from 0% arises due to non-cyclical types of unemployment.
Market price	In economics, market price is the economic price for which a good or service is offered in the marketplace. It is of interest mainly in the study of microeconomics. Market value and market price are equal only under conditions of market efficiency, equilibrium, and rational expectations.
International trade	International trade is the exchange of capital, goods, and services across international borders or territories. In most countries, such trade represents a significant share of gross domestic product (GDP). While international trade has been present throughout much of history, its economic, social, and political importance has been on the rise in recent centuries.
Rent control	Rent control is a system of laws, administered by a court or a public authority, which limits the changes that can be made in the price of renting a house or other real property. Usually the objective is to limit the price that would result from the market, where inequality of bargaining power between landlords and tenants produces continually escalating prices. Regulation of rents is most frequently seen in residential housing.
Black market	A black market or underground economy is the market in which goods or services are traded illegally. The key distinction of a black market trade is that the transaction itself is illegal. The goods or services may or may not themselves be illegal to own, or to trade through other, legal channels.
Price floor	A price floor is a government- or group-imposed price control or limit on how low a price can be charged for a product.

3. Demand, Supply, and Market Equilibrium

	A price floor must be greater than the equilibrium price in order to be effective.
Primary market	The primary market is the part of the capital market that deals with issuing of new securities. Companies, governments or public sector institutions can obtain funds through the sale of a new stock or bond issues through primary market. This is typically done through an investment bank or finance syndicate of securities dealers.
Secondary market	The secondary market, is also called aftermarket, is the financial market in which previously issued financial instruments such as stock, bonds, options, and futures are bought and sold. Another frequent usage of 'secondary market' is to refer to loans which are sold by a mortgage bank to investors such as Fannie Mae and Freddie Mac. The term 'secondary market' is also used to refer to the market for any used goods or assets, or an alternative use for an existing product or asset where the customer base is the second market (for example, corn has been traditionally used primarily for food production and feedstock, but a 'second' or 'third' market has developed for use in ethanol production).
Misery index	The misery index is an economic indicator, created by economist Arthur Okun, and found by adding the unemployment rate to the inflation rate. It is assumed that both a higher rate of unemployment and a worsening of inflation create economic and social costs for a country.

1. A _____ is a government- or group-imposed price control or limit on how low a price can be charged for a product. A _____ must be greater than the equilibrium price in order to be effective.

   a. Capital control
   b. Doctrine of parity
   c. Price floor
   d. Flour War

2. . In economics, the _____ of a good or service is the gain from an increase or loss from a decrease in the consumption of that good or service. Economists sometimes speak of a law of diminishing _____, meaning that the first unit of consumption of a good or service yields more utility than the second and subsequent units, with a continuing reduction for greater amounts. The marginal decision rule states that a good or service should be consumed at a quantity at which the _____ is equal to the marginal cost.

   a. Baker cube

b. Marginal utility

c. Biological standard of living

d. Bodily integrity

3. _____ are goods that have a zero cross elasticity of demand. Changes in the price of one good will have no effect on the demand of an _____(s). For example, a person's demand for nails is independent of his or her demand for bread, since they are two unrelated types of goods.

a. Independent goods

b. Case

c. Common good

d. Credence good

4. A _____ is a form of exchange which provides services for stock brokers and traders to trade stocks, bonds, and other securities. _____s also provide facilities for issue and redemption of securities and other financial instruments, and capital events including the payment of income and dividends. Securities traded on a _____ include stock issued by companies, unit trusts, derivatives, pooled investment products and bonds.

a. Stock exchange

b. Barbell strategy

c. BATS Chi-X Europe

d. Bellwether

5. In economics, an _____ is a good that decreases in demand when consumer income rises, unlike normal goods, for which the opposite is observed. Normal goods are those for which consumers' demand increases when their income increases. This would be the opposite of a superior good, one that is often associated with wealth and the wealthy, whereas an _____ is often associated with lower socio-economic groups.

a. Bad

b. Case

c. Inferior good

d. Credence good

---

1. c
2. b
3. a
4. a
5. c

You can take the complete Chapter Practice Test

for 3. Demand, Supply, and Market Equilibrium
on all key terms, persons, places, and concepts.

Online 99 Cents

http://www.JustTheFacts101.com

Use www.JustTheFacts101.com for all your study needs

including Facts101's online interactive problem solving labs in

chemistry, statistics, mathematics, and more.

4. Market Failures: Public Goods and Externalities

CHAPTER OUTLINE: KEY TERMS, PEOPLE, PLACES, CONCEPTS

Market failure

Allocative efficiency

Productive efficiency

Interest rate

Private good

Public good

Rivalry

Pay for performance

Inflation

Free riding

Product

Monopoly

Natural monopoly

Externality

Public sector

Air pollution

Coase theorem

Pollution

Laffer curve

Carbon dioxide

Carbon dioxide emissions

4. Market Failures: Public Goods and Externalities

CHAPTER OUTLINE: KEY TERMS, PEOPLE, PLACES, CONCEPTS

	Adverse selection
	Moral hazard
	Social security
	Price elasticity
	Elasticity
	Short run

CHAPTER HIGHLIGHTS & NOTES: KEY TERMS, PEOPLE, PLACES, CONCEPTS

Market failure	Market failure is a concept within economic theory describing when the allocation of goods and services by a free market is not efficient. That is, there exists another conceivable outcome where a market participant may be made better-off without making someone else worse-off. (The outcome is not Pareto optimal).
Allocative efficiency	Allocative efficiency is a type of economic efficiency in which economy/producers produce only those types of goods and services that are more desirable in the society and also in high demand. According to the formula the point of allocative efficiency is a point where price is equal to marginal cost (P=MC)or (MC=MR). At this point the social surplus is maximized with no deadweight loss, or the value society puts on that level of output produced minus the value of resources used to achieve that level, yet can be applied to other things such as level of pollution.
Productive efficiency	Productive efficiency occurs when the economy is using all of its resources efficiently. The concept is illustrated on a production possibility frontier (PPF) where all points on the curve are points of maximum productive efficiency. An equilibrium may be productively efficient without being allocatively efficient-- i.e. it may result in a distribution of goods where social welfare is not maximized.
Interest rate	An interest rate is the rate at which interest is paid by a borrower for the use of money that they borrow from a lender (creditor). Specifically, the interest rate is a percent of principal (P) paid a certain amount of times (m) per period (usually quoted per annum).

4. Market Failures: Public Goods and Externalities

Private good	A private good is defined in economics as 'an item that yields positive benefits to people' that is excludable, i.e. its owners can exercise private property rights, preventing those who have not paid for it from using the good or consuming its benefits; and rivalrous, i.e. consumption by one necessarily prevents that of another. A private good, as an economic resource is scarce, which can cause competition for it.The market demand curve for a private good is a horizontal summation of individual demand curves. Unlike public goods, private goods are less likely to have the free rider problem.
Public good	In economics, a public good is a good that is both non-excludable and non-rivalrous in that individuals cannot be effectively excluded from use and where use by one individual does not reduce availability to others. Examples of public goods include fresh air, knowledge, lighthouses, national defense, flood control systems and street lighting. Public goods that are available everywhere are sometimes referred to as global public goods.
Rivalry	In economics, rivalry is a characteristic of a good. A good can be placed along a continuum ranging from rivalrous (rival) to non-rival. The same characteristic is sometimes referred to as subtractable or non-subtractable.
Pay for performance	Pay for performance is an emerging movement in health insurance . Providers under this arrangement are rewarded for meeting pre-established targets for delivery of healthcare services. This is a fundamental change from fee for service payment.
Inflation	In economics, inflation is a sustained increase in the general price level of goods and services in an economy over a period of time. When the general price level rises, each unit of currency buys fewer goods and services. Consequently, inflation reflects a reduction in the purchasing power per unit of money - a loss of real value in the medium of exchange and unit of account within the economy.
Free riding	Free riding is a term used in the stock-trading world to describe the practice of buying shares or other securities without actually having the capital to cover the trade. This is possible when recently bought or sold shares are unsettled, and therefore have not been paid for. Since stock transactions usually settle after three business days, a crafty trader can buy a stock and sell it the following day (or the same day), without ever having sufficient funds in the account.
Product	In marketing, a product is anything that can be offered to a market that might satisfy a want or need. In retailing, products are called merchandise. In manufacturing, products are bought as raw materials and sold as finished goods.

Monopoly	A monopoly (from Greek monos μ???? + polein p??e?? (to sell)) exists when a specific person or enterprise is the only supplier of a particular commodity (this contrasts with a monopsony which relates to a single entity's control of a market to purchase a good or service, and with oligopoly which consists of a few entities dominating an industry). Monopolies are thus characterized by a lack of economic competition to produce the good or service and a lack of viable substitute goods. The verb 'monopolize' refers to the process by which a company gains the ability to raise prices or exclude competitors.
Natural monopoly	A monopoly is a firm which is the only one producing and selling a particular product. A natural monopoly is a monopoly in an industry in which it is most efficient (involving the lowest long-run average cost) for production to be concentrated in a single firm. This market situation gives the largest supplier in an industry, often the first supplier in a market, an overwhelming cost advantage over other actual and potential competitors, so a natural monopoly situation generally leads to an actual monopoly.
Externality	In economics, an externality is the cost or benefit that affects a party who did not choose to incur that cost or benefit.
	For example, manufacturing activities that cause air pollution impose health and clean-up costs on the whole society, whereas the neighbors of an individual who chooses to fire-proof his home may benefit from a reduced risk of a fire spreading to their own houses. If external costs exist, such as pollution, the producer may choose to produce more of the product than would be produced if the producer were required to pay all associated environmental costs.
Public sector	The public sector refers to the part of the economy concerned with providing various government services. The composition of the public sector varies by country, but in most countries the public sector includes such services as the military, police, public transit and care of public roads, public education, along with healthcare and those working for the government itself, such as elected officials. The public sector might provide services that a non-payer cannot be excluded from (such as street lighting), services which benefit all of society rather than just the individual who uses the service.
Air pollution	Air pollution is the introduction of chemicals, particulates, biological materials, or other harmful materials into the Earth's atmosphere, possibly causing disease, death to humans, damage to other living organisms such as food crops, or the natural or built environment.
	The atmosphere is a complex natural gaseous system that is essential to support life on planet Earth. Stratospheric ozone depletion due to air pollution has long been recognized as a threat to human health as well as to the Earth's ecosystems.
Coase theorem	In law and economics, the Coase theorem describes the economic efficiency of an economic allocation or outcome in the presence of externalities.

4. Market Failures: Public Goods and Externalities

	The theorem states that if trade in an externality is possible and there are sufficiently low transaction costs, bargaining will lead to an efficient outcome regardless of the initial allocation of property. In practice, obstacles to bargaining or poorly defined property rights can prevent Coasian bargaining.
Pollution	Pollution is the introduction of contaminants into the natural environment that cause adverse change. Pollution can take the form of chemical substances or energy, such as noise, heat or light. Pollutants, the components of pollution, can be either foreign substances/energies or naturally occurring contaminants.
Laffer curve	In economics, the Laffer curve is a representation of the relationship between possible rates of taxation and the resulting levels of government revenue. It illustrates the concept of taxable income elasticity--i.e., taxable income will change in response to changes in the rate of taxation. It postulates that no tax revenue will be raised at the extreme tax rates of 0% and 100% and that there must be at least one rate where tax revenue would be a non-zero maximum.
Carbon dioxide	Carbon dioxide is a naturally occurring chemical compound composed of 2 oxygen atoms each covalently double bonded to a single carbon atom. It is a gas at standard temperature and pressure and exists in Earth's atmosphere in this state, as a trace gas at a concentration of 0.04 per cent (400 ppm) by volume, as of 2014. As part of the carbon cycle, plants, algae, and cyanobacteria use light energy to photosynthesize carbohydrate from carbon dioxide and water, with oxygen produced as a waste product.
Carbon dioxide emissions	This is a list of sovereign states and territories by carbon dioxide emissions due to certain forms of human activity. The data presented below corresponds to emissions in 2008. The data was collected by the United States Department of Energy's Carbon Dioxide Information Analysis Center (CDIAC) for the United Nations. The data only considers carbon dioxide emissions from the burning of fossil fuels and cement manufacture, but not emissions from land use, land-use change and forestry.
Adverse selection	Adverse selection, anti-selection, or negative selection is a term used in economics, insurance, risk management, and statistics. It refers to a market process in which undesired results occur when buyers and sellers have asymmetric information (access to different information); the 'bad' products or services are more likely to be selected. For example, a bank that sets one price for all of its checking account customers runs the risk of being adversely selected against by its low-balance, high-activity (and hence least profitable) customers.
Moral hazard	In economic theory, a moral hazard is a situation where a party will have a tendency to take risks because the costs that could result will not be felt by the party taking the risk. In other words, it is a tendency to be more willing to take a risk, knowing that the potential costs or burdens of taking such risk will be borne, in whole or in part, by others.

Social security	Social security is a concept enshrined in Article 22 of the Universal Declaration of Human Rights which states, Everyone, as a member of society, has the right to social security and is entitled to realization, through national effort and international co-operation and in accordance with the organization and resources of each State, of the economic, social and cultural rights indispensable for his dignity and the free development of his personality. In simple terms, the signatories agree that society in which a person lives should help them to develop and to make the most of all the advantages (culture, work, social welfare) which are offered to them in the country. Social security may also refer to the action programs of government intended to promote the welfare of the population through assistance measures guaranteeing access to sufficient resources for food and shelter and to promote health and well-being for the population at large and potentially vulnerable segments such as children, the elderly, the sick and the unemployed.
Price elasticity	Price elasticity of demand is a measure used in economics to show the responsiveness, or elasticity, of the quantity demanded of a good or service to a change in its price. More precisely, it gives the percentage change in quantity demanded in response to a one percent change in price (ceteris paribus, i.e. holding constant all the other determinants of demand, such as income). Price elasticities are almost always negative, although analysts tend to ignore the sign even though this can lead to ambiguity.
Elasticity	In economics, elasticity is the measurement of how responsive an economic variable is to a change in another. For example:•'If I lower the price of my product, how much more will I sell?'•'If I raise the price of one good, how will that affect sales of this other good?'•'If we learn that a resource is becoming scarce, will people scramble to acquire it?' An elastic variable (or elasticity value greater than 1) is one which responds more than proportionally to changes in other variables. In contrast, an inelastic variable (or elasticity value less than 1) is one which changes less than proportionally in response to changes in other variables.
Short run	In microeconomics, the long run is the conceptual time period in which there are no fixed factors of production as to changing the output level by changing the capital stock or by entering or leaving an industry. The long run contrasts with the short run, in which some factors are variable and others are fixed, constraining entry or exit from an industry. In macroeconomics, the long run is the period when the general price level, contractual wage rates, and expectations adjust fully to the state of the economy, in contrast to the short run when these variables may not fully adjust.

4. Market Failures: Public Goods and Externalities

1. In economics, an _____ is the cost or benefit that affects a party who did not choose to incur that cost or benefit.

   For example, manufacturing activities that cause air pollution impose health and clean-up costs on the whole society, whereas the neighbors of an individual who chooses to fire-proof his home may benefit from a reduced risk of a fire spreading to their own houses. If external costs exist, such as pollution, the producer may choose to produce more of the product than would be produced if the producer were required to pay all associated environmental costs.

   a. Bank of Natural Capital
   b. Externality
   c. Boat sharing
   d. Buy Quiet

2. In marketing, a _____ is anything that can be offered to a market that might satisfy a want or need. In retailing, _____s are called merchandise. In manufacturing, _____s are bought as raw materials and sold as finished goods.

   a. Back office
   b. Balanced scorecard
   c. Product
   d. Boutique manufacturing

3. _____ is a concept within economic theory describing when the allocation of goods and services by a free market is not efficient. That is, there exists another conceivable outcome where a market participant may be made better-off without making someone else worse-off. (The outcome is not Pareto optimal).

   a. Bank Transfer Day
   b. Bankruptcy
   c. Base effect
   d. Market failure

4. . _____ is a concept enshrined in Article 22 of the Universal Declaration of Human Rights which states, Everyone, as a member of society, has the right to _____ and is entitled to realization, through national effort and international co-operation and in accordance with the organization and resources of each State, of the economic, social and cultural rights indispensable for his dignity and the free development of his personality. In simple terms, the signatories agree that society in which a person lives should help them to develop and to make the most of all the advantages (culture, work, social welfare) which are offered to them in the country.

   _____ may also refer to the action programs of government intended to promote the welfare of the population through assistance measures guaranteeing access to sufficient resources for food and shelter and to promote health and well-being for the population at large and potentially vulnerable segments such as children, the elderly, the sick and the unemployed.

   a. Baker cube
   b. Social security
   c. Biological standard of living

5. _____ is a type of economic efficiency in which economy/producers produce only those types of goods and services that are more desirable in the society and also in high demand. According to the formula the point of _____ is a point where price is equal to marginal cost (P=MC)or (MC=MR). At this point the social surplus is maximized with no deadweight loss, or the value society puts on that level of output produced minus the value of resources used to achieve that level, yet can be applied to other things such as level of pollution.

a. Fuel protests in the United Kingdom
b. Bachelor tax
c. Banking Cash Transaction Tax
d. Allocative efficiency

1. b
2. c
3. d
4. b
5. d

You can take the complete Chapter Practice Test

for 4. Market Failures: Public Goods and Externalities
on all key terms, persons, places, and concepts.

Online 99 Cents

http://www.JustTheFacts101.com

Use www.JustTheFacts101.com for all your study needs

including Facts101's online interactive problem solving labs in

chemistry, statistics, mathematics, and more.

5. Government's Role and Government Failure

CHAPTER OUTLINE: KEY TERMS, PEOPLE, PLACES, CONCEPTS

Market failure

Private sector

Interest rate

Market system

Government failure

Aggregation problem

Collective action

Baby Boomers

Inefficiency

Bank of England

Bank of Japan

Business cycle

Central bank

European Central Bank

Fiscal policy

Monetary policy

Public choice

Freedom

Health insurance

Stabilization policy

Deregulation

	Regulatory capture
	Intervention
	Corruption
	Income
	Loan guarantee
	National income
	Product
	Specialization
	Emergency management
	Private good
	Public good
	Logrolling
	Paradox of voting

Market failure	Market failure is a concept within economic theory describing when the allocation of goods and services by a free market is not efficient. That is, there exists another conceivable outcome where a market participant may be made better-off without making someone else worse-off. (The outcome is not Pareto optimal).
Private sector	The private sector is that part of the economy, sometimes referred to as the citizen sector, which is run by private individuals or groups, usually as a means of enterprise for profit, and is not controlled by the state .
Interest rate	An interest rate is the rate at which interest is paid by a borrower for the use of money that they borrow from a lender (creditor). Specifically, the interest rate is a percent of principal (P) paid a certain amount of times (m) per period (usually quoted per annum). For example, a small company borrows capital from a bank to buy new assets for its business, and in return the lender receives interest at a predetermined interest rate for deferring the use of funds and instead lending it to the borrower.
Market system	A market system is any systematic process enabling many market players to bid and ask: helping bidders and sellers interact and make deals. It is not just the price mechanism but the entire system of regulation, qualification, credentials, reputations and clearing that surrounds that mechanism and makes it operate in a social context. Because a market system relies on the assumption that players are constantly involved and unequally enabled, a market system is distinguished specifically from a voting system where candidates seek the support of voters on a less regular basis.
Government failure	Government failure is the public-sector analogy to market failure and occurs when government intervention causes a more inefficient allocation of goods and resources than would occur without that intervention. In not comparing realized inadequacies of market outcomes against those of potential interventions, one writer describes the 'anatomy' of market failure as providing 'only limited help in prescribing therapies for government success.' The government's failure to intervene in a market failure that would result in a socially preferable mix of output is similarly referred to as passive government failure. Just as with market failures, different kinds of government failures describe corresponding economic distortions.
Aggregation problem	An aggregate in economics is a summary measure describing a market or economy. The aggregation problem refers to the difficulty of treating an empirical or theoretical aggregate as if it reacted like a less-aggregated measure, say, about behavior of an individual agent as described in general microeconomic theory. Examples of aggregates in micro- and macroeconomics relative to less aggregated counterparts are:•food vs. apples•the price level and real GDP vs. the price and quantity of apples•the capital stock for the economy vs. the value of computers of a certain type and the value of steam shovels•the money supply vs.

5. Government`s Role and Government Failure

paper currency•the general unemployment rate vs. the unemployment rate of civil engineers.

Standard theory uses simple assumptions to derive general, and commonly accepted, results such as the law of demand to explain market behavior.

Collective action	Collective action is traditionally defined as any action taken together by a group of people whose goal is to enhance their status and achieve a common objective. It is enacted by a representative of the group. It is a term that has formulations and theories in many areas of the social sciences including psychology, sociology, political science and economics.
Baby Boomers	Baby boomers are people born during the demographic Post-World War II baby boom between the years 1946 and 1964. According to the U.S. Census Bureau, the term 'baby boomer' is also used in a cultural context. Therefore, it is impossible to achieve broad consensus of a precise date definition, even within a given territory. Different groups, organizations, individuals, and scholars may have widely varying opinions on what constitutes a baby boomer, both technically and culturally.
Inefficiency	The term inefficiency has several meanings depending on the context in which its used:•Distributive Inefficiency - refers to the inefficient distribution of income and wealth within a society. Decreasing marginal utilities of wealth suggests that more egalitarian distributions of wealth are more efficient than unegalitarian distributions. Distributive inefficiency is often associated with economic inequality.•Economic inefficiency - refers to a situation where 'we could be doing a better job,' i.e., attaining our goals at lower cost.
Bank of England	The Bank of England, formally the Governor and Company of the Bank of England, is the central bank of the United Kingdom and the model on which most modern central banks have been based. Established in 1694, it is the second oldest central bank in the world, after the Sveriges Riksbank, and the world's 8th oldest bank. It was established to act as the English Government's banker, and is still the banker for the Government of the United Kingdom.
Bank of Japan	The Bank of Japan is the central bank of Japan. The Bank is often called Nichigin for short. It has its headquarters in Chuo, Tokyo.
Business cycle	The term business cycle refers fluctuations in aggregate production, trade and activity over several months or years in a market economy. The business cycle is the upward and downward movements of levels of gross domestic product (GDP) and refers to the period of expansions and contractions in the level of economic activities (business fluctuations) around its long-term growth trend.

5. Government`s Role and Government Failure

Central bank	A central bank, reserve bank, or monetary authority is an institution that manages a state's currency, money supply, and interest rates. Central banks also usually oversee the commercial banking system of their respective countries. In contrast to a commercial bank, a central bank possesses a monopoly on increasing the amount of money in the nation, and usually also prints the national currency, which usually serves as the nation's legal tender.
European Central Bank	The European Central Bank is the central bank for the euro and administers the monetary policy of the Eurozone, which consists of 18 EU member states and is one of the largest currency areas in the world. It is one of the world's most important central banks and is one of the seven institutions of the European Union (EU) listed in the Treaty on European Union (TEU). The capital stock of the bank is owned by the central banks of all 28 EU member states.
Fiscal policy	In economics and political science, fiscal policy is the use of government revenue collection and expenditure (spending) to influence the economy, or else it involves the government changing the levels of taxation and government spending in order to influence Aggregrate Demand and the level of economic activity. The two main instruments of fiscal policy are changes in the level and composition of taxation and government spending in various sectors. These changes can affect the following macroeconomic variables in an economy:•Aggregate demand and the level of economic activity;•The distribution of income;•The pattern of resource allocation within the government sector and relative to the private sector. Fiscal policy refers to the use of the government budget to influence economic activity.
Monetary policy	Monetary policy is the process by which the monetary authority of a country controls the supply of money, often targeting a rate of interest for the purpose of promoting economic growth and stability. The official goals usually include relatively stable prices and low unemployment. Monetary economics provides insight into how to craft optimal monetary policy.
Public choice	Public choice theory has been described as 'the use of economic tools to deal with traditional problems of political science'. Its content includes the study of political behavior. In political science, it is the subset of positive political theory that models voters, politicians, and bureaucrats as mainly self-interested.
Freedom	Freedom is a London-based anarchist newspaper published monthly by Freedom Press ceasing print publication in 2014. The paper was started in 1886 by volunteers including Peter Kropotkin and Charlotte Wilson and continues to 2014 as an unpaid project. Originally, the subtitle was 'A Journal of Anarchist Socialism.' The title was changed to 'A Journal of Anarchist Communism' in June 1889. Today it is unlabelled.
Health insurance	Health insurance is insurance against the risk of incurring medical expenses among individuals.

5. Government's Role and Government Failure

	By estimating the overall risk of health care and health system expenses, among a targeted group, an insurer can develop a routine finance structure, such as a monthly premium or payroll tax, to ensure that money is available to pay for the health care benefits specified in the insurance agreement. The benefit is administered by a central organization such as a government agency, private business, or not-for-profit entity.
Stabilization policy	A stabilization policy is a package or set of measures introduced to stabilize a financial system or economy. The term can refer to policies in two distinct sets of circumstances: business cycle stabilization and crisis stabilization.
Deregulation	Deregulation is the process of removing or reducing state regulations. It is therefore opposite of regulation, which refers to the process of the government regulating certain activities.
Regulatory capture	Regulatory capture is a form of political corruption that occurs when a regulatory agency, created to act in the public interest, instead advances the commercial or special concerns of interest groups that dominate the industry or sector it is charged with regulating. Regulatory capture is a form of government failure; it creates an opening for firms to behave in ways injurious to the public (e.g., producing negative externalities). The agencies are called 'captured agencies'.
Intervention	Intervention, in terms of international law, is the term for the use of force by one country or sovereign state in the internal or external affairs of another. In most cases, intervention is considered to be an unlawfu. l
Corruption	In philosophical, theological, or moral discussions, corruption is spiritual or moral impurity or deviation from an ideal. Corruption may include many activities including bribery and embezzlement. Government, or 'political', corruption occurs when an office-holder or other governmental employee acts in an official capacity for personal gain.
Income	Income is the consumption and savings opportunity gained by an entity within a specified timeframe, which is generally expressed in monetary terms. However, for households and individuals, 'income is the sum of all the wages, salaries, profits, interests payments, rents and other forms of earnings received... in a given period of time.'
	In the field of public economics, the term may refer to the accumulation of both monetary and non-monetary consumption ability, with the former (monetary) being used as a proxy for total income.
Loan guarantee	A loan guarantee, in finance, is a promise by one party to assume the debt obligation of a borrower if that borrower defaults. A guarantee can be limited or unlimited, making the guarantor liable for only a portion or all of the debt.
	Guarantor mortgages are popular with young borrowers who do not have a large deposit saved and need to borrow 100% of the property value to purchase a property.

5. Government`s Role and Government Failure

National income	A variety of measures of national income and output are used in economics to estimate total economic activity in a country or region, including gross domestic product, gross national product (GNP), net national income and adjusted national income. All are specially concerned with counting the total amount of goods and services produced within some 'boundary'. The boundary is usually defined by geography or citizenship, and may also restrict the goods and services that are counted.
Product	In marketing, a product is anything that can be offered to a market that might satisfy a want or need. In retailing, products are called merchandise. In manufacturing, products are bought as raw materials and sold as finished goods.
Specialization	Specialization is the separation of tasks within a system. In a multicellular creature, cells are specialized for functions such as bone construction or oxygen transport. In capitalist societies, individual workers specialize for functions such as building construction or gasoline transport.
Emergency management	Disaster management (or emergency management) is the term used to designate the efforts of communities or businesses to plan for and coordinate all personnel and materials required to either mitigate the effects of, or recover from, natural or man-made disasters, or acts of terrorism. Disaster management does not avert or eliminate the threats, although their study is an important part of the field. Events covered by disaster management include acts of terrorism, industrial sabotage, fire, natural disasters (such as earthquakes, hurricanes, etc)., public disorder, industrial accidents, and communication failures.
Private good	A private good is defined in economics as 'an item that yields positive benefits to people' that is excludable, i.e. its owners can exercise private property rights, preventing those who have not paid for it from using the good or consuming its benefits; and rivalrous, i.e. consumption by one necessarily prevents that of another. A private good, as an economic resource is scarce, which can cause competition for it. The market demand curve for a private good is a horizontal summation of individual demand curves. Unlike public goods, private goods are less likely to have the free rider problem.
Public good	In economics, a public good is a good that is both non-excludable and non-rivalrous in that individuals cannot be effectively excluded from use and where use by one individual does not reduce availability to others. Examples of public goods include fresh air, knowledge, lighthouses, national defense, flood control systems and street lighting. Public goods that are available everywhere are sometimes referred to as global public goods.
Logrolling	Logrolling is the trading of favors, or quid pro quo, such as vote trading by legislative members to obtain passage of actions of interest to each legislative member. In an academic context, the Nuttall Encyclopedia describes logrolling as 'mutual praise by authors of each other's work.' In organizational analysis, it refers to a practice in which different organizations promote each other's agendas, each in the expectation that the other will reciprocate.

5. Government`s Role and Government Failure

Paradox of voting	The paradox of voting, also called Downs paradox, is that for a rational, self-interested voter, the costs of voting will normally exceed the expected benefits. Because the chance of exercising the pivotal vote (i.e., in an otherwise tied election) is minuscule compared to any realistic estimate of the private individual benefits of the different possible outcomes, the expected benefits of voting are less than the costs. The fact that people do vote is a problem for public choice theory, first observed by Anthony Downs.

1. An _____ is the rate at which interest is paid by a borrower for the use of money that they borrow from a lender (creditor). Specifically, the _____ is a percent of principal (P) paid a certain amount of times (m) per period (usually quoted per annum). For example, a small company borrows capital from a bank to buy new assets for its business, and in return the lender receives interest at a predetermined _____ for deferring the use of funds and instead lending it to the borrower.

   a. Bernanke doctrine
   b. Discretionary policy
   c. Interest rate
   d. Battle of Annaberg

2. _____ is traditionally defined as any action taken together by a group of people whose goal is to enhance their status and achieve a common objective. It is enacted by a representative of the group. It is a term that has formulations and theories in many areas of the social sciences including psychology, sociology, political science and economics.

   a. Banking lobby
   b. Bundling
   c. Bureaucratic drift
   d. Collective action

3. . _____ is the public-sector analogy to market failure and occurs when government intervention causes a more inefficient allocation of goods and resources than would occur without that intervention. In not comparing realized inadequacies of market outcomes against those of potential interventions, one writer describes the 'anatomy' of market failure as providing 'only limited help in prescribing therapies for government success.'

   The government's failure to intervene in a market failure that would result in a socially preferable mix of output is similarly referred to as passive _____. Just as with market failures, different kinds of _____s describe corresponding economic distortions.

   a. Bank Transfer Day

b. Bankruptcy

c. Base effect

d. Government failure

4. _____ is a form of political corruption that occurs when a regulatory agency, created to act in the public interest, instead advances the commercial or special concerns of interest groups that dominate the industry or sector it is charged with regulating. _____ is a form of government failure; it creates an opening for firms to behave in ways injurious to the public (e.g., producing negative externalities). The agencies are called 'captured agencies'.

a. Bio-inspired computing

b. Regulatory capture

c. Collaborative filtering

d. Collective behavior

5. The term _____ refers fluctuations in aggregate production, trade and activity over several months or years in a market economy.

The _____ is the upward and downward movements of levels of gross domestic product (GDP) and refers to the period of expansions and contractions in the level of economic activities (business fluctuations) around its long-term growth trend.

These fluctuations occur around a long-term growth trend, and typically involve shifts over time between periods of relatively rapid economic growth (an expansion or boom), and periods of relative stagnation or decline (a contraction or recession).

a. Business cycle

b. Battle of Annaberg

c. Freikorps Lichtschlag

d. Freikorps Oberland

1. c
2. d
3. d
4. b
5. a

You can take the complete Chapter Practice Test

for 5. Government`s Role and Government Failure
on all key terms, persons, places, and concepts.

Online 99 Cents

http://www.JustTheFacts101.com

Use www.JustTheFacts101.com for all your study needs

including Facts101's online interactive problem solving labs in

chemistry, statistics, mathematics, and more.

6. Elasticity

CHAPTER OUTLINE: KEY TERMS, PEOPLE, PLACES, CONCEPTS

Elasticity

Price elasticity

Total revenue

Demand curve

Lump-sum tax

Monopoly

Collective bargaining

Phillips curve

Short run

Inflation

Cross elasticity of demand

Complementary good

Independent goods

Substitute good

Pricing

Income elasticity of demand

Inferior good

Normal good

6. Elasticity

Elasticity	In economics, elasticity is the measurement of how responsive an economic variable is to a change in another. For example:•'If I lower the price of my product, how much more will I sell?'•'If I raise the price of one good, how will that affect sales of this other good?'•'If we learn that a resource is becoming scarce, will people scramble to acquire it?'
	An elastic variable (or elasticity value greater than 1) is one which responds more than proportionally to changes in other variables. In contrast, an inelastic variable (or elasticity value less than 1) is one which changes less than proportionally in response to changes in other variables.
Price elasticity	Price elasticity of demand is a measure used in economics to show the responsiveness, or elasticity, of the quantity demanded of a good or service to a change in its price. More precisely, it gives the percentage change in quantity demanded in response to a one percent change in price (ceteris paribus, i.e. holding constant all the other determinants of demand, such as income).
	Price elasticities are almost always negative, although analysts tend to ignore the sign even though this can lead to ambiguity.
Total revenue	Total revenue is the total receipts of a firm from the sale of any given quantity of a product.
	It can be calculated as the selling price of the firm's product times the quantity sold, i.e. total revenue = price × quantity, or letting TR be the total revenue function: $$TR(Q) = P(Q) \times Q$$ where Q is the quantity of output sold, and P(Q) is the inverse demand function (the demand function solved out for price in terms of quantity demanded).
Demand curve	In economics, the demand curve is the graph depicting the relationship between the price of a certain commodity and the amount of it that consumers are willing and able to purchase at that given price. It is a graphic representation of a demand schedule. The demand curve for all consumers together follows from the demand curve of every individual consumer: the individual demands at each price are added together.
Lump-sum tax	A lump-sum tax is a tax that is a fixed amount, no matter the change in circumstance of the taxed entity. (A lump-sum subsidy or lump-sum redistribution is defined similarly).
	It is one of the various modes used for taxation: income, things owned (property taxes), money spent (sales taxes), miscellaneous (excise taxes).

6. Elasticity

Monopoly	A monopoly (from Greek monos μ???? + polein p??e?? (to sell)) exists when a specific person or enterprise is the only supplier of a particular commodity (this contrasts with a monopsony which relates to a single entity's control of a market to purchase a good or service, and with oligopoly which consists of a few entities dominating an industry). Monopolies are thus characterized by a lack of economic competition to produce the good or service and a lack of viable substitute goods. The verb 'monopolize' refers to the process by which a company gains the ability to raise prices or exclude competitors.
Collective bargaining	Collaborative bargaining is a style of negotiation which recognises the interests of the other party and emphasises cooperation between them. It was especially promoted, practised and studied in the negotiations between school districts and teaching unions in the USA in the 1990s. It is compared and contrasted with more adversarial models of collective bargaining in which the parties may regard each other as enemies.
Phillips curve	In economics, the Phillips curve is a historical inverse relationship between rates of unemployment and corresponding rates of inflation that result in an economy. Stated simply, decreased unemployment, (i.e., increased levels of employment) in an economy will correlate with higher rates of inflation. While there is a short run tradeoff between unemployment and inflation, it has not been observed in the long run.
Short run	In microeconomics, the long run is the conceptual time period in which there are no fixed factors of production as to changing the output level by changing the capital stock or by entering or leaving an industry. The long run contrasts with the short run, in which some factors are variable and others are fixed, constraining entry or exit from an industry. In macroeconomics, the long run is the period when the general price level, contractual wage rates, and expectations adjust fully to the state of the economy, in contrast to the short run when these variables may not fully adjust.
Inflation	In economics, inflation is a sustained increase in the general price level of goods and services in an economy over a period of time. When the general price level rises, each unit of currency buys fewer goods and services. Consequently, inflation reflects a reduction in the purchasing power per unit of money - a loss of real value in the medium of exchange and unit of account within the economy.
Cross elasticity of demand	In economics, the cross elasticity of demand or cross-price elasticity of demand measures the responsiveness of the demand for a good to a change in the price of another good. It is measured as the percentage change in demand for the first good that occurs in response to a percentage change in price of the second good. For example, if, in response to a 10% increase in the price of fuel, the demand of new cars that are fuel inefficient decreased by 20%, the cross elasticity of demand would be:

6. Elasticity

Complementary good	In economics, a complementary good is a good with a negative cross elasticity of demand, in contrast to a substitute good. This means a good's demand is increased when the price of another good is decreased. Conversely, the demand for a good is decreased when the price of another good is increased.
Independent goods	Independent goods are goods that have a zero cross elasticity of demand. Changes in the price of one good will have no effect on the demand of an independent good. For example, a person's demand for nails is independent of his or her demand for bread, since they are two unrelated types of goods.
Substitute good	In economics, one way that two or more goods can be classified is by examining the relationship of the demand schedules when the price of one good changes. This relationship between demand schedules leads to classification of goods as either substitutes or complements. Substitute goods are goods which, as a result of changed conditions, may replace each other in use (or consumption).
Pricing	Pricing is the process of determining what a company will receive in exchange for its product. Pricing factors are manufacturing cost, market place, competition, market condition, brand, and quality of product. Pricing is also a key variable in microeconomic price allocation theory.
Income elasticity of demand	In economics, income elasticity of demand measures the responsiveness of the demand for a good to a change in the income of the people demanding the good, ceteris paribus. It is calculated as the ratio of the percentage change in demand to the percentage change in income. For example, if, in response to a 10% increase in income, the demand for a good increased by 20%, the income elasticity of demand would be 20%/10% = 2.
Inferior good	In economics, an inferior good is a good that decreases in demand when consumer income rises, unlike normal goods, for which the opposite is observed. Normal goods are those for which consumers' demand increases when their income increases. This would be the opposite of a superior good, one that is often associated with wealth and the wealthy, whereas an inferior good is often associated with lower socio-economic groups.
Normal good	In economics, normal goods are any goods for which demand increases when income increases, and falls when income decreases but price remains constant, i.e. with a positive income elasticity of demand. The term does not necessarily refer to the quality of the good, but an abnormal good would clearly not be in demand, except for possibly lower socioeconomic groups. In particular, when the price of a normal good is zero, the demand is infinite.

6. Elasticity

1. In economics, the _____ is a historical inverse relationship between rates of unemployment and corresponding rates of inflation that result in an economy. Stated simply, decreased unemployment, (i.e., increased levels of employment) in an economy will correlate with higher rates of inflation.

   While there is a short run tradeoff between unemployment and inflation, it has not been observed in the long run.

   a. Beveridge curve
   b. Budget constraint
   c. Cost curve
   d. Phillips curve

2. In economics, an _____ is a good that decreases in demand when consumer income rises, unlike normal goods, for which the opposite is observed. Normal goods are those for which consumers' demand increases when their income increases. This would be the opposite of a superior good, one that is often associated with wealth and the wealthy, whereas an _____ is often associated with lower socio-economic groups.

   a. Bad
   b. Case
   c. Inferior good
   d. Credence good

3. _____ is the total receipts of a firm from the sale of any given quantity of a product.

   It can be calculated as the selling price of the firm's product times the quantity sold, i.e. _____ = price × quantity, or letting TR be the _____ function: $TR(Q) = P(Q) \times Q$

   where Q is the quantity of output sold, and P(Q) is the inverse demand function (the demand function solved out for price in terms of quantity demanded).

   a. Base period
   b. Total revenue
   c. Blanket order
   d. Bond

4. . In economics, the _____ is the graph depicting the relationship between the price of a certain commodity and the amount of it that consumers are willing and able to purchase at that given price. It is a graphic representation of a demand schedule. The _____ for all consumers together follows from the _____ of every individual consumer: the individual demands at each price are added together.

   a. Beveridge curve
   b. Budget constraint
   c. Cost curve

5. In economics, _____ is the measurement of how responsive an economic variable is to a change in another. For example:•'If I lower the price of my product, how much more will I sell?'•'If I raise the price of one good, how will that affect sales of this other good?'•'If we learn that a resource is becoming scarce, will people scramble to acquire it?'

An elastic variable (or _____ value greater than 1) is one which responds more than proportionally to changes in other variables. In contrast, an inelastic variable (or _____ value less than 1) is one which changes less than proportionally in response to changes in other variables.

a. Elasticity
b. Bliss point
c. Club good
d. Conjectural variation

1. d
2. c
3. b
4. d
5. a

7. Utility Maximization

	Demand curve
	Marginal utility
	Utility
	Budget constraint
	Consumer choice
	Health insurance
	Opportunity cost
	Cardinal utility
	Indifference curve
	Marginal rate of substitution

Demand curve	In economics, the demand curve is the graph depicting the relationship between the price of a certain commodity and the amount of it that consumers are willing and able to purchase at that given price. It is a graphic representation of a demand schedule. The demand curve for all consumers together follows from the demand curve of every individual consumer: the individual demands at each price are added together.
Marginal utility	In economics, the marginal utility of a good or service is the gain from an increase or loss from a decrease in the consumption of that good or service. Economists sometimes speak of a law of diminishing marginal utility, meaning that the first unit of consumption of a good or service yields more utility than the second and subsequent units, with a continuing reduction for greater amounts. The marginal decision rule states that a good or service should be consumed at a quantity at which the marginal utility is equal to the marginal cost.
Utility	Utility, or usefulness, is the ability of something to satisfy needs or wants.

7. Utility Maximization

Utility is an important concept in economics and game theory, because it represents satisfaction experienced by the consumer of a good. Not coincidentally, a good is something that satisfies human wants and provides utility, for example, to a consumer making a purchase.

Budget constraint

A budget constraint represents all the combinations of goods and services that a consumer may purchase given current prices within his or her given income. Consumer theory uses the concepts of a budget constraint and a preference map to analyze consumer choices. Both concepts have a ready graphical representation in the two-good case.

Consumer choice

In microeconomics, the theory of consumer choice relates preferences to consumption expenditures; ultimately, this relationship between preferences and consumption expenditures is used to relate preferences to consumer demand curves. The link between personal preferences, consumption, and the demand curve is one of the most closely studied relations in economics. Consumer choice theory is a way of analyzing how consumers may achieve equilibrium between preferences and expenditures by maximizing utility as subject to consumer budget constraints.

Health insurance

Health insurance is insurance against the risk of incurring medical expenses among individuals. By estimating the overall risk of health care and health system expenses, among a targeted group, an insurer can develop a routine finance structure, such as a monthly premium or payroll tax, to ensure that money is available to pay for the health care benefits specified in the insurance agreement. The benefit is administered by a central organization such as a government agency, private business, or not-for-profit entity.

Opportunity cost

In microeconomic theory, the opportunity cost of a choice is the value of the best alternative forgone, in a situation in which a choice needs to be made between several mutually exclusive alternatives given limited resources. Assuming the best choice is made, it is the 'cost' incurred by not enjoying the benefit that would be had by taking the second best choice available. The New Oxford American Dictionary defines it as 'the loss of potential gain from other alternatives when one alternative is chosen'.

Cardinal utility

In economics, a cardinal utility function or scale is a utility index that preserves preference orderings uniquely up to positive affine transformations. Two utility indices are related by an affine transformation if for every value $u(x_1)$ of one index u, occurring at quantity x_1 of the goods bundle being evaluated, the corresponding value $v(x_1)$ of the other index v satisfies a relationship of the form $v(x_1) = au(x_1) + b$,

for fixed constants a and b. Thus the utility functions themselves are related by $v(x) = au(x) + b.$

The two indices differ only with respect to scale and origin.

7. Utility Maximization

Indifference curve	In microeconomic theory, an indifference curve is a graph showing different bundles of goods between which a consumer is indifferent. That is, at each point on the curve, the consumer has no preference for one bundle over another. One can equivalently refer to each point on the indifference curve as rendering the same level of utility (satisfaction) for the consumer.
Marginal rate of substitution	In economics, the marginal rate of substitution is the rate at which a consumer is ready to give up one good in exchange for another good while maintaining the same level of utility. At consumption levels, our marginal rates of substitution are identical.

1. In economics, the _____ is the graph depicting the relationship between the price of a certain commodity and the amount of it that consumers are willing and able to purchase at that given price. It is a graphic representation of a demand schedule. The _____ for all consumers together follows from the _____ of every individual consumer: the individual demands at each price are added together.

   a. Beveridge curve
   b. Demand curve
   c. Cost curve
   d. Fuel protests in the United Kingdom

2. In economics, a _____ function or scale is a utility index that preserves preference orderings uniquely up to positive affine transformations. Two utility indices are related by an affine transformation if for every value $u(x_1)$ of one index u, occurring at quantity x_1 of the goods bundle being evaluated, the corresponding value $v(x_1)$ of the other index v satisfies a relationship of the form $v(x_1) = au(x_1) + b$,

   for fixed constants a and b. Thus the utility functions themselves are related by $v(x) = au(x) + b.$

   The two indices differ only with respect to scale and origin.

   a. Fuel protests in the United Kingdom
   b. Battle of Annaberg
   c. Cardinal utility
   d. Freikorps Oberland

3. In economics, the _____ is the rate at which a consumer is ready to give up one good in exchange for another good while maintaining the same level of utility. At consumption levels, our marginal rates of substitution are identical.

    a. Budget set
    b. Marginal rate of substitution
    c. Consumer service
    d. Consumption

4. _____, or usefulness, is the ability of something to satisfy needs or wants. _____ is an important concept in economics and game theory, because it represents satisfaction experienced by the consumer of a good. Not coincidentally, a good is something that satisfies human wants and provides _____, for example, to a consumer making a purchase.

    a. Fuel protests in the United Kingdom
    b. Battle of Annaberg
    c. Freikorps Lichtschlag
    d. Utility

5. In economics, the _____ of a good or service is the gain from an increase or loss from a decrease in the consumption of that good or service. Economists sometimes speak of a law of diminishing _____, meaning that the first unit of consumption of a good or service yields more utility than the second and subsequent units, with a continuing reduction for greater amounts. The marginal decision rule states that a good or service should be consumed at a quantity at which the _____ is equal to the marginal cost.

    a. Marginal utility
    b. Bereavement benefit
    c. Biological standard of living
    d. Bodily integrity

1. b
2. c
3. b
4. d
5. a

You can take the complete Chapter Practice Test

for 7. Utility Maximization
on all key terms, persons, places, and concepts.

Online 99 Cents

http://www.JustTheFacts101.com

Use www.JustTheFacts101.com for all your study needs

including Facts101's online interactive problem solving labs in

chemistry, statistics, mathematics, and more.

8. Behavioral Economics

CHAPTER OUTLINE: KEY TERMS, PEOPLE, PLACES, CONCEPTS

	Behavioral economics
	Neoclassical economics
	Interest rate
	Prospect theory
	Hedonism
	Loss aversion
	Adverse selection
	Mental accounting
	Accounting
	Market system
	Poverty

CHAPTER HIGHLIGHTS & NOTES: KEY TERMS, PEOPLE, PLACES, CONCEPTS

Behavioral economics	Behavioral economics and the related field, behavioral finance, study the effects of social, cognitive, and emotional factors on the economic decisions of individuals and institutions and the consequences for market prices, returns, and the resource allocation. The fields are primarily concerned with the bounds of rationality of economic agents. Behavioral models typically integrate insights from psychology with microeconomic theory; in so doing, these behavioral models cover a range of concepts, methods, and fields.
Neoclassical economics	Neoclassical economics is a term variously used for approaches to economics focusing on the determination of prices, outputs, and income distributions in markets through supply and demand, often mediated through a hypothesized maximization of utility by income-constrained individuals and of profits by cost-constrained firms employing available information and factors of production, in accordance with rational choice theory.

	Neoclassical economics dominates microeconomics, and together with Keynesian economics forms the neoclassical synthesis which dominates mainstream economics today. Although neoclassical economics has gained widespread acceptance by contemporary economists, there have been many critiques of neoclassical economics, often incorporated into newer versions of neoclassical theory.
Interest rate	An interest rate is the rate at which interest is paid by a borrower for the use of money that they borrow from a lender (creditor). Specifically, the interest rate is a percent of principal (P) paid a certain amount of times (m) per period (usually quoted per annum). For example, a small company borrows capital from a bank to buy new assets for its business, and in return the lender receives interest at a predetermined interest rate for deferring the use of funds and instead lending it to the borrower.
Prospect theory	Prospect theory is a behavioral economic theory that describes the way people choose between probabilistic alternatives that involve risk, where the probabilities of outcomes are known. The theory states that people make decisions based on the potential value of losses and gains rather than the final outcome, and that people evaluate these losses and gains using certain heuristics. The model is descriptive: it tries to model real-life choices, rather than optimal decisions.
Hedonism	Hedonism is a school of thought that argues that pleasure is the only intrinsic good. In very simple terms, a hedonist strives to maximize net pleasure (pleasure minus pain).
	Ethical hedonism is the idea that all people have the right to do everything in their power to achieve the greatest amount of pleasure possible to them.
Loss aversion	In economics and decision theory, loss aversion refers to people's tendency to strongly prefer avoiding losses to acquiring gains. Some studies suggest that losses are twice as powerful, psychologically, as gains. Loss aversion was first demonstrated by Amos Tversky and Daniel Kahneman.
Adverse selection	Adverse selection, anti-selection, or negative selection is a term used in economics, insurance, risk management, and statistics. It refers to a market process in which undesired results occur when buyers and sellers have asymmetric information (access to different information); the 'bad' products or services are more likely to be selected. For example, a bank that sets one price for all of its checking account customers runs the risk of being adversely selected against by its low-balance, high-activity (and hence least profitable) customers.
Mental accounting	A concept first named by Richard Thaler, mental accounting attempts to describe the process whereby people code, categorize and evaluate economic outcomes.

8. Behavioral Economics

	One detailed application of mental accounting, the behavioral life cycle hypothesis (Shefrin & Thaler, 1988), posits that people mentally frame assets as belonging to either current income, current wealth or future income and this has implications for their behavior as the accounts are largely non-fungible and marginal propensity to consume out of each account is different.
Accounting	Accounting, or accountancy, is the measurement, processing and communication of financial information about economic entities. Accounting, which has been called the 'language of business', measures the results of an organization's economic activities and conveys this information to a variety of users including investors, creditors, management, and regulators. Practitioners of accounting are known as accountants.
Market system	A market system is any systematic process enabling many market players to bid and ask: helping bidders and sellers interact and make deals. It is not just the price mechanism but the entire system of regulation, qualification, credentials, reputations and clearing that surrounds that mechanism and makes it operate in a social context. Because a market system relies on the assumption that players are constantly involved and unequally enabled, a market system is distinguished specifically from a voting system where candidates seek the support of voters on a less regular basis.
Poverty	Poverty is general scarcity or dearth, or the state of one who lacks a certain amount of material possessions or money. Absolute poverty or destitution refers to the deprivation of basic human needs, which commonly includes food, water, sanitation, clothing, shelter, health care and education. Relative poverty is defined contextually as economic inequality in the location or society in which people live.

1. . A _____ is any systematic process enabling many market players to bid and ask: helping bidders and sellers interact and make deals. It is not just the price mechanism but the entire system of regulation, qualification, credentials, reputations and clearing that surrounds that mechanism and makes it operate in a social context.

   Because a _____ relies on the assumption that players are constantly involved and unequally enabled, a _____ is distinguished specifically from a voting system where candidates seek the support of voters on a less regular basis.

   a. Market system
   b. Breadwinner model
   c. British International Political Economy

2. _____ is a term variously used for approaches to economics focusing on the determination of prices, outputs, and income distributions in markets through supply and demand, often mediated through a hypothesized maximization of utility by income-constrained individuals and of profits by cost-constrained firms employing available information and factors of production, in accordance with rational choice theory.

_____ dominates microeconomics, and together with Keynesian economics forms the neoclassical synthesis which dominates mainstream economics today. Although _____ has gained widespread acceptance by contemporary economists, there have been many critiques of _____, often incorporated into newer versions of neoclassical theory.

a. Fuel protests in the United Kingdom
b. Neoclassical economics
c. Freikorps Lichtschlag
d. Freikorps Oberland

3. _____ is a behavioral economic theory that describes the way people choose between probabilistic alternatives that involve risk, where the probabilities of outcomes are known. The theory states that people make decisions based on the potential value of losses and gains rather than the final outcome, and that people evaluate these losses and gains using certain heuristics. The model is descriptive: it tries to model real-life choices, rather than optimal decisions.

a. Behavioral clustering
b. Blissful ignorance effect
c. Prospect theory
d. Canadian Index of Consumer Confidence

4. In economics and decision theory, _____ refers to people's tendency to strongly prefer avoiding losses to acquiring gains. Some studies suggest that losses are twice as powerful, psychologically, as gains. _____ was first demonstrated by Amos Tversky and Daniel Kahneman.

a. Loss aversion
b. Blissful ignorance effect
c. Buzz monitoring
d. Canadian Index of Consumer Confidence

5. . _____ is a school of thought that argues that pleasure is the only intrinsic good. In very simple terms, a hedonist strives to maximize net pleasure (pleasure minus pain).

Ethical _____ is the idea that all people have the right to do everything in their power to achieve the greatest amount of pleasure possible to them.

a. Consequentialism
b. Hedonism
c. The Collected Works of Jeremy Bentham

1. a
2. b
3. c
4. a
5. b

You can take the complete Chapter Practice Test

for 8. Behavioral Economics
on all key terms, persons, places, and concepts.

Online 99 Cents

http://www.JustTheFacts101.com

Use www.JustTheFacts101.com for all your study needs

including Facts101's online interactive problem solving labs in

chemistry, statistics, mathematics, and more.

9. Businesses and the Costs of Production

CHAPTER OUTLINE: KEY TERMS, PEOPLE, PLACES, CONCEPTS

Economic cost

Explicit cost

Implicit cost

Opportunity cost

Marginal utility

Long run

Phillips curve

Aggregate supply

Income

Instability

Diminishing returns

Marginal product

Production

Expression

Fixed cost

Total cost

Variable cost

Average fixed cost

Marginal cost

Sunk costs

Product

9. Businesses and the Costs of Production

CHAPTER OUTLINE: KEY TERMS, PEOPLE, PLACES, CONCEPTS

_____	Cost curve
_____	Economies of scale
_____	Diseconomies of scale
_____	Capital
_____	Specialization
_____	Minimum efficient scale
_____	Natural monopoly
_____	Interest rate
_____	Industrial Revolution
_____	Economic growth
_____	Health care
_____	Market price

CHAPTER HIGHLIGHTS & NOTES: KEY TERMS, PEOPLE, PLACES, CONCEPTS

Economic cost	The economic cost of a decision depends on both the cost of the alternative chosen and the benefit that the best alternative would have provided if chosen. Economic cost differs from accounting cost because it includes opportunity cost. As an example, consider the economic cost of attending college.
Explicit cost	An explicit cost is a direct payment made to others in the course of running a business, such as wage, rent and materials, as opposed to implicit costs, which are those where no actual payment is made. It is possible still to underestimate these costs, however: for example, pension contributions and other 'perks' must be taken into account when considering the cost of labour.

9. Businesses and the Costs of Production

Implicit cost	In economics, an implicit cost, also called an imputed cost, implied cost, or notional cost, is the opportunity cost equal to what a firm must give up in order to use factors which it neither purchases nor hires. It is the opposite of an explicit cost, which is borne directly. In other words, an implicit cost is any cost that results from using an asset instead of renting, selling, or lending it.
Opportunity cost	In microeconomic theory, the opportunity cost of a choice is the value of the best alternative forgone, in a situation in which a choice needs to be made between several mutually exclusive alternatives given limited resources. Assuming the best choice is made, it is the 'cost' incurred by not enjoying the benefit that would be had by taking the second best choice available. The New Oxford American Dictionary defines it as 'the loss of potential gain from other alternatives when one alternative is chosen'.
Marginal utility	In economics, the marginal utility of a good or service is the gain from an increase or loss from a decrease in the consumption of that good or service. Economists sometimes speak of a law of diminishing marginal utility, meaning that the first unit of consumption of a good or service yields more utility than the second and subsequent units, with a continuing reduction for greater amounts. The marginal decision rule states that a good or service should be consumed at a quantity at which the marginal utility is equal to the marginal cost.
Long run	In microeconomics, the long run is the conceptual time period in which there are no fixed factors of production as to changing the output level by changing the capital stock or by entering or leaving an industry. The long run contrasts with the short run, in which some factors are variable and others are fixed, constraining entry or exit from an industry. In macroeconomics, the long run is the period when the general price level, contractual wage rates, and expectations adjust fully to the state of the economy, in contrast to the short run when these variables may not fully adjust.
Phillips curve	In economics, the Phillips curve is a historical inverse relationship between rates of unemployment and corresponding rates of inflation that result in an economy. Stated simply, decreased unemployment, (i.e., increased levels of employment) in an economy will correlate with higher rates of inflation.

While there is a short run tradeoff between unemployment and inflation, it has not been observed in the long run. |
| Aggregate supply | In economics, aggregate supply is the total supply of goods and services that firms in a national economy plan on selling during a specific time period. It is the total amount of goods and services that firms are willing to sell at a given price level in an economy. |
| Income | Income is the consumption and savings opportunity gained by an entity within a specified timeframe, which is generally expressed in monetary terms. However, for households and individuals, 'income is the sum of all the wages, salaries, profits, interests payments, rents and other forms of earnings received... in a given period of time.' |

9. Businesses and the Costs of Production

	In the field of public economics, the term may refer to the accumulation of both monetary and non-monetary consumption ability, with the former (monetary) being used as a proxy for total income.
Instability	In numerous fields of study, the component of instability within a system is generally characterized by some of the outputs or internal states growing without bounds. Not all systems that are not stable are unstable; systems can also be marginally stable or exhibit limit cycle behavior.
	In control theory, a system is unstable if any of the roots of its characteristic equation has real part greater than zero (or if zero is a repeated root).
Diminishing returns	In economics, diminishing returns is the decrease in the marginal (per-unit) output of a production process as the amount of a single factor of production is increased, while the amounts of all other factors of production stay constant.
	The law of diminishing returns states that in all productive processes, adding more of one factor of production, while holding all others constant ('ceteris paribus'), will at some point yield lower per-unit returns. The law of diminishing returns does not imply that adding more of a factor will decrease the total production, a condition known as negative returns, though in fact this is common.
Marginal product	In economics and in particular neoclassical economics, the marginal product or marginal physical product of an input is the extra output that can be produced by using one more unit of the input (for instance, the difference in output when a firm's labor usage is increased from five to six units), assuming that the quantities of no other inputs to production change.
	The marginal product of a given input can be expressed as $$MP = \frac{\Delta Y}{\Delta X}$$ where ΔX is the change in the firm's use of the input (conventionally a one-unit change) and ΔY is the change in quantity of output produced. Note that the quantity Y of the 'product' is typically defined ignoring external costs and benefits.
Production	Production is a process of combining various material inputs and immaterial inputs in order to make something for consumption (the output). It is the act of creating output, a good or service which has value and contributes to the utility of individuals. Economic well-being is created in a production process, meaning all economic activities that aim directly or indirectly to satisfy human needs.
Expression	In mathematics, an expression is a finite combination of symbols that is well-formed according to rules that depend on the context.

Symbols can designate numbers (constants), variables, operations, functions, and other mathematical symbols, as well as punctuation, symbols of grouping, and other syntactic symbols. The use of expressions can range from the simple: $0 + 0$

to the complex: $$f(a) + \sum_{k=1}^{n} \frac{1}{k!} \frac{d^k}{dt^k}\bigg|_{t=0} f(u(t)) + \int_0^1 \frac{(1-t)^n}{n!} \frac{d^{n+1}}{dt^{n+1}} f(u(t))\, dt.$$

We can think of algebraic expressions as generalizations of common arithmetic operations that are formed by combining numbers, variables, and mathematical operations.

Fixed cost

In economics, fixed costs, indirect costs or overheads are business expenses that are not dependent on the level of goods or services produced by the business. They tend to be time-related, such as salaries or rents being paid per month, and are often referred to as overhead costs. This is in contrast to variable costs, which are volume-related (and are paid per quantity produced).

Total cost

In economics, and cost accounting, total cost describes the total economic cost of production and is made up of variable costs, which vary according to the quantity of a good produced and include inputs such as labor and raw materials, plus fixed costs, which are independent of the quantity of a good produced and include inputs (capital) that cannot be varied in the short term, such as buildings and machinery. Total cost in economics includes the total opportunity cost of each factor of production as part of its fixed or variable costs.

The rate at which total cost changes as the amount produced changes is called marginal cost.

Variable cost

Variable costs are costs that change in proportion to the good or service that a business produces. Variable costs are also the sum of marginal costs over all units produced. They can also be considered normal costs.

Average fixed cost

In economics, average fixed cost is the fixed costs of production (FC) divided by the quantity (Q) of output produced. Fixed costs are those costs that must be incurred in fixed quantity regardless of the level of output produced.

$$AFC = \frac{FC}{Q}.$$

Average fixed cost is a per-unit-of-output measure of fixed costs.

Marginal cost

In economics and finance, marginal cost is the change in the total cost that arises when the quantity produced has an increment by unit. That is, it is the cost of producing one more unit of a good.

9. Businesses and the Costs of Production

Sunk costs	In economics and business decision-making, a sunk cost is a retrospective cost that has already been incurred and cannot be recovered. Sunk costs are sometimes contrasted with prospective costs, which are future costs that may be incurred or changed if an action is taken. Both retrospective and prospective costs may be either fixed (continuous for as long as the business is in operation and unaffected by output volume) or variable (dependent on volume) costs.
Product	In marketing, a product is anything that can be offered to a market that might satisfy a want or need. In retailing, products are called merchandise. In manufacturing, products are bought as raw materials and sold as finished goods.
Cost curve	In economics, a cost curve is a graph of the costs of production as a function of total quantity produced. In a free market economy, productively efficient firms use these curves to find the optimal point of production (minimizing cost), and profit maximizing firms can use them to decide output quantities to achieve those aims. There are various types of cost curves, all related to each other, including total and average cost curves, and marginal ('for each additional unit') cost curves, which are equal to the differential of the total cost curves.
Economies of scale	In microeconomics, economies of scale are the cost advantages that enterprises obtain due to size, output, or scale of operation, with cost per unit of output generally decreasing with increasing scale as fixed costs are spread out over more units of output. Often operational efficiency is also greater with increasing scale, leading to lower variable cost as well. Economies of scale apply to a variety of organizational and business situations and at various levels, such as a business or manufacturing unit, plant or an entire enterprise.
Diseconomies of scale	Diseconomies of scale are the forces that cause larger firms and governments to produce goods and services at increased per-unit costs. The concept is the opposite of economies of scale.
Capital	In economics, capital goods, real capital, or capital assets are already-produced durable goods or any non-financial asset that is used in production of goods or services. Capital goods are not significantly consumed in the production process though they may depreciate. How a capital good or is maintained or returned to its pre-production state varies with the type of capital involved.
Specialization	Specialization is the separation of tasks within a system. In a multicellular creature, cells are specialized for functions such as bone construction or oxygen transport. In capitalist societies, individual workers specialize for functions such as building construction or gasoline transport.

9. Businesses and the Costs of Production

CHAPTER HIGHLIGHTS & NOTES: KEY TERMS, PEOPLE, PLACES, CONCEPTS

Minimum efficient scale	In industrial organization, the minimum efficient scale or efficient scale of production is the lowest point where the plant (or firm) can produce such that its long run average costs are minimized.
Natural monopoly	A monopoly is a firm which is the only one producing and selling a particular product. A natural monopoly is a monopoly in an industry in which it is most efficient (involving the lowest long-run average cost) for production to be concentrated in a single firm. This market situation gives the largest supplier in an industry, often the first supplier in a market, an overwhelming cost advantage over other actual and potential competitors, so a natural monopoly situation generally leads to an actual monopoly.
Interest rate	An interest rate is the rate at which interest is paid by a borrower for the use of money that they borrow from a lender (creditor). Specifically, the interest rate is a percent of principal (P) paid a certain amount of times (m) per period (usually quoted per annum). For example, a small company borrows capital from a bank to buy new assets for its business, and in return the lender receives interest at a predetermined interest rate for deferring the use of funds and instead lending it to the borrower.
Industrial Revolution	The Industrial Revolution was the transition to new manufacturing processes in the period from about 1760 to sometime between 1820 and 1840. This transition included going from hand production methods to machines, new chemical manufacturing and iron production processes, improved efficiency of water power, the increasing use of steam power and the development of machine tools. It also included the change from wood and other bio-fuels to coal.
	Textiles were the dominant industry of the Industrial Revolution in terms of employment, value of output and capital invested.
Economic growth	Economic growth is the increase in the market value of the goods and services produced by an economy over time. It is conventionally measured as the percent rate of increase in real gross domestic product, or real GDP. Of more importance is the growth of the ratio of GDP to population (GDP per capita), which is also called per capita income. An increase in per capita income is referred to as intensive growth.
Health care	Health care is the diagnosis, treatment, and prevention of disease, illness, injury, and other physical and mental impairments in human beings. Health care is delivered by practitioners in allied health, dentistry, midwifery-obstetrics, medicine, nursing, optometry, pharmacy, psychology and other care providers. It refers to the work done in providing primary care, secondary care, and tertiary care, as well as in public health.
Market price	In economics, market price is the economic price for which a good or service is offered in the marketplace. It is of interest mainly in the study of microeconomics. Market value and market price are equal only under conditions of market efficiency, equilibrium, and rational expectations.

9. Businesses and the Costs of Production

1. In microeconomic theory, the _____ of a choice is the value of the best alternative forgone, in a situation in which a choice needs to be made between several mutually exclusive alternatives given limited resources. Assuming the best choice is made, it is the 'cost' incurred by not enjoying the benefit that would be had by taking the second best choice available. The New Oxford American Dictionary defines it as 'the loss of potential gain from other alternatives when one alternative is chosen'.

   a. Opportunity cost
   b. Bliss point
   c. Club good
   d. Conjectural variation

2. In economics, a _____ is a graph of the costs of production as a function of total quantity produced. In a free market economy, productively efficient firms use these curves to find the optimal point of production (minimizing cost), and profit maximizing firms can use them to decide output quantities to achieve those aims. There are various types of _____s, all related to each other, including total and average _____s, and marginal ('for each additional unit') _____s, which are equal to the differential of the total _____s.

   a. Beveridge curve
   b. Budget constraint
   c. Cost curve
   d. Battle of Annaberg

3. In economics, _____ is the fixed costs of production (FC) divided by the quantity (Q) of output produced. Fixed costs are those costs that must be incurred in fixed quantity regardless of the level of output produced.

$$AFC = \frac{FC}{Q}.$$

   _____ is a per-unit-of-output measure of fixed costs.

   a. Fuel protests in the United Kingdom
   b. Battle of Annaberg
   c. Average fixed cost
   d. Freikorps Oberland

4. . In economics, an _____, also called an imputed cost, implied cost, or notional cost, is the opportunity cost equal to what a firm must give up in order to use factors which it neither purchases nor hires. It is the opposite of an explicit cost, which is borne directly. In other words, an _____ is any cost that results from using an asset instead of renting, selling, or lending it.

   a. Base period
   b. Benefit incidence
   c. Implicit cost

5. In microeconomics, _____ are the cost advantages that enterprises obtain due to size, output, or scale of operation, with cost per unit of output generally decreasing with increasing scale as fixed costs are spread out over more units of output.

Often operational efficiency is also greater with increasing scale, leading to lower variable cost as well.

_____ apply to a variety of organizational and business situations and at various levels, such as a business or manufacturing unit, plant or an entire enterprise.

a. Capacity utilization
b. Constant elasticity of transformation
c. Economies of scale
d. Diseconomies of scale

---

1. a
2. c
3. c
4. c
5. c

You can take the complete Chapter Practice Test

for 9. Businesses and the Costs of Production
on all key terms, persons, places, and concepts.

Online 99 Cents

http://www.JustTheFacts101.com

Use www.JustTheFacts101.com for all your study needs

including Facts101's online interactive problem solving labs in

chemistry, statistics, mathematics, and more.

10. Pure Competition in the Short Run

CHAPTER OUTLINE: KEY TERMS, PEOPLE, PLACES, CONCEPTS

_____ Market structure

_____ Monopolistic competition

_____ Oligopoly

_____ Free entry

_____ Exit

_____ Total revenue

_____ Expression

_____ Marginal revenue

_____ Revenue

_____ Phillips curve

_____ Profit maximization

_____ Short run

_____ Total cost

_____ Production

_____ Price level

10. Pure Competition in the Short Run

CHAPTER HIGHLIGHTS & NOTES: KEY TERMS, PEOPLE, PLACES, CONCEPTS

Market structure	In economics, market structure is the number of firms producing identical products which are homogeneous.
Monopolistic competition	Monopolistic competition is a type of imperfect competition such that many producers sell products that are differentiated from one another and hence are not perfect substitutes. In monopolistic competition, a firm takes the prices charged by its rivals as given and ignores the impact of its own prices on the prices of other firms. In the presence of coercive government, monopolistic competition will fall into government-granted monopoly.
Oligopoly	An oligopoly is a market form in which a market or industry is dominated by a small number of sellers . Oligopolies can result from various forms of collusion which reduce competition and lead to higher prices for consumers. With few sellers, each oligopolist is likely to be aware of the actions of the others.
Free entry	In economics, free entry is a condition in which firms can freely enter the market for an economic good by establishing production and beginning to sell the product. Free entry is implied by the perfect competition assumption that there are an unlimited number of buyers and sellers in a market. In conditions in which there is not a natural monopoly caused by unlimited economies of scale, free entry prevents any existing firm from maintaining a monopoly, which would restrict output and charge a higher price than a multi-firm market would.
Exit	Exit, in economics, means opting out of future transactions.
Total revenue	Total revenue is the total receipts of a firm from the sale of any given quantity of a product. It can be calculated as the selling price of the firm's product times the quantity sold, i.e. total revenue = price × quantity, or letting TR be the total revenue function: $$TR(Q) = P(Q) \times Q$$ where Q is the quantity of output sold, and P(Q) is the inverse demand function (the demand function solved out for price in terms of quantity demanded).
Expression	In mathematics, an expression is a finite combination of symbols that is well-formed according to rules that depend on the context. Symbols can designate numbers (constants), variables, operations, functions, and other mathematical symbols, as well as punctuation, symbols of grouping, and other syntactic symbols. The use of expressions can range from the simple: $0 + 0$ to the complex:

10. Pure Competition in the Short Run

CHAPTER HIGHLIGHTS & NOTES: KEY TERMS, PEOPLE, PLACES, CONCEPTS

$$\left. f(a) + \sum_{k=1}^{n} \frac{1}{k!} \frac{d^k}{dt^k} \right|_{t=0} f(u(t)) + \int_{0}^{1} \frac{(1-t)^n}{n!} \frac{d^{n+1}}{dt^{n+1}} f(u(t)) \, dt.$$

We can think of algebraic expressions as generalizations of common arithmetic operations that are formed by combining numbers, variables, and mathematical operations.

Marginal revenue	In microeconomics, marginal revenue is the additional revenue that will be generated by increasing product sales by 1 unit. It can also be described as the unit revenue the last item sold has generated for the firm. In a perfectly competitive market, the additional revenue generated by selling an additional unit of a good is equal to the price the firm is able to charge the buyer of the good.
Revenue	In business, revenue or turnover is income that a company receives from its normal business activities, usually from the sale of goods and services to customers. In many countries, revenue is referred to as turnover. Some companies receive revenue from interest, royalties, or other fees.
Phillips curve	In economics, the Phillips curve is a historical inverse relationship between rates of unemployment and corresponding rates of inflation that result in an economy. Stated simply, decreased unemployment, (i.e., increased levels of employment) in an economy will correlate with higher rates of inflation.
	While there is a short run tradeoff between unemployment and inflation, it has not been observed in the long run.
Profit maximization	In economics, profit maximization is the short run or long run process by which a firm determines the price and output level that returns the greatest profit. There are several approaches to this problem. The total revenue-total cost perspective relies on the fact that profit equals revenue minus cost and focuses on maximizing this difference, and the marginal revenue-marginal cost perspective is based on the fact that total profit reaches its maximum point where marginal revenue equals marginal cost.
Short run	In microeconomics, the long run is the conceptual time period in which there are no fixed factors of production as to changing the output level by changing the capital stock or by entering or leaving an industry. The long run contrasts with the short run, in which some factors are variable and others are fixed, constraining entry or exit from an industry. In macroeconomics, the long run is the period when the general price level, contractual wage rates, and expectations adjust fully to the state of the economy, in contrast to the short run when these variables may not fully adjust.

10. Pure Competition in the Short Run

Total cost	In economics, and cost accounting, total cost describes the total economic cost of production and is made up of variable costs, which vary according to the quantity of a good produced and include inputs such as labor and raw materials, plus fixed costs, which are independent of the quantity of a good produced and include inputs (capital) that cannot be varied in the short term, such as buildings and machinery. Total cost in economics includes the total opportunity cost of each factor of production as part of its fixed or variable costs. The rate at which total cost changes as the amount produced changes is called marginal cost.
Production	Production is a process of combining various material inputs and immaterial inputs in order to make something for consumption (the output). It is the act of creating output, a good or service which has value and contributes to the utility of individuals. Economic well-being is created in a production process, meaning all economic activities that aim directly or indirectly to satisfy human needs.
Price level	The general price level is a hypothetical measure of overall prices for some set of goods and services, in a given region during a given interval, normalized relative to some base set. Typically, a price level is approximated with a price index.

1. In economics, _____ is the number of firms producing identical products which are homogeneous.

   a. Fuel protests in the United Kingdom
   b. Battle of Annaberg
   c. Market structure
   d. Freikorps Oberland

2. . In economics, _____ is a condition in which firms can freely enter the market for an economic good by establishing production and beginning to sell the product.

   _____ is implied by the perfect competition assumption that there are an unlimited number of buyers and sellers in a market. In conditions in which there is not a natural monopoly caused by unlimited economies of scale, _____ prevents any existing firm from maintaining a monopoly, which would restrict output and charge a higher price than a multi-firm market would.

   a. Countervailing power
   b. Dorfman-Steiner Theorem
   c. Free entry

10. Pure Competition in the Short Run

3. In business, _____ or turnover is income that a company receives from its normal business activities, usually from the sale of goods and services to customers. In many countries, _____ is referred to as turnover. Some companies receive _____ from interest, royalties, or other fees.

   a. Revenue
   b. Bliss point
   c. Club good
   d. Conjectural variation

4. _____ is a type of imperfect competition such that many producers sell products that are differentiated from one another and hence are not perfect substitutes. In _____, a firm takes the prices charged by its rivals as given and ignores the impact of its own prices on the prices of other firms. In the presence of coercive government, _____ will fall into government-granted monopoly.

   a. Cellophane paradox
   b. Monopolistic competition
   c. Deregulation
   d. Disequilibrium

5. An _____ is a market form in which a market or industry is dominated by a small number of sellers . _____ (ies) can result from various forms of collusion which reduce competition and lead to higher prices for consumers.

   With few sellers, each oligopolist is likely to be aware of the actions of the others.

   a. Oligopoly
   b. Competition
   c. Deregulation
   d. Disequilibrium

1. c
2. c
3. a
4. b
5. a

You can take the complete Chapter Practice Test

for 10. Pure Competition in the Short Run
on all key terms, persons, places, and concepts.

Online 99 Cents

http://www.JustTheFacts101.com

Use www.JustTheFacts101.com for all your study needs

including Facts101's online interactive problem solving labs in

chemistry, statistics, mathematics, and more.

11. Pure Competition in the Long Run

CHAPTER OUTLINE: KEY TERMS, PEOPLE, PLACES, CONCEPTS

Phillips curve

Long run

Free entry

Opportunity cost

Cost approach

Exit

Price level

Profit maximization

Interest rate

Allocative efficiency

Productive efficiency

Market system

Creative destruction

Life expectancy

11. Pure Competition in the Long Run

Phillips curve	In economics, the Phillips curve is a historical inverse relationship between rates of unemployment and corresponding rates of inflation that result in an economy. Stated simply, decreased unemployment, (i.e., increased levels of employment) in an economy will correlate with higher rates of inflation. While there is a short run tradeoff between unemployment and inflation, it has not been observed in the long run.
Long run	In microeconomics, the long run is the conceptual time period in which there are no fixed factors of production as to changing the output level by changing the capital stock or by entering or leaving an industry. The long run contrasts with the short run, in which some factors are variable and others are fixed, constraining entry or exit from an industry. In macroeconomics, the long run is the period when the general price level, contractual wage rates, and expectations adjust fully to the state of the economy, in contrast to the short run when these variables may not fully adjust.
Free entry	In economics, free entry is a condition in which firms can freely enter the market for an economic good by establishing production and beginning to sell the product. Free entry is implied by the perfect competition assumption that there are an unlimited number of buyers and sellers in a market. In conditions in which there is not a natural monopoly caused by unlimited economies of scale, free entry prevents any existing firm from maintaining a monopoly, which would restrict output and charge a higher price than a multi-firm market would.
Opportunity cost	In microeconomic theory, the opportunity cost of a choice is the value of the best alternative forgone, in a situation in which a choice needs to be made between several mutually exclusive alternatives given limited resources. Assuming the best choice is made, it is the 'cost' incurred by not enjoying the benefit that would be had by taking the second best choice available. The New Oxford American Dictionary defines it as 'the loss of potential gain from other alternatives when one alternative is chosen'.
Cost approach	In real estate appraisal, the cost approach is one of three basic valuation methods. The others are market, or sale comparison, and income. The fundamental premise of the cost approach is that a potential user of real estate won't, or shouldn't, pay more for a property than it would cost to build an equivalent.
Exit	Exit, in economics, means opting out of future transactions.
Price level	The general price level is a hypothetical measure of overall prices for some set of goods and services, in a given region during a given interval, normalized relative to some base set. Typically, a price level is approximated with a price index.

Profit maximization	In economics, profit maximization is the short run or long run process by which a firm determines the price and output level that returns the greatest profit. There are several approaches to this problem. The total revenue-total cost perspective relies on the fact that profit equals revenue minus cost and focuses on maximizing this difference, and the marginal revenue-marginal cost perspective is based on the fact that total profit reaches its maximum point where marginal revenue equals marginal cost.
Interest rate	An interest rate is the rate at which interest is paid by a borrower for the use of money that they borrow from a lender (creditor). Specifically, the interest rate is a percent of principal (P) paid a certain amount of times (m) per period (usually quoted per annum). For example, a small company borrows capital from a bank to buy new assets for its business, and in return the lender receives interest at a predetermined interest rate for deferring the use of funds and instead lending it to the borrower.
Allocative efficiency	Allocative efficiency is a type of economic efficiency in which economy/producers produce only those types of goods and services that are more desirable in the society and also in high demand. According to the formula the point of allocative efficiency is a point where price is equal to marginal cost (P=MC)or (MC=MR). At this point the social surplus is maximized with no deadweight loss, or the value society puts on that level of output produced minus the value of resources used to achieve that level, yet can be applied to other things such as level of pollution.
Productive efficiency	Productive efficiency occurs when the economy is using all of its resources efficiently. The concept is illustrated on a production possibility frontier (PPF) where all points on the curve are points of maximum productive efficiency. An equilibrium may be productively efficient without being allocatively efficient-- i.e. it may result in a distribution of goods where social welfare is not maximized.
Market system	A market system is any systematic process enabling many market players to bid and ask: helping bidders and sellers interact and make deals. It is not just the price mechanism but the entire system of regulation, qualification, credentials, reputations and clearing that surrounds that mechanism and makes it operate in a social context. Because a market system relies on the assumption that players are constantly involved and unequally enabled, a market system is distinguished specifically from a voting system where candidates seek the support of voters on a less regular basis.
Creative destruction	Creative destruction, sometimes known as Schumpeter's gale, is a term in economics which has since the 1950s become most readily identified with the Austrian American economist Joseph Schumpeter's theory of economic innovation and business cycle. Creative destruction describes the 'process of industrial mutation that incessantly revolutionizes the economic structure from within, incessantly destroying the old one, incessantly creating a new one.'

11. Pure Competition in the Long Run

The German Marxist sociologist Werner Sombart who has been credited with the first use of these terms in his work Krieg und Kapitalismus ('War and Capitalism', 1913). In the earlier work of Marx, however, the idea of creative destruction or annihilation (German: Vernichtung) implies not only that capitalism destroys and reconfigures previous economic orders, but also that it must ceaselessly devalue existing wealth (whether through war, dereliction, or regular and periodic economic crises) in order to clear the ground for the creation of new wealth.

Life expectancy	Life expectancy is the expected number of years of life remaining at a given age. It is denoted by e_x, which means the average number of subsequent years of life for someone now aged x, according to a particular mortality experience. Because life expectancy is an average, a particular person may well die many years before or many years after their 'expected' survival.

1. _____ is the expected number of years of life remaining at a given age. It is denoted by e_x, which means the average number of subsequent years of life for someone now aged x, according to a particular mortality experience. Because _____ is an average, a particular person may well die many years before or many years after their 'expected' survival.

   a. Baby boom
   b. Birth rate
   c. Childfree
   d. Life expectancy

2. The general _____ is a hypothetical measure of overall prices for some set of goods and services, in a given region during a given interval, normalized relative to some base set. Typically, a _____ is approximated with a price index.

   a. Price level
   b. Care work
   c. Cash collection
   d. Commercial location development

3. . _____ is a type of economic efficiency in which economy/producers produce only those types of goods and services that are more desirable in the society and also in high demand. According to the formula the point of _____ is a point where price is equal to marginal cost (P=MC)or (MC=MR). At this point the social surplus is maximized with no deadweight loss, or the value society puts on that level of output produced minus the value of resources used to achieve that level, yet can be applied to other things such as level of pollution.

a. Allocative efficiency
b. Bachelor tax
c. Banking Cash Transaction Tax
d. Brick tax

4. In microeconomics, the _____ is the conceptual time period in which there are no fixed factors of production as to changing the output level by changing the capital stock or by entering or leaving an industry. The _____ contrasts with the short run, in which some factors are variable and others are fixed, constraining entry or exit from an industry. In macroeconomics, the _____ is the period when the general price level, contractual wage rates, and expectations adjust fully to the state of the economy, in contrast to the short run when these variables may not fully adjust.

a. Long run
b. Fuel protests in the United Kingdom
c. Battle of Annaberg
d. Demand curve

5. In economics, the _____ is a historical inverse relationship between rates of unemployment and corresponding rates of inflation that result in an economy. Stated simply, decreased unemployment, (i.e., increased levels of employment) in an economy will correlate with higher rates of inflation.

While there is a short run tradeoff between unemployment and inflation, it has not been observed in the long run.

a. Beveridge curve
b. Budget constraint
c. Phillips curve
d. Demand curve

1. d

2. a

3. a

4. a

5. c

12. Pure Monopoly

_____ | Barriers to entry

_____ | First Data

_____ | Western Union

_____ | Monopoly

_____ | Pricing

_____ | Natural monopoly

_____ | Economies of scale

_____ | Federal Communications Commission

_____ | Leverage

_____ | Collusion

_____ | Fiscal policy

_____ | Intellectual property

_____ | Marginal revenue

_____ | Revenue

_____ | Price elasticity

_____ | Total revenue

_____ | Elasticity

_____ | Productive efficiency

_____ | Interest rate

_____ | Allocative efficiency

_____ | Income

12. Pure Monopoly

CHAPTER OUTLINE: KEY TERMS, PEOPLE, PLACES, CONCEPTS

	Minimum efficient scale
	National income
	Network effect
	Product
	Transfer payment
	X-inefficiency
	Total cost
	Lenovo
	Multinational corporation
	Panasonic
	Price discrimination
	Occupational segregation

CHAPTER HIGHLIGHTS & NOTES: KEY TERMS, PEOPLE, PLACES, CONCEPTS

Barriers to entry	In theories of competition in economics, barriers to entry, also known as barrier to entry, are obstacles that make it difficult to enter a given market. The term can refer to hindrances a firm faces in trying to enter a market or industry--such as government regulation and patents, or a large, established firm taking advantage of economies of scale--or those an individual faces in trying to gain entrance to a profession--such as education or licensing requirements. Because barriers to entry protect incumbent firms and restrict competition in a market, they can contribute to distortionary prices.
First Data	First Data Corporation is a global payment processing company headquartered in Atlanta, Georgia, United States. First Data is a provider of electronic commerce and payment solutions.

12. Pure Monopoly

Western Union	The Western Union Company is a financial services and communications company based in the United States. Its North American headquarters is in Meridian, Colorado, though the postal designation of nearby Englewood is used in its mailing address. Up until it discontinued the service in 2006, Western Union was the best-known U.S. company in the business of exchanging telegrams.
Monopoly	A monopoly (from Greek monos μ???? + polein p??e?? (to sell)) exists when a specific person or enterprise is the only supplier of a particular commodity (this contrasts with a monopsony which relates to a single entity's control of a market to purchase a good or service, and with oligopoly which consists of a few entities dominating an industry). Monopolies are thus characterized by a lack of economic competition to produce the good or service and a lack of viable substitute goods. The verb 'monopolize' refers to the process by which a company gains the ability to raise prices or exclude competitors.
Pricing	Pricing is the process of determining what a company will receive in exchange for its product. Pricing factors are manufacturing cost, market place, competition, market condition, brand, and quality of product. Pricing is also a key variable in microeconomic price allocation theory.
Natural monopoly	A monopoly is a firm which is the only one producing and selling a particular product. A natural monopoly is a monopoly in an industry in which it is most efficient (involving the lowest long-run average cost) for production to be concentrated in a single firm. This market situation gives the largest supplier in an industry, often the first supplier in a market, an overwhelming cost advantage over other actual and potential competitors, so a natural monopoly situation generally leads to an actual monopoly.
Economies of scale	In microeconomics, economies of scale are the cost advantages that enterprises obtain due to size, output, or scale of operation, with cost per unit of output generally decreasing with increasing scale as fixed costs are spread out over more units of output. Often operational efficiency is also greater with increasing scale, leading to lower variable cost as well. Economies of scale apply to a variety of organizational and business situations and at various levels, such as a business or manufacturing unit, plant or an entire enterprise.
Federal Communications Commission	The Federal Communications Commission is an independent agency of the United States government, created by Congressional statute to regulate interstate and international communications by radio, television, wire, satellite, and cable in all 50 states, the District of Columbia and U.S. territories. The Federal Communications Commission works towards six goals in the areas of broadband, competition, the spectrum, the media, public safety and homeland security. The Commission is also in the process of modernizing itself.

12. Pure Monopoly

Leverage	In finance, leverage is a general term for any technique to multiply gains and losses. Most often this involves buying more of an asset by using borrowed funds. The belief is that the income from the asset will be more than the pay for the cost of borrowing.
Collusion	Collusion is an agreement between two or more parties, sometimes illegal and therefore secretive, to limit open competition by deceiving, misleading, or defrauding others of their legal rights, or to obtain an objective forbidden by law typically by defrauding or gaining an unfair advantage. It is an agreement among firms or individuals to divide a market, set prices, limit production or limit opportunities. It can involve 'wage fixing, kickbacks, or misrepresenting the independence of the relationship between the colluding parties'.
Fiscal policy	In economics and political science, fiscal policy is the use of government revenue collection and expenditure (spending) to influence the economy, or else it involves the government changing the levels of taxation and government spending in order to influence Aggregrate Demand and the level of economic activity. The two main instruments of fiscal policy are changes in the level and composition of taxation and government spending in various sectors. These changes can affect the following macroeconomic variables in an economy:•Aggregate demand and the level of economic activity;•The distribution of income;•The pattern of resource allocation within the government sector and relative to the private sector.

Fiscal policy refers to the use of the government budget to influence economic activity. |
Intellectual property	Intellectual property rights are the legally recognized exclusive rights to creations of the mind. Under intellectual property law, owners are granted certain exclusive rights to a variety of intangible assets, such as musical, literary, and artistic works; discoveries and inventions; and words, phrases, symbols, and designs. Common types of intellectual property rights include copyright, trademarks, patents, industrial design rights, trade dress, and in some jurisdictions trade secrets.
Marginal revenue	In microeconomics, marginal revenue is the additional revenue that will be generated by increasing product sales by 1 unit. It can also be described as the unit revenue the last item sold has generated for the firm. In a perfectly competitive market, the additional revenue generated by selling an additional unit of a good is equal to the price the firm is able to charge the buyer of the good.
Revenue	In business, revenue or turnover is income that a company receives from its normal business activities, usually from the sale of goods and services to customers. In many countries, revenue is referred to as turnover. Some companies receive revenue from interest, royalties, or other fees.
Price elasticity	Price elasticity of demand is a measure used in economics to show the responsiveness, or elasticity, of the quantity demanded of a good or service to a change in its price. More precisely, it gives the percentage change in quantity demanded in response to a one percent change in price (ceteris paribus, i.e. holding constant all the other determinants of demand, such as income).

12. Pure Monopoly

Total revenue	Total revenue is the total receipts of a firm from the sale of any given quantity of a product. It can be calculated as the selling price of the firm's product times the quantity sold, i.e. total revenue = price × quantity, or letting TR be the total revenue function: $$TR(Q) = P(Q) \times Q$$ where Q is the quantity of output sold, and P(Q) is the inverse demand function (the demand function solved out for price in terms of quantity demanded).
Elasticity	In economics, elasticity is the measurement of how responsive an economic variable is to a change in another. For example:•'If I lower the price of my product, how much more will I sell?'•'If I raise the price of one good, how will that affect sales of this other good?'•'If we learn that a resource is becoming scarce, will people scramble to acquire it?' An elastic variable (or elasticity value greater than 1) is one which responds more than proportionally to changes in other variables. In contrast, an inelastic variable (or elasticity value less than 1) is one which changes less than proportionally in response to changes in other variables.
Productive efficiency	Productive efficiency occurs when the economy is using all of its resources efficiently. The concept is illustrated on a production possibility frontier (PPF) where all points on the curve are points of maximum productive efficiency. An equilibrium may be productively efficient without being allocatively efficient-- i.e. it may result in a distribution of goods where social welfare is not maximized.
Interest rate	An interest rate is the rate at which interest is paid by a borrower for the use of money that they borrow from a lender (creditor). Specifically, the interest rate is a percent of principal (P) paid a certain amount of times (m) per period (usually quoted per annum). For example, a small company borrows capital from a bank to buy new assets for its business, and in return the lender receives interest at a predetermined interest rate for deferring the use of funds and instead lending it to the borrower.
Allocative efficiency	Allocative efficiency is a type of economic efficiency in which economy/producers produce only those types of goods and services that are more desirable in the society and also in high demand. According to the formula the point of allocative efficiency is a point where price is equal to marginal cost (P=MC)or (MC=MR). At this point the social surplus is maximized with no deadweight loss, or the value society puts on that level of output produced minus the value of resources used to achieve that level, yet can be applied to other things such as level of pollution.
Income	Income is the consumption and savings opportunity gained by an entity within a specified timeframe, which is generally expressed in monetary terms.

	However, for households and individuals, 'income is the sum of all the wages, salaries, profits, interests payments, rents and other forms of earnings received... in a given period of time.' In the field of public economics, the term may refer to the accumulation of both monetary and non-monetary consumption ability, with the former (monetary) being used as a proxy for total income.
Minimum efficient scale	In industrial organization, the minimum efficient scale or efficient scale of production is the lowest point where the plant (or firm) can produce such that its long run average costs are minimized.
National income	A variety of measures of national income and output are used in economics to estimate total economic activity in a country or region, including gross domestic product, gross national product (GNP), net national income and adjusted national income. All are specially concerned with counting the total amount of goods and services produced within some 'boundary'. The boundary is usually defined by geography or citizenship, and may also restrict the goods and services that are counted.
Network effect	In economics and business, a network effect is the effect that one user of a good or service has on the value of that product to other people. When network effect is present, the value of a product or service is dependent on the number of others using it. The classic example is the telephone.
Product	In marketing, a product is anything that can be offered to a market that might satisfy a want or need. In retailing, products are called merchandise. In manufacturing, products are bought as raw materials and sold as finished goods.
Transfer payment	In economics, a transfer payment is a redistribution of income in the market system. These payments are considered to be non-exhaustive because they do not directly absorb resources or create output. In other words, the transfer is made without any exchange of goods or services.
X-inefficiency	X-inefficiency is the difference between efficient behavior of businesses assumed or implied by economic theory and their observed behavior in practice. It occurs when technical-efficiency is not being achieved due to a lack of competitive pressure. The concepts of x-inefficiency were introduced by Harvey Leibenstein.
Total cost	In economics, and cost accounting, total cost describes the total economic cost of production and is made up of variable costs, which vary according to the quantity of a good produced and include inputs such as labor and raw materials, plus fixed costs, which are independent of the quantity of a good produced and include inputs (capital) that cannot be varied in the short term, such as buildings and machinery. Total cost in economics includes the total opportunity cost of each factor of production as part of its fixed or variable costs. The rate at which total cost changes as the amount produced changes is called marginal cost.

12. Pure Monopoly

Lenovo	Lenovo Group Ltd. is a Chinese multinational technology company with headquarters in Beijing, China, and Morrisville, North Carolina, United States. It designs, develops, manufactures and sells personal computers, tablet computers, smartphones, workstations, servers, electronic storage devices, IT management software and smart televisions.
Multinational corporation	A multinational corporation or multinational enterprise (MNE) are organizations that own or control production or services facilities in one or more countries other than the home country. For example, when a corporation that is registered in more than one country or that has operations in more than one country may be attributed as MNC. Usually, it is a large corporation which both produces and sells goods or services in various countries. It can also be referred to as an international corporation.
Panasonic	Panasonic is the principal brand name of the Japanese electronics manufacturer Panasonic Corporation. The company sells a wide range of products under the brand worldwide, including plasma and LCD televisions, DVD and Blu-ray Disc recorders and players, camcorders, telephones, vacuum cleaners, microwave ovens, shavers, projectors, digital cameras, batteries, laptop computers (under the sub-brand Toughbook), CD players and home stereo equipment, fax machines, scanners, printers, electronic white-boards, electronic components and semiconductors. The brand uses the marketing slogan 'Ideas for Life'.
Price discrimination	Price discrimination or price differentiation is a pricing strategy where identical or largely similar goods or services are transacted at different prices by the same provider in different markets or territories. Price differentiation is distinguished from product differentiation by the more substantial difference in production cost for the differently priced products involved in the latter strategy. Price differentiation essentially relies on the variation in the customers' willingness to pay.
Occupational segregation	Occupational segregation is the distribution of people based upon demographic characteristics, most often gender, both across and within occupations and jobs. Occupational segregation levels differ on a basis of perfect segregation and integration. Perfect segregation occurs where any given occupation employs only one group.

12. Pure Monopoly

1. The _____ Company is a financial services and communications company based in the United States. Its North American headquarters is in Meridian, Colorado, though the postal designation of nearby Englewood is used in its mailing address. Up until it discontinued the service in 2006, _____ was the best-known U.S. company in the business of exchanging telegrams.

   a. Pemex
   b. Western Union
   c. Fuel protests in the United Kingdom
   d. Battle of Annaberg

2. A monopoly is a firm which is the only one producing and selling a particular product. A _____ is a monopoly in an industry in which it is most efficient (involving the lowest long-run average cost) for production to be concentrated in a single firm. This market situation gives the largest supplier in an industry, often the first supplier in a market, an overwhelming cost advantage over other actual and potential competitors, so a _____ situation generally leads to an actual monopoly.

   a. Coercive monopoly
   b. Common-pool resource
   c. Free rider problem
   d. Natural monopoly

3. In economics and political science, _____ is the use of government revenue collection and expenditure (spending) to influence the economy, or else it involves the government changing the levels of taxation and government spending in order to influence Aggregate Demand and the level of economic activity. The two main instruments of _____ are changes in the level and composition of taxation and government spending in various sectors. These changes can affect the following macroeconomic variables in an economy:•Aggregate demand and the level of economic activity;•The distribution of income;•The pattern of resource allocation within the government sector and relative to the private sector.

   _____ refers to the use of the government budget to influence economic activity.

   a. Barnett formula
   b. Budget freeze
   c. Fiscal policy
   d. California Municipal Treasurers Association

4. . A _____ (from Greek monos μ???? + polein p??e?? (to sell)) exists when a specific person or enterprise is the only supplier of a particular commodity (this contrasts with a monopsony which relates to a single entity's control of a market to purchase a good or service, and with oligopoly which consists of a few entities dominating an industry). _____(ies) are thus characterized by a lack of economic competition to produce the good or service and a lack of viable substitute goods. The verb 'monopolize' refers to the process by which a company gains the ability to raise prices or exclude competitors.

   a. Monopoly
   b. Competition
   c. Deregulation

12. Pure Monopoly

5. _____ Corporation is a global payment processing company headquartered in Atlanta, Georgia, United States. _____ is a provider of electronic commerce and payment solutions. The company's portfolio includes merchant transaction processing services; credit, debit, private-label, gift, payroll and other prepaid card offerings; fraud protection and authentication solutions, credit reporting agency services (through _____ Merchant Services Corporation); electronic check acceptance services through TeleCheck; as well as Internet commerce and mobile payment solutions.

   a. 1LINK
   b. First Data
   c. BACHO record format
   d. Bankgiro

---

1. b
2. d
3. c
4. a
5. b

---

13. Monopolistic Competition and Oligopoly

CHAPTER OUTLINE: KEY TERMS, PEOPLE, PLACES, CONCEPTS

	Game theory
	Monopolistic competition
	Product
	Collusion
	Adverse selection
	Brain drain
	Exit
	Herfindahl index
	Demand curve
	Phillips curve
	Allocative efficiency
	Productive efficiency
	Interest rate
	Product market
	Variable cost
	Clinique
	Oligopoly
	Economic growth
	Economies of scale
	Menu cost
	International trade

13. Monopolistic Competition and Oligopoly

	Diversity
	Incentive
	Kinked demand
	Cartel
	OPEC
	Panasonic
	Production
	Recession
	Pricing
	Barriers to entry
	First-mover advantage

CHAPTER HIGHLIGHTS & NOTES: KEY TERMS, PEOPLE, PLACES, CONCEPTS

Game theory	Game theory is a study of strategic decision making. Specifically, it is 'the study of mathematical models of conflict and cooperation between intelligent rational decision-makers'. An alternative term suggested 'as a more descriptive name for the discipline' is interactive decision theory.
Monopolistic competition	Monopolistic competition is a type of imperfect competition such that many producers sell products that are differentiated from one another and hence are not perfect substitutes. In monopolistic competition, a firm takes the prices charged by its rivals as given and ignores the impact of its own prices on the prices of other firms. In the presence of coercive government, monopolistic competition will fall into government-granted monopoly.
Product	In marketing, a product is anything that can be offered to a market that might satisfy a want or need. In retailing, products are called merchandise.

Collusion	Collusion is an agreement between two or more parties, sometimes illegal and therefore secretive, to limit open competition by deceiving, misleading, or defrauding others of their legal rights, or to obtain an objective forbidden by law typically by defrauding or gaining an unfair advantage. It is an agreement among firms or individuals to divide a market, set prices, limit production or limit opportunities. It can involve 'wage fixing, kickbacks, or misrepresenting the independence of the relationship between the colluding parties'.
Adverse selection	Adverse selection, anti-selection, or negative selection is a term used in economics, insurance, risk management, and statistics. It refers to a market process in which undesired results occur when buyers and sellers have asymmetric information (access to different information); the 'bad' products or services are more likely to be selected. For example, a bank that sets one price for all of its checking account customers runs the risk of being adversely selected against by its low-balance, high-activity (and hence least profitable) customers.
Brain drain	Brain drain, or human capital flight, is a buzzword that describes the departure or emigration of individuals with technical skills or knowledge from organizations, industries, or geographical regions. Brain drain is common among developing nations, such as many former African colonies, the island nations of the Caribbean, and in centralized economies such as former East Germany and the Soviet Union. China and India have recently been documented as the world leaders in brain drain.
Exit	Exit, in economics, means opting out of future transactions.
Herfindahl index	The Herfindahl index is a measure of the size of firms in relation to the industry and an indicator of the amount of competition among them. Named after economists Orris C. Herfindahl and Albert O. Hirschman, it is an economic concept widely applied in competition law, antitrust and also technology management. It is defined as the sum of the squares of the market shares of the 50 largest firms (or summed over all the firms if there are fewer than 50) within the industry, where the market shares are expressed as fractions.
Demand curve	In economics, the demand curve is the graph depicting the relationship between the price of a certain commodity and the amount of it that consumers are willing and able to purchase at that given price. It is a graphic representation of a demand schedule. The demand curve for all consumers together follows from the demand curve of every individual consumer: the individual demands at each price are added together.
Phillips curve	In economics, the Phillips curve is a historical inverse relationship between rates of unemployment and corresponding rates of inflation that result in an economy. Stated simply, decreased unemployment, (i.e., increased levels of employment) in an economy will correlate with higher rates of inflation.

13. Monopolistic Competition and Oligopoly

Allocative efficiency	Allocative efficiency is a type of economic efficiency in which economy/producers produce only those types of goods and services that are more desirable in the society and also in high demand. According to the formula the point of allocative efficiency is a point where price is equal to marginal cost (P=MC)or (MC=MR). At this point the social surplus is maximized with no deadweight loss, or the value society puts on that level of output produced minus the value of resources used to achieve that level, yet can be applied to other things such as level of pollution.
Productive efficiency	Productive efficiency occurs when the economy is using all of its resources efficiently. The concept is illustrated on a production possibility frontier (PPF) where all points on the curve are points of maximum productive efficiency. An equilibrium may be productively efficient without being allocatively efficient-- i.e. it may result in a distribution of goods where social welfare is not maximized.
Interest rate	An interest rate is the rate at which interest is paid by a borrower for the use of money that they borrow from a lender (creditor). Specifically, the interest rate is a percent of principal (P) paid a certain amount of times (m) per period (usually quoted per annum). For example, a small company borrows capital from a bank to buy new assets for its business, and in return the lender receives interest at a predetermined interest rate for deferring the use of funds and instead lending it to the borrower.
Product market	Product market is where goods and services produced by businesses are sold to households. The households use the income they receive from the sale of resources to purchase the products. The money they spend is returned to the businesses as revenue.
Variable cost	Variable costs are costs that change in proportion to the good or service that a business produces. Variable costs are also the sum of marginal costs over all units produced. They can also be considered normal costs.
Clinique	Clinique Laboratories, LLC is a manufacturer of skincare, cosmetics, toiletries and fragrances, owned by the Estée Lauder Corporation.
Oligopoly	An oligopoly is a market form in which a market or industry is dominated by a small number of sellers . Oligopolies can result from various forms of collusion which reduce competition and lead to higher prices for consumers. With few sellers, each oligopolist is likely to be aware of the actions of the others.
Economic growth	Economic growth is the increase in the market value of the goods and services produced by an economy over time. It is conventionally measured as the percent rate of increase in real gross domestic product, or real GDP. Of more importance is the growth of the ratio of GDP to population (GDP per capita), which is also called per capita income. An increase in per capita income is referred to as intensive growth.

Economies of scale	In microeconomics, economies of scale are the cost advantages that enterprises obtain due to size, output, or scale of operation, with cost per unit of output generally decreasing with increasing scale as fixed costs are spread out over more units of output.
	Often operational efficiency is also greater with increasing scale, leading to lower variable cost as well.
	Economies of scale apply to a variety of organizational and business situations and at various levels, such as a business or manufacturing unit, plant or an entire enterprise.
Menu cost	In economics, a menu cost is the cost to a firm resulting from changing its prices. The name stems from the cost of restaurants literally printing new menus, but economists use it to refer to the costs of changing nominal prices in general. In this broader definition, menu costs might include updating computer systems, re-tagging items, and hiring consultants to develop new pricing strategies as well as the literal costs of printing menus.
International trade	International trade is the exchange of capital, goods, and services across international borders or territories. In most countries, such trade represents a significant share of gross domestic product (GDP). While international trade has been present throughout much of history, its economic, social, and political importance has been on the rise in recent centuries.
Diversity	The 'business case for diversity' stem from the progression of the models of diversity within the workplace since the 1960s. The original model for diversity was situated around affirmative action drawing strength from the law and a need to comply with equal opportunity employment objectives. This compliance-based model gave rise to the idea that tokenism was the reason an individual was hired into a company when they differed from the dominant group.
Incentive	An incentive is something that motivates an individual to perform an action. The study of incentive structures is central to the study of all economic activities (both in terms of individual decision-making and in terms of co-operation and competition within a larger institutional structure). Economic analysis, then, of the differences between societies (and between different organizations within a society) largely amounts to characterizing the differences in incentive structures faced by individuals involved in these collective efforts.
Kinked demand	The kinked demand curve theory is an economic theory regarding oligopoly and monopolistic competition. When it was created, the idea fundamentally challenged classical economic tenets such as efficient markets and rapidly changing prices, ideas that underlie basic supply and demand models. Kinked demand was an initial attempt to explain sticky prices.
Cartel	A cartel is a formal 'agreement' among competing firms. It is a formal organization of producers and manufacturers that agree to fix prices, marketing, and production.

13. Monopolistic Competition and Oligopoly

OPEC	OPEC is an international organization whose mission is to coordinate the policies of the oil-producing countries. The goal is to secure a steady income to the member states and to secure supply of oil to consumers.
	OPEC is an intergovernmental organization that was created at the Baghdad Conference on 10-14 September 1960, by Iraq, Kuwait, Iran, Saudi Arabia and Venezuela.
Panasonic	Panasonic is the principal brand name of the Japanese electronics manufacturer Panasonic Corporation. The company sells a wide range of products under the brand worldwide, including plasma and LCD televisions, DVD and Blu-ray Disc recorders and players, camcorders, telephones, vacuum cleaners, microwave ovens, shavers, projectors, digital cameras, batteries, laptop computers (under the sub-brand Toughbook), CD players and home stereo equipment, fax machines, scanners, printers, electronic white-boards, electronic components and semiconductors.
	The brand uses the marketing slogan 'Ideas for Life'.
Production	Production is a process of combining various material inputs and immaterial inputs in order to make something for consumption (the output). It is the act of creating output, a good or service which has value and contributes to the utility of individuals. Economic well-being is created in a production process, meaning all economic activities that aim directly or indirectly to satisfy human needs.
Recession	In economics, a recession is a business cycle contraction. It is a general slowdown in economic activity. Macroeconomic indicators such as GDP (gross domestic product), investment spending, capacity utilization, household income, business profits, and inflation fall, while bankruptcies and the unemployment rate rise.
Pricing	Pricing is the process of determining what a company will receive in exchange for its product. Pricing factors are manufacturing cost, market place, competition, market condition, brand, and quality of product. Pricing is also a key variable in microeconomic price allocation theory.
Barriers to entry	In theories of competition in economics, barriers to entry, also known as barrier to entry, are obstacles that make it difficult to enter a given market. The term can refer to hindrances a firm faces in trying to enter a market or industry--such as government regulation and patents, or a large, established firm taking advantage of economies of scale--or those an individual faces in trying to gain entrance to a profession--such as education or licensing requirements.
	Because barriers to entry protect incumbent firms and restrict competition in a market, they can contribute to distortionary prices.
First-mover advantage	In business, economics, or marketing, first-mover advantage, or First mover advantage, is the advantage gained by the initial significant occupant of a market segment. It may be also referred to as Technological Leadership.

1. _____, or human capital flight, is a buzzword that describes the departure or emigration of individuals with technical skills or knowledge from organizations, industries, or geographical regions. _____ is common among developing nations, such as many former African colonies, the island nations of the Caribbean, and in centralized economies such as former East Germany and the Soviet Union. China and India have recently been documented as the world leaders in _____.

    a. Bendigo Petition
    b. Charcuterie
    c. Brain drain
    d. Brandenburger Gold Coast

2. In economics, the _____ is a historical inverse relationship between rates of unemployment and corresponding rates of inflation that result in an economy. Stated simply, decreased unemployment, (i.e., increased levels of employment) in an economy will correlate with higher rates of inflation.

    While there is a short run tradeoff between unemployment and inflation, it has not been observed in the long run.

    a. Beveridge curve
    b. Budget constraint
    c. Phillips curve
    d. Demand curve

3. _____ is a study of strategic decision making. Specifically, it is 'the study of mathematical models of conflict and cooperation between intelligent rational decision-makers'. An alternative term suggested 'as a more descriptive name for the discipline' is interactive decision theory.

    a. Game theory
    b. Fixed-point theorem
    c. Fuel protests in the United Kingdom
    d. Battle of Annaberg

4. In theories of competition in economics, _____, also known as barrier to entry, are obstacles that make it difficult to enter a given market. The term can refer to hindrances a firm faces in trying to enter a market or industry--such as government regulation and patents, or a large, established firm taking advantage of economies of scale--or those an individual faces in trying to gain entrance to a profession--such as education or licensing requirements.

    Because _____ protect incumbent firms and restrict competition in a market, they can contribute to distortionary prices.

    a. Fuel protests in the United Kingdom
    b. Barriers to entry
    c. Freikorps Lichtschlag
    d. Freikorps Oberland

13. Monopolistic Competition and Oligopoly

5. _____ is a type of imperfect competition such that many producers sell products that are differentiated from one another and hence are not perfect substitutes. In _____, a firm takes the prices charged by its rivals as given and ignores the impact of its own prices on the prices of other firms. In the presence of coercive government, _____ will fall into government-granted monopoly.

   a. Monopolistic competition
   b. Competition
   c. Deregulation
   d. Disequilibrium

1. c
2. c
3. a
4. b
5. a

14. The Demand for Resources

CHAPTER OUTLINE: KEY TERMS, PEOPLE, PLACES, CONCEPTS

_____ | Derived demand

_____ | Income

_____ | Marginal product

_____ | Marginal revenue

_____ | Product market

_____ | Residual claimant

_____ | Pricing

_____ | Product

_____ | Productivity

_____ | Monopolistic competition

_____ | Complementary good

_____ | Quantitative easing

_____ | Economic growth

_____ | Labor demand

_____ | Elasticity

_____ | Great Recession

_____ | Recession

_____ | Total cost

_____ | Marginal cost

_____ | Lorenz curve

_____ | Income distribution

_____ | Automated teller machine _____

_____ | Consumer Financial Protection Bureau _____

CHAPTER HIGHLIGHTS & NOTES: KEY TERMS, PEOPLE, PLACES, CONCEPTS

Derived demand	Derived demand is a term in economics, where demand for a factor of production or intermediate good occurs as a result of the demand for another intermediate or final good. In other words, if the demand for a good such as wheat increases, then the productivity increases, which leads to an increase in labor. This may occur as the former is a part of production of the second.
Income	Income is the consumption and savings opportunity gained by an entity within a specified timeframe, which is generally expressed in monetary terms. However, for households and individuals, 'income is the sum of all the wages, salaries, profits, interests payments, rents and other forms of earnings received... in a given period of time.'
	In the field of public economics, the term may refer to the accumulation of both monetary and non-monetary consumption ability, with the former (monetary) being used as a proxy for total income.
Marginal product	In economics and in particular neoclassical economics, the marginal product or marginal physical product of an input is the extra output that can be produced by using one more unit of the input (for instance, the difference in output when a firm's labor usage is increased from five to six units), assuming that the quantities of no other inputs to production change.

The marginal product of a given input can be expressed as
$$MP = \frac{\Delta Y}{\Delta X}$$

where ΔX is the change in the firm's use of the input (conventionally a one-unit change) and ΔY is the change in quantity of output produced. Note that the quantity Y of the 'product' is typically defined ignoring external costs and benefits.

Marginal revenue	In microeconomics, marginal revenue is the additional revenue that will be generated by increasing product sales by 1 unit. It can also be described as the unit revenue the last item sold has generated for the firm.

CHAPTER HIGHLIGHTS & NOTES: KEY TERMS, PEOPLE, PLACES, CONCEPTS

Product market	Product market is where goods and services produced by businesses are sold to households. The households use the income they receive from the sale of resources to purchase the products. The money they spend is returned to the businesses as revenue.
Residual claimant	In economics, the residual claimant is the agent who receives the net income . Residual claimancy is generally required in order for there to be moral hazard, which is a problem typical of information asymmetry. This is specifically the case for the principal-agent problem.
Pricing	Pricing is the process of determining what a company will receive in exchange for its product. Pricing factors are manufacturing cost, market place, competition, market condition, brand, and quality of product. Pricing is also a key variable in microeconomic price allocation theory.
Product	In marketing, a product is anything that can be offered to a market that might satisfy a want or need. In retailing, products are called merchandise. In manufacturing, products are bought as raw materials and sold as finished goods.
Productivity	Productivity is the ratio of output to inputs in production; it is an average measure of the efficiency of production. Efficiency of production means production's capability to create incomes which is measured by the formula real output value minus real input value. Increasing national productivity can raise living standards because more real income improves people's ability to purchase goods and services, enjoy leisure, improve housing and education and contribute to social and environmental programs.
Monopolistic competition	Monopolistic competition is a type of imperfect competition such that many producers sell products that are differentiated from one another and hence are not perfect substitutes. In monopolistic competition, a firm takes the prices charged by its rivals as given and ignores the impact of its own prices on the prices of other firms. In the presence of coercive government, monopolistic competition will fall into government-granted monopoly.
Complementary good	In economics, a complementary good is a good with a negative cross elasticity of demand, in contrast to a substitute good. This means a good's demand is increased when the price of another good is decreased. Conversely, the demand for a good is decreased when the price of another good is increased.
Quantitative easing	Quantitative easing is an unconventional monetary policy used by central banks to stimulate the economy when standard monetary policy has become ineffective. A central bank implements quantitative easing by buying specified amounts of financial assets from commercial banks and other private institutions, thus raising the prices of those financial assets and lowering their yield, while simultaneously increasing the monetary base.

14. The Demand for Resources

Economic growth	Economic growth is the increase in the market value of the goods and services produced by an economy over time. It is conventionally measured as the percent rate of increase in real gross domestic product, or real GDP. Of more importance is the growth of the ratio of GDP to population (GDP per capita), which is also called per capita income. An increase in per capita income is referred to as intensive growth.
Labor demand	In economics, labor demand refers to the number of hours of hiring that an employer is willing to do based on the various exogenous variables it is faced with, such as the wage rate, the unit cost of capital, the market-determined selling price of its output, etc. The function specifying the quantity of labor that would be demanded at any of various possible values of these exogenous variables is called the labor demand function.
Elasticity	In economics, elasticity is the measurement of how responsive an economic variable is to a change in another. For example:•'If I lower the price of my product, how much more will I sell?'•'If I raise the price of one good, how will that affect sales of this other good?'•'If we learn that a resource is becoming scarce, will people scramble to acquire it?'
	An elastic variable (or elasticity value greater than 1) is one which responds more than proportionally to changes in other variables. In contrast, an inelastic variable (or elasticity value less than 1) is one which changes less than proportionally in response to changes in other variables.
Great Recession	The Great Recession was a global economic decline in the late 2000s. According to aggregated national data, a worldwide recession began in Q3-2008 and ended in Q1-2009.
	It is related to a liquidity crisis, commonly being dated to have started when several central banks had to step in with liquidity lending to the interbank lending market on 9 August 2007. This was a response to a situation where BNP Paribas temporarily had to block money withdrawals from three hedge funds--citing a 'complete evaporation of liquidity'.
Recession	In economics, a recession is a business cycle contraction. It is a general slowdown in economic activity. Macroeconomic indicators such as GDP (gross domestic product), investment spending, capacity utilization, household income, business profits, and inflation fall, while bankruptcies and the unemployment rate rise.
Total cost	In economics, and cost accounting, total cost describes the total economic cost of production and is made up of variable costs, which vary according to the quantity of a good produced and include inputs such as labor and raw materials, plus fixed costs, which are independent of the quantity of a good produced and include inputs (capital) that cannot be varied in the short term, such as buildings and machinery. Total cost in economics includes the total opportunity cost of each factor of production as part of its fixed or variable costs.

Marginal cost	In economics and finance, marginal cost is the change in the total cost that arises when the quantity produced has an increment by unit. That is, it is the cost of producing one more unit of a good. In general terms, marginal cost at each level of production includes any additional costs required to produce the next unit.
Lorenz curve	In economics, the Lorenz curve is a graphical representation of the cumulative distribution function of the empirical probability distribution of wealth, and was developed by Max O. Lorenz in 1905 for representing inequality of the wealth distribution.
	The curve is a graph showing the proportion of the distribution assumed by the bottom y% of the values, although this is not rigorously true for a finite population . It is often used to represent income distribution, where it shows for the bottom x% of households, what percentage y% of the total income they have.
Income distribution	In economics, income distribution is how a nation's total GDP is distributed amongst its population.
	Income and distribution has always been a central concern of economic theory and economic policy. Classical economists such as Adam Smith, Thomas Malthus and David Ricardo were mainly concerned with factor income distribution, that is, the distribution of income between the main factors of production, land, labour and capital.
Automated teller machine	An automated teller machine or automatic teller machine. (American, Australian, Singaporean, Indian, and Hiberno-English), also known as an automated banking machine (ABM) (Canadian English), cash machine, cashpoint, cashline or hole in the wall (British, South African, and Sri Lankan English), is an electronic telecommunications device that enables the clients of a financial institution to perform financial transactions without the need for a cashier, human clerk or bank teller.
	On most modern Automated teller machines, the customer is identified by inserting a plastic Automated teller machine card with a magnetic stripe or a plastic smart card with a chip that contains a unique card number and some security information such as an expiration date or CVVC (CVV).
Consumer Financial Protection Bureau	The Consumer Financial Protection Bureau is an independent agency of the United States government responsible for consumer protection in the financial sector. Its jurisdiction includes banks, credit unions, securities firms, payday lenders, mortgage-servicing operations, foreclosure relief services, debt collectors and other financial companies operating in the United States.
	The Consumer Financial Protection Bureau's creation was authorized by the Dodd-Frank Wall Street Reform and Consumer Protection Act, whose passage in 2010 was a legislative response to the financial crisis of 2007-08 and the subsequent Great Recession.

14. The Demand for Resources

1. In economics and finance, _____ is the change in the total cost that arises when the quantity produced has an increment by unit. That is, it is the cost of producing one more unit of a good. In general terms, _____ at each level of production includes any additional costs required to produce the next unit.

    a. Marginal cost
    b. Bliss point
    c. Club good
    d. Conjectural variation

2. _____ is the consumption and savings opportunity gained by an entity within a specified timeframe, which is generally expressed in monetary terms. However, for households and individuals, '_____ is the sum of all the wages, salaries, profits, interests payments, rents and other forms of earnings received... in a given period of time.'

    In the field of public economics, the term may refer to the accumulation of both monetary and non-monetary consumption ability, with the former (monetary) being used as a proxy for total _____.

    a. Fuel protests in the United Kingdom
    b. Income
    c. Freikorps Lichtschlag
    d. Freikorps Oberland

3. _____ is a type of imperfect competition such that many producers sell products that are differentiated from one another and hence are not perfect substitutes. In _____, a firm takes the prices charged by its rivals as given and ignores the impact of its own prices on the prices of other firms. In the presence of coercive government, _____ will fall into government-granted monopoly.

    a. Cellophane paradox
    b. Competition
    c. Monopolistic competition
    d. Disequilibrium

4. _____ is the increase in the market value of the goods and services produced by an economy over time. It is conventionally measured as the percent rate of increase in real gross domestic product, or real GDP. Of more importance is the growth of the ratio of GDP to population (GDP per capita), which is also called per capita income. An increase in per capita income is referred to as intensive growth.

    a. Baker cube
    b. Bereavement benefit
    c. Economic growth
    d. Bodily integrity

5. . _____ is a term in economics, where demand for a factor of production or intermediate good occurs as a result of the demand for another intermediate or final good.

In other words, if the demand for a good such as wheat increases, then the productivity increases, which leads to an increase in labor. This may occur as the former is a part of production of the second.

a. Business ecosystem
b. Center for Business and Economic Research
c. Derived demand
d. Consumer economy

1. a
2. b
3. c
4. c
5. c

You can take the complete Chapter Practice Test

for 14. The Demand for Resources
on all key terms, persons, places, and concepts.

Online 99 Cents

http://www.JustTheFacts101.com

Use www.JustTheFacts101.com for all your study needs

including Facts101's online interactive problem solving labs in

chemistry, statistics, mathematics, and more.

15. Wage Determination

CHAPTER OUTLINE: KEY TERMS, PEOPLE, PLACES, CONCEPTS

_____ Real wage

_____ Production

_____ Economic growth

_____ Productivity

_____ Wage ratio

_____ Phillips curve

_____ Monopsony

_____ Great Recession

_____ Recession

_____ Equilibrium wage

_____ Product

_____ Product market

_____ Bilateral monopoly

_____ Fair Labor Standards Act

_____ Minimum wage

_____ Demand curve

_____ Marginal revenue

_____ Labor demand

_____ Human capital

_____ Income

_____ National income

	Efficiency wage
	Government failure
	Occupational segregation
	Pay for performance
	Royalties
	Conflict of interest
	Profit sharing
	Federation
	Independent union
	Agency shop
	Closed shop
	Collective bargaining
	Open shop
	Featherbedding
	Lockout
	National Labor Relations Act
	Work rule
	Interest rate

15. Wage Determination

Real wage	The term real wages refers to wages that have been adjusted for inflation, or, equivalently, wages in terms of the amount of goods and services that can be bought. This term is used in contrast to nominal wages or unadjusted wages. Because it has been adjusted to account for changes in the prices of goods and services, real wages provide a clearer representation of an individual's wages in terms of what they can afford to buy with those wages - specifically, in terms of the amount of goods and services that can be bought.
Production	Production is a process of combining various material inputs and immaterial inputs in order to make something for consumption (the output). It is the act of creating output, a good or service which has value and contributes to the utility of individuals. Economic well-being is created in a production process, meaning all economic activities that aim directly or indirectly to satisfy human needs.
Economic growth	Economic growth is the increase in the market value of the goods and services produced by an economy over time. It is conventionally measured as the percent rate of increase in real gross domestic product, or real GDP. Of more importance is the growth of the ratio of GDP to population (GDP per capita), which is also called per capita income. An increase in per capita income is referred to as intensive growth.
Productivity	Productivity is the ratio of output to inputs in production; it is an average measure of the efficiency of production. Efficiency of production means production's capability to create incomes which is measured by the formula real output value minus real input value. Increasing national productivity can raise living standards because more real income improves people's ability to purchase goods and services, enjoy leisure, improve housing and education and contribute to social and environmental programs.
Wage ratio	In economics, the wage ratio refers to the ratio of the top salaries in a group to the bottom salaries. It is a measure of wage dispersion.
Phillips curve	In economics, the Phillips curve is a historical inverse relationship between rates of unemployment and corresponding rates of inflation that result in an economy. Stated simply, decreased unemployment, (i.e., increased levels of employment) in an economy will correlate with higher rates of inflation. While there is a short run tradeoff between unemployment and inflation, it has not been observed in the long run.
Monopsony	In economics, a monopsony (from Ancient Greek μ???? 'single' + ?????a (opsonía) 'purchase') is a market form in which only one buyer interfaces with many sellers.

15. Wage Determination

	The microeconomic theory of imperfect competition assumes the monopsonist can dictate terms to its suppliers, as the only purchaser of a good or service, much in the same manner that a monopolist is said to control the market for its buyers in a monopoly, in which only one seller faces many buyers.
	In addition to its use in microeconomic theory, monopsony and monopsonist are descriptive terms often used to describe a market where a single buyer substantially controls the market as the major purchaser of goods and services.
Great Recession	The Great Recession was a global economic decline in the late 2000s. According to aggregated national data, a worldwide recession began in Q3-2008 and ended in Q1-2009.
	It is related to a liquidity crisis, commonly being dated to have started when several central banks had to step in with liquidity lending to the interbank lending market on 9 August 2007. This was a response to a situation where BNP Paribas temporarily had to block money withdrawals from three hedge funds--citing a 'complete evaporation of liquidity'.
Recession	In economics, a recession is a business cycle contraction. It is a general slowdown in economic activity. Macroeconomic indicators such as GDP (gross domestic product), investment spending, capacity utilization, household income, business profits, and inflation fall, while bankruptcies and the unemployment rate rise.
Equilibrium wage	In economics, the equilibrium wage is the wage rate that produces neither an excess supply of workers nor an excess demand for workers and labor market. See economic equilibrium.
Product	In marketing, a product is anything that can be offered to a market that might satisfy a want or need. In retailing, products are called merchandise. In manufacturing, products are bought as raw materials and sold as finished goods.
Product market	Product market is where goods and services produced by businesses are sold to households. The households use the income they receive from the sale of resources to purchase the products. The money they spend is returned to the businesses as revenue.
Bilateral monopoly	In a bilateral monopoly there is both a monopoly and monopsony (a single buyer) in the same market.
	In such, market price and output will be determined by forces like bargaining power of both buyer and seller. A bilateral monopoly model is often used in situations where the switching costs of both sides are prohibitively high.

15. Wage Determination

Fair Labor Standards Act	The Fair Labor Standards Act of 1938 is a federal statute of the United States. The Fair Labor Standards Act introduced a maximum 44-hour seven-day workweek, established a national minimum wage, guaranteed 'time-and-a-half' for overtime in certain jobs, and prohibited most employment of minors in 'oppressive child labor', a term that is defined in the statute. It applies to employees engaged in interstate commerce or employed by an enterprise engaged in commerce or in the production of goods for commerce, unless the employer can claim an exemption from coverage.
Minimum wage	A minimum wage is the lowest hourly, daily or monthly remuneration that employers may legally pay to workers. Equivalently, it is the lowest wage at which workers may sell their labor. Although minimum wage laws are in effect in many jurisdictions, differences of opinion exist about the benefits and drawbacks of a minimum wage.
Demand curve	In economics, the demand curve is the graph depicting the relationship between the price of a certain commodity and the amount of it that consumers are willing and able to purchase at that given price. It is a graphic representation of a demand schedule. The demand curve for all consumers together follows from the demand curve of every individual consumer: the individual demands at each price are added together.
Marginal revenue	In microeconomics, marginal revenue is the additional revenue that will be generated by increasing product sales by 1 unit. It can also be described as the unit revenue the last item sold has generated for the firm. In a perfectly competitive market, the additional revenue generated by selling an additional unit of a good is equal to the price the firm is able to charge the buyer of the good.
Labor demand	In economics, labor demand refers to the number of hours of hiring that an employer is willing to do based on the various exogenous variables it is faced with, such as the wage rate, the unit cost of capital, the market-determined selling price of its output, etc. The function specifying the quantity of labor that would be demanded at any of various possible values of these exogenous variables is called the labor demand function.
Human capital	Human capital is the stock of competencies, knowledge, habits, social and personality attributes, including creativity, cognitive abilities, embodied in the ability to perform labor so as to produce economic value. It is an aggregate economic view of the human being acting within economies, which is an attempt to capture the social, biological, cultural and psychological complexity as they interact in explicit and/or economic transactions. Many theories explicitly connect investment in human capital development to education, and the role of human capital in economic development, productivity growth, and innovation has frequently been cited as a justification for government subsidies for education and job skills training.
Income	Income is the consumption and savings opportunity gained by an entity within a specified timeframe, which is generally expressed in monetary terms.

15. Wage Determination

	However, for households and individuals, 'income is the sum of all the wages, salaries, profits, interests payments, rents and other forms of earnings received... in a given period of time.'
	In the field of public economics, the term may refer to the accumulation of both monetary and non-monetary consumption ability, with the former (monetary) being used as a proxy for total income.
National income	A variety of measures of national income and output are used in economics to estimate total economic activity in a country or region, including gross domestic product, gross national product (GNP), net national income and adjusted national income. All are specially concerned with counting the total amount of goods and services produced within some 'boundary'. The boundary is usually defined by geography or citizenship, and may also restrict the goods and services that are counted.
Efficiency wage	In labor economics, the efficiency wage hypothesis argues that wages, at least in some markets, form in a way that is not market-clearing. Specifically, it points to the incentive for managers to pay their employees more than the market-clearing wage in order to increase their productivity or efficiency, or reduce costs associated with turnover, in industries where the costs of replacing labor is high. This increased labor productivity and/or decreased costs pay for the higher wages.
Government failure	Government failure is the public-sector analogy to market failure and occurs when government intervention causes a more inefficient allocation of goods and resources than would occur without that intervention. In not comparing realized inadequacies of market outcomes against those of potential interventions, one writer describes the 'anatomy' of market failure as providing 'only limited help in prescribing therapies for government success.'
	The government's failure to intervene in a market failure that would result in a socially preferable mix of output is similarly referred to as passive government failure. Just as with market failures, different kinds of government failures describe corresponding economic distortions.
Occupational segregation	Occupational segregation is the distribution of people based upon demographic characteristics, most often gender, both across and within occupations and jobs. Occupational segregation levels differ on a basis of perfect segregation and integration. Perfect segregation occurs where any given occupation employs only one group.
Pay for performance	Pay for performance is an emerging movement in health insurance . Providers under this arrangement are rewarded for meeting pre-established targets for delivery of healthcare services. This is a fundamental change from fee for service payment.
Royalties	A royalty (sometimes, running royalties, or private sector taxes) is a usage-based payment made by one party to another (the 'licensor') for the right to ongoing use of an asset, sometimes an intellectual property (IP). Royalties are typically agreed upon as a percentage of gross or net revenues derived from the use of an asset or a fixed price per unit sold of an item of such, but there are also other modes and metrics of compensation.

15. Wage Determination

Conflict of interest	A conflict of interest is a situation occuring when an individual or organization is involved in multiple interests, one of which could possibly corrupt the motivation. The presence of a conflict of interest is independent of the occurrence of impropriety. Therefore, a conflict of interest can be discovered and voluntarily defused before any corruption occurs.
Profit sharing	Profit sharing refers to various incentive plans introduced by businesses that provide direct or indirect payments to employees that depend on company's profitability in addition to employees' regular salary and bonuses. In publicly traded companies these plans typically amount to allocation of shares to employees. The profit sharing plans are based on predetermined economic sharing rules that define the split of gains between the company as a principal and the employee as an agent.
Federation	A federation, also known as a federal state, is a political entity characterized by a union of partially self-governing states or regions under a central (federal) government. In a federation, the self-governing status of the component states, as well as the division of power between them and the central government, are typically constitutionally entrenched and may not be altered by a unilateral decision of either party, the states or the federal political body. The governmental or constitutional structure found in a federation is known as federalism.
Independent union	An independent union is a trade union that represents workers in one plant or company and is free of employer control. (This includes a union representing workers in more than one plant located in two or more states but employed by the same employer). A national independent union is a union of a national character not affiliated with the AFL or CIO; a local independent union is one of a local character not affiliated with the international union having jurisdiction over that branch of industry.
Agency shop	An agency shop is a form of union security agreement where the employer may hire union or non-union workers, and employees need not join the union in order to remain employed. However, the non-union worker must pay a fee to cover collective bargaining costs. The fee paid by non-union members under the agency shop is known as the 'agency fee.' Where the agency shop is illegal, as is common in labor law governing American public sector unions, a 'fair share provision' may be agreed to by the union and the employer.
Closed shop	A pre-entry closed shop is a form of union security agreement under which the employer agrees to hire union members only, and employees must remain members of the union at all times in order to remain employed. A post-entry closed shop is an agreement requiring all employees to join the union if they are not already members.

15. Wage Determination

Collective bargaining	Collaborative bargaining is a style of negotiation which recognises the interests of the other party and emphasises cooperation between them. It was especially promoted, practised and studied in the negotiations between school districts and teaching unions in the USA in the 1990s. It is compared and contrasted with more adversarial models of collective bargaining in which the parties may regard each other as enemies.
Open shop	An open shop is a place of employment at which one is not required to join or financially support a union as a condition of hiring or continued employment. Open shop is also known as a merit shop.
Featherbedding	Featherbedding is the practice of hiring more workers than are needed to perform a given job, or to adopt work procedures which appear pointless, complex and time-consuming merely to employ additional workers. The term 'make-work' is sometimes used as a synonym for featherbedding. The term 'featherbedding' is usually used by management to describe behaviors and rules sought by workers.
Lockout	A lockout is a temporary work stoppage or denial of employment initiated by the management of a company during a labor dispute. This is different from a strike, in which employees refuse to work. It is usually implemented by simply refusing to admit employees onto company premises, and may include actions such as changing locks and hiring security guards for the premises.
National Labor Relations Act	The National Labor Relations Act of 1935 29 U.S.C. § 151-169 (also known as the Wagner Act after NY Senator Robert F. Wagner) is a foundational statute of US labor law which guarantees basic rights of private sector employees to organize into trade unions, engage in collective bargaining for better terms and conditions at work, and take collective action including strike if necessary. The act also created the National Labor Relations Board, which conducts elections that can require employers to engage in collective bargaining with labor unions (also known as trade unions). The Act does not apply to workers who are covered by the Railway Labor Act, agricultural employees, domestic employees, supervisors, federal, state or local government workers, independent contractors and some close relatives of individual employers.
Work rule	A work rule is a negotiated stipulation in a labor contract that limits the conditions under which management may direct the performance of labor.
Interest rate	An interest rate is the rate at which interest is paid by a borrower for the use of money that they borrow from a lender (creditor). Specifically, the interest rate is a percent of principal (P) paid a certain amount of times (m) per period (usually quoted per annum). For example, a small company borrows capital from a bank to buy new assets for its business, and in return the lender receives interest at a predetermined interest rate for deferring the use of funds and instead lending it to the borrower.

15. Wage Determination

1. A variety of measures of _____ and output are used in economics to estimate total economic activity in a country or region, including gross domestic product, gross national product (GNP), net _____ and adjusted _____. All are specially concerned with counting the total amount of goods and services produced within some 'boundary'. The boundary is usually defined by geography or citizenship, and may also restrict the goods and services that are counted.

   a. National income
   b. Battle of Annaberg
   c. Freikorps Lichtschlag
   d. Freikorps Oberland

2. In economics, the _____ is the graph depicting the relationship between the price of a certain commodity and the amount of it that consumers are willing and able to purchase at that given price. It is a graphic representation of a demand schedule. The _____ for all consumers together follows from the _____ of every individual consumer: the individual demands at each price are added together.

   a. Demand curve
   b. Budget constraint
   c. Cost curve
   d. Fuel protests in the United Kingdom

3. A _____ is a situation occuring when an individual or organization is involved in multiple interests, one of which could possibly corrupt the motivation.

   The presence of a _____ is independent of the occurrence of impropriety. Therefore, a _____ can be discovered and voluntarily defused before any corruption occurs.

   a. Bayesian probability
   b. Conflict of interest
   c. Biofact
   d. Biological determinism

4. In a _____ there is both a monopoly and monopsony (a single buyer) in the same market.

   In such, market price and output will be determined by forces like bargaining power of both buyer and seller. A _____ model is often used in situations where the switching costs of both sides are prohibitively high.

   a. Bilateral monopoly
   b. Fuel protests in the United Kingdom
   c. Battle of Annaberg
   d. Freikorps Lichtschlag

5. . An _____ is the rate at which interest is paid by a borrower for the use of money that they borrow from a lender (creditor).

15. Wage Determination

Specifically, the _____ is a percent of principal (P) paid a certain amount of times (m) per period (usually quoted per annum). For example, a small company borrows capital from a bank to buy new assets for its business, and in return the lender receives interest at a predetermined _____ for deferring the use of funds and instead lending it to the borrower.

a. Bernanke doctrine
b. Interest rate
c. Fuel protests in the United Kingdom
d. Battle of Annaberg

1. a
2. a
3. b
4. a
5. b

You can take the complete Chapter Practice Test

for 15. Wage Determination
on all key terms, persons, places, and concepts.

Online 99 Cents

http://www.JustTheFacts101.com

Use www.JustTheFacts101.com for all your study needs

including Facts101's online interactive problem solving labs in

chemistry, statistics, mathematics, and more.

16. Rent, Interest, and Profit

CHAPTER OUTLINE: KEY TERMS, PEOPLE, PLACES, CONCEPTS

Economic rent

Land Economics

Allocative efficiency

Laffer curve

Market system

Private property

Quality

Single tax

Federal funds

Interest rate

Loanable funds

Compound interest

Future value

Present value

Capital

OPEC

Real interest rate

Production

Explicit cost

Implicit cost

Residual claimant

16. Rent, Interest, and Profit

CHAPTER OUTLINE: KEY TERMS, PEOPLE, PLACES, CONCEPTS

	Annual percentage rate
	Truth in Lending Act
	Great Recession
	Income
	Recession
	Income distribution
	Pricing

CHAPTER HIGHLIGHTS & NOTES: KEY TERMS, PEOPLE, PLACES, CONCEPTS

Economic rent	In economics, economic rent is any payment to a factor of production in excess of its opportunity cost. Economic rent should not be confounded or confused with opportunity cost, producer surplus, or normal profit in that all of these other terms involve productive human action. Economic rent is the cost of non-produced inputs or advantages; the result of natural or contrived exclusivity.
Land Economics	Land Economics is a peer-reviewed academic journal dedicated to the study of land use, natural resources, public utilities, housing, and urban land issues. The journal was established in 1925 by the founder of the American Economic Association, Richard T. Ely (University of Wisconsin). Land Economics covers such topics as transportation, energy, urban and rural land use, housing, environmental quality, public utilities, and natural resources.
Allocative efficiency	Allocative efficiency is a type of economic efficiency in which economy/producers produce only those types of goods and services that are more desirable in the society and also in high demand. According to the formula the point of allocative efficiency is a point where price is equal to marginal cost (P=MC)or (MC=MR). At this point the social surplus is maximized with no deadweight loss, or the value society puts on that level of output produced minus the value of resources used to achieve that level, yet can be applied to other things such as level of pollution.
Laffer curve	In economics, the Laffer curve is a representation of the relationship between possible rates of taxation and the resulting levels of government revenue. It illustrates the concept of taxable income elasticity--i.e., taxable income will change in response to changes in the rate of taxation.

16. Rent, Interest, and Profit

Market system	A market system is any systematic process enabling many market players to bid and ask: helping bidders and sellers interact and make deals. It is not just the price mechanism but the entire system of regulation, qualification, credentials, reputations and clearing that surrounds that mechanism and makes it operate in a social context. Because a market system relies on the assumption that players are constantly involved and unequally enabled, a market system is distinguished specifically from a voting system where candidates seek the support of voters on a less regular basis.
Private property	Private property is a legal designation of the ownership of property by non-governmental legal entities. Private property is distinguishable from public property, which is owned by a state entity; and collective property, which is owned by a group of non-governmental entities. Private property is further distinguished from personal property, which refers to property for personal use and consumption.
Quality	Quality in business, engineering and manufacturing has a pragmatic interpretation as the non-inferiority or superiority of something; it is also defined as fitness for purpose. Quality is a perceptual, conditional, and somewhat subjective attribute and may be understood differently by different people. Consumers may focus on the specification quality of a product/service, or how it compares to competitors in the marketplace.
Single tax	A single tax system is a system of taxation based primarily or exclusively on one tax, typically chosen for its special properties. The original proposal for a single tax, and consequently the one most commonly known and referred to as a 'single tax', is the Georgist proposal for a tax system based exclusively on land value taxes. More recently others have made proposals for a single tax based on other revenue models such as the FairTax proposal which is based on a consumption tax.
Federal funds	In the United States, federal funds are overnight borrowings between banks and other entities to maintain their bank reserves at the Federal Reserve. Banks keep reserves at Federal Reserve Banks to meet their reserve requirements and to clear financial transactions. Transactions in the federal funds market enable depository institutions with reserve balances in excess of reserve requirements to lend reserves to institutions with reserve deficiencies.
Interest rate	An interest rate is the rate at which interest is paid by a borrower for the use of money that they borrow from a lender (creditor). Specifically, the interest rate is a percent of principal (P) paid a certain amount of times (m) per period (usually quoted per annum). For example, a small company borrows capital from a bank to buy new assets for its business, and in return the lender receives interest at a predetermined interest rate for deferring the use of funds and instead lending it to the borrower.

16. Rent, Interest, and Profit

Loanable funds	In economics, the loanable funds market is a hypothetical market that brings savers and borrowers together, also bringing together the money available in commercial banks and lending institutions available for firms and households to finance expenditures, either investments or consumption. Savers supply the loanable funds; for instance, buying bonds will transfer their money to the institution issuing the bond, which can be a firm or government. In return, borrowers demand loanable funds; when an institution sells a bond, it is demanding loanable funds.
Compound interest	Compound interest arises when interest is added to the principal of a deposit or loan, so that, from that moment on, the interest that has been added also earns interest. This addition of interest to the principal is called compounding. A bank account, for example, may have its interest compounded every year: in this case, an account with $1000 initial principal and 20% interest per year would have a balance of $1200 at the end of the first year, $1440 at the end of the second year, and so on.
Future value	Future value is the value of an asset at a specific date. It measures the nominal future sum of money that a given sum of money is 'worth' at a specified time in the future assuming a certain interest rate, or more generally, rate of return; it is the present value multiplied by the accumulation function. The value does not include corrections for inflation or other factors that affect the true value of money in the future.
Present value	Present value, also known as present discounted value, is a future amount of money that has been discounted to reflect its current value, as if it existed today. The present value is always less than or equal to the future value because money has interest-earning potential, a characteristic referred to as the time value of money. Time value can be described with the simplified phrase, "A dollar today is worth more than a dollar tomorrow".
Capital	In economics, capital goods, real capital, or capital assets are already-produced durable goods or any non-financial asset that is used in production of goods or services. Capital goods are not significantly consumed in the production process though they may depreciate. How a capital good or is maintained or returned to its pre-production state varies with the type of capital involved.
OPEC	OPEC is an international organization whose mission is to coordinate the policies of the oil-producing countries. The goal is to secure a steady income to the member states and to secure supply of oil to consumers. OPEC is an intergovernmental organization that was created at the Baghdad Conference on 10-14 September 1960, by Iraq, Kuwait, Iran, Saudi Arabia and Venezuela.
Real interest rate	The real interest rate is the rate of interest an investor expects to receive after allowing for inflation.

	It can be described more formally by the Fisher equation, which states that the real interest rate is approximately the nominal interest rate minus the inflation rate. If, for example, an investor were able to lock in a 5% interest rate for the coming year and anticipated a 2% rise in prices, they would expect to earn a real interest rate of 3%.
Production	Production is a process of combining various material inputs and immaterial inputs in order to make something for consumption (the output). It is the act of creating output, a good or service which has value and contributes to the utility of individuals. Economic well-being is created in a production process, meaning all economic activities that aim directly or indirectly to satisfy human needs.
Explicit cost	An explicit cost is a direct payment made to others in the course of running a business, such as wage, rent and materials, as opposed to implicit costs, which are those where no actual payment is made. It is possible still to underestimate these costs, however: for example, pension contributions and other 'perks' must be taken into account when considering the cost of labour. Explicit costs are taken into account along with implicit ones when considering economic profit.
Implicit cost	In economics, an implicit cost, also called an imputed cost, implied cost, or notional cost, is the opportunity cost equal to what a firm must give up in order to use factors which it neither purchases nor hires. It is the opposite of an explicit cost, which is borne directly. In other words, an implicit cost is any cost that results from using an asset instead of renting, selling, or lending it.
Residual claimant	In economics, the residual claimant is the agent who receives the net income . Residual claimancy is generally required in order for there to be moral hazard, which is a problem typical of information asymmetry. This is specifically the case for the principal-agent problem.
Annual percentage rate	The term annual percentage rate of charge, corresponding sometimes to a nominal Annual percentage rate and sometimes to an effective Annual percentage rate (or EAPR), describes the interest rate for a whole year (annualized), rather than just a monthly fee/rate, as applied on a loan, mortgage loan, credit card, etc. It is a finance charge expressed as an annual rate. Those terms have formal, legal definitions in some countries or legal jurisdictions, but in general:•The nominal Annual percentage rate is the simple-interest rate (for a year).•The effective Annual percentage rate is the fee+compound interest rate (calculated across a year). In some areas, the annual percentage rate is the simplified counterpart to the effective interest rate that the borrower will pay on a loan.
Truth in Lending Act	The Truth in Lending Act of 1968 is United States federal law designed to promote the informed use of consumer credit, by requiring disclosures about its terms and cost to standardize the manner in which costs associated with borrowing are calculated and disclosed.

16. Rent, Interest, and Profit

CHAPTER HIGHLIGHTS & NOTES: KEY TERMS, PEOPLE, PLACES, CONCEPTS

	Truth in Lending Act also gives consumers the right to cancel certain credit transactions that involve a lien on a consumer's principal dwelling, regulates certain credit card practices, and provides a means for fair and timely resolution of credit billing disputes. With the exception of certain high-cost mortgage loans, Truth in Lending Act does not regulate the charges that may be imposed for consumer credit.
Great Recession	The Great Recession was a global economic decline in the late 2000s. According to aggregated national data, a worldwide recession began in Q3-2008 and ended in Q1-2009. It is related to a liquidity crisis, commonly being dated to have started when several central banks had to step in with liquidity lending to the interbank lending market on 9 August 2007. This was a response to a situation where BNP Paribas temporarily had to block money withdrawals from three hedge funds--citing a 'complete evaporation of liquidity'.
Income	Income is the consumption and savings opportunity gained by an entity within a specified timeframe, which is generally expressed in monetary terms. However, for households and individuals, 'income is the sum of all the wages, salaries, profits, interests payments, rents and other forms of earnings received... in a given period of time.' In the field of public economics, the term may refer to the accumulation of both monetary and non-monetary consumption ability, with the former (monetary) being used as a proxy for total income.
Recession	In economics, a recession is a business cycle contraction. It is a general slowdown in economic activity. Macroeconomic indicators such as GDP (gross domestic product), investment spending, capacity utilization, household income, business profits, and inflation fall, while bankruptcies and the unemployment rate rise.
Income distribution	In economics, income distribution is how a nation's total GDP is distributed amongst its population. Income and distribution has always been a central concern of economic theory and economic policy. Classical economists such as Adam Smith, Thomas Malthus and David Ricardo were mainly concerned with factor income distribution, that is, the distribution of income between the main factors of production, land, labour and capital.
Pricing	Pricing is the process of determining what a company will receive in exchange for its product. Pricing factors are manufacturing cost, market place, competition, market condition, brand, and quality of product. Pricing is also a key variable in microeconomic price allocation theory.

1. _____ is a legal designation of the ownership of property by non-governmental legal entities. _____ is distinguishable from public property, which is owned by a state entity; and collective property, which is owned by a group of non-governmental entities. _____ is further distinguished from personal property, which refers to property for personal use and consumption.

   a. Capital
   b. Chiefdom
   c. Classical liberalism
   d. Private property

2. _____ in business, engineering and manufacturing has a pragmatic interpretation as the non-inferiority or superiority of something; it is also defined as fitness for purpose. _____ is a perceptual, conditional, and somewhat subjective attribute and may be understood differently by different people. Consumers may focus on the specification _____ of a product/service, or how it compares to competitors in the marketplace.

   a. 100 Best Workplaces in Europe
   b. Career portfolio
   c. CESG Claims Tested Mark
   d. Quality

3. In economics, an _____, also called an imputed cost, implied cost, or notional cost, is the opportunity cost equal to what a firm must give up in order to use factors which it neither purchases nor hires. It is the opposite of an explicit cost, which is borne directly. In other words, an _____ is any cost that results from using an asset instead of renting, selling, or lending it.

   a. Base period
   b. Implicit cost
   c. Blanket order
   d. Bond

4. In economics, _____ is how a nation's total GDP is distributed amongst its population.

   Income and distribution has always been a central concern of economic theory and economic policy. Classical economists such as Adam Smith, Thomas Malthus and David Ricardo were mainly concerned with factor _____, that is, the distribution of income between the main factors of production, land, labour and capital.

   a. Income distribution
   b. Battle of Annaberg
   c. Freikorps Lichtschlag
   d. Freikorps Oberland

5. . In economics, _____ is any payment to a factor of production in excess of its opportunity cost.

16. Rent, Interest, and Profit

_____ should not be confounded or confused with opportunity cost, producer surplus, or normal profit in that all of these other terms involve productive human action. _____ is the cost of non-produced inputs or advantages; the result of natural or contrived exclusivity.

a. Economic rent
b. Care work
c. Cash collection
d. Commercial location development

1. d
2. d
3. b
4. a
5. a

You can take the complete Chapter Practice Test

for 16. Rent, Interest, and Profit
on all key terms, persons, places, and concepts.

Online 99 Cents

http://www.JustTheFacts101.com

Use www.JustTheFacts101.com for all your study needs

including Facts101's online interactive problem solving labs in

chemistry, statistics, mathematics, and more.

17. Natural Resource and Energy Economics

CHAPTER OUTLINE: KEY TERMS, PEOPLE, PLACES, CONCEPTS

Demographic transition

Industrial Revolution

Total cost

Income

National income

Product

Residual claimant

Great Recession

Recession

Interest rate

Abound Solar

Air pollution

Carbon dioxide

Carbon dioxide emissions

Pollution

Natural resource economics

Present value

Commercial bank

Property rights

Economic growth

Quality

17. Natural Resource and Energy Economics

	Tragedy of the commons

Demographic transition	Demographic transition refers to the transition from high birth and death rates to low birth and death rates as a country develops from a pre-industrial to an industrialized economic system. This is typically demonstrated through a demographic transition model (DTM). The theory is based on an interpretation of demographic history developed in 1929 by the American demographer Warren Thompson (1887-1973).
Industrial Revolution	The Industrial Revolution was the transition to new manufacturing processes in the period from about 1760 to sometime between 1820 and 1840. This transition included going from hand production methods to machines, new chemical manufacturing and iron production processes, improved efficiency of water power, the increasing use of steam power and the development of machine tools. It also included the change from wood and other bio-fuels to coal. Textiles were the dominant industry of the Industrial Revolution in terms of employment, value of output and capital invested.
Total cost	In economics, and cost accounting, total cost describes the total economic cost of production and is made up of variable costs, which vary according to the quantity of a good produced and include inputs such as labor and raw materials, plus fixed costs, which are independent of the quantity of a good produced and include inputs (capital) that cannot be varied in the short term, such as buildings and machinery. Total cost in economics includes the total opportunity cost of each factor of production as part of its fixed or variable costs. The rate at which total cost changes as the amount produced changes is called marginal cost.
Income	Income is the consumption and savings opportunity gained by an entity within a specified timeframe, which is generally expressed in monetary terms. However, for households and individuals, 'income is the sum of all the wages, salaries, profits, interests payments, rents and other forms of earnings received... in a given period of time.' In the field of public economics, the term may refer to the accumulation of both monetary and non-monetary consumption ability, with the former (monetary) being used as a proxy for total income.

17. Natural Resource and Energy Economics

National income	A variety of measures of national income and output are used in economics to estimate total economic activity in a country or region, including gross domestic product, gross national product (GNP), net national income and adjusted national income. All are specially concerned with counting the total amount of goods and services produced within some 'boundary'. The boundary is usually defined by geography or citizenship, and may also restrict the goods and services that are counted.
Product	In marketing, a product is anything that can be offered to a market that might satisfy a want or need. In retailing, products are called merchandise. In manufacturing, products are bought as raw materials and sold as finished goods.
Residual claimant	In economics, the residual claimant is the agent who receives the net income . Residual claimancy is generally required in order for there to be moral hazard, which is a problem typical of information asymmetry. This is specifically the case for the principal-agent problem.
Great Recession	The Great Recession was a global economic decline in the late 2000s. According to aggregated national data, a worldwide recession began in Q3-2008 and ended in Q1-2009. It is related to a liquidity crisis, commonly being dated to have started when several central banks had to step in with liquidity lending to the interbank lending market on 9 August 2007. This was a response to a situation where BNP Paribas temporarily had to block money withdrawals from three hedge funds--citing a 'complete evaporation of liquidity'.
Recession	In economics, a recession is a business cycle contraction. It is a general slowdown in economic activity. Macroeconomic indicators such as GDP (gross domestic product), investment spending, capacity utilization, household income, business profits, and inflation fall, while bankruptcies and the unemployment rate rise.
Interest rate	An interest rate is the rate at which interest is paid by a borrower for the use of money that they borrow from a lender (creditor). Specifically, the interest rate is a percent of principal (P) paid a certain amount of times (m) per period (usually quoted per annum). For example, a small company borrows capital from a bank to buy new assets for its business, and in return the lender receives interest at a predetermined interest rate for deferring the use of funds and instead lending it to the borrower.
Abound Solar	Abound Solar was a manufacturer of cadmium telluride thin-film photovoltaic modules based in the United States. It owns production facility in Longmont, Colorado. The company was incorporated as AVA Solar in 2007 and was rebranded as Abound Solar in March 2009. In 2010 Abound received a $400 million loan from the U.S. government.

17. Natural Resource and Energy Economics

Air pollution	Air pollution is the introduction of chemicals, particulates, biological materials, or other harmful materials into the Earth's atmosphere, possibly causing disease, death to humans, damage to other living organisms such as food crops, or the natural or built environment.
	The atmosphere is a complex natural gaseous system that is essential to support life on planet Earth. Stratospheric ozone depletion due to air pollution has long been recognized as a threat to human health as well as to the Earth's ecosystems.
Carbon dioxide	Carbon dioxide is a naturally occurring chemical compound composed of 2 oxygen atoms each covalently double bonded to a single carbon atom. It is a gas at standard temperature and pressure and exists in Earth's atmosphere in this state, as a trace gas at a concentration of 0.04 per cent (400 ppm) by volume, as of 2014.
	As part of the carbon cycle, plants, algae, and cyanobacteria use light energy to photosynthesize carbohydrate from carbon dioxide and water, with oxygen produced as a waste product.
Carbon dioxide emissions	This is a list of sovereign states and territories by carbon dioxide emissions due to certain forms of human activity. The data presented below corresponds to emissions in 2008. The data was collected by the United States Department of Energy's Carbon Dioxide Information Analysis Center (CDIAC) for the United Nations. The data only considers carbon dioxide emissions from the burning of fossil fuels and cement manufacture, but not emissions from land use, land-use change and forestry.
Pollution	Pollution is the introduction of contaminants into the natural environment that cause adverse change. Pollution can take the form of chemical substances or energy, such as noise, heat or light. Pollutants, the components of pollution, can be either foreign substances/energies or naturally occurring contaminants.
Natural resource economics	Natural resource economics deals with the supply, demand, and allocation of the Earth's natural resources. One main objective of natural resource economics is to better understand the role of natural resources in the economy in order to develop more sustainable methods of managing those resources to ensure their availability to future generations. Resource economists study interactions between economic and natural systems, with the goal of developing a sustainable and efficient economy.
Present value	Present value, also known as present discounted value, is a future amount of money that has been discounted to reflect its current value, as if it existed today. The present value is always less than or equal to the future value because money has interest-earning potential, a characteristic referred to as the time value of money. Time value can be described with the simplified phrase, "A dollar today is worth more than a dollar tomorrow".

Commercial bank	A commercial bank is a type of bank that provides services such as accepting deposits, making business loans, and offering basic investment products. Commercial bank can also refer to a bank or a division of a bank that mostly deals with deposits and loans from corporations or large businesses, as opposed to individual members of the public. In the US the term commercial bank was often used to distinguish it from an investment bank due to differences in bank regulation.
Property rights	Property rights are theoretical constructs in economics for determining how a resource is used and owned. Resources can be owned (the subject of property) by individuals, associations or governments. Property rights can be viewed as an attribute of an economic good.
Economic growth	Economic growth is the increase in the market value of the goods and services produced by an economy over time. It is conventionally measured as the percent rate of increase in real gross domestic product, or real GDP. Of more importance is the growth of the ratio of GDP to population (GDP per capita), which is also called per capita income. An increase in per capita income is referred to as intensive growth.
Quality	Quality in business, engineering and manufacturing has a pragmatic interpretation as the non-inferiority or superiority of something; it is also defined as fitness for purpose. Quality is a perceptual, conditional, and somewhat subjective attribute and may be understood differently by different people. Consumers may focus on the specification quality of a product/service, or how it compares to competitors in the marketplace.
Tragedy of the commons	The tragedy of the commons is an economics theory by Garrett Hardin, according to which individuals, acting independently and rationally according to each one's self-interest, behave contrary to the whole group's long-term best interests by depleting some common resource. The concept is often cited in connection with sustainable development, meshing economic growth and environmental protection, as well as in the debate over global warming. 'Commons' can include the atmosphere, oceans, rivers, fish stocks, national parks and any other shared resource.

17. Natural Resource and Energy Economics

1. _____ refers to the transition from high birth and death rates to low birth and death rates as a country develops from a pre-industrial to an industrialized economic system. This is typically demonstrated through a _____ model (DTM). The theory is based on an interpretation of demographic history developed in 1929 by the American demographer Warren Thompson (1887-1973).

   a. Baby boom
   b. Birth rate
   c. Demographic transition
   d. Cost of raising a child

2. The _____ was the transition to new manufacturing processes in the period from about 1760 to sometime between 1820 and 1840. This transition included going from hand production methods to machines, new chemical manufacturing and iron production processes, improved efficiency of water power, the increasing use of steam power and the development of machine tools. It also included the change from wood and other bio-fuels to coal.

   Textiles were the dominant industry of the _____ in terms of employment, value of output and capital invested.

   a. Bendigo Petition
   b. Bacon
   c. Industrial Revolution
   d. Commercial Revolution

3. _____ is the consumption and savings opportunity gained by an entity within a specified timeframe, which is generally expressed in monetary terms. However, for households and individuals, '_____ is the sum of all the wages, salaries, profits, interests payments, rents and other forms of earnings received... in a given period of time.'

   In the field of public economics, the term may refer to the accumulation of both monetary and non-monetary consumption ability, with the former (monetary) being used as a proxy for total _____.

   a. Fuel protests in the United Kingdom
   b. Battle of Annaberg
   c. Income
   d. Freikorps Oberland

4. In marketing, a _____ is anything that can be offered to a market that might satisfy a want or need. In retailing, _____s are called merchandise. In manufacturing, _____s are bought as raw materials and sold as finished goods.

   a. Back office
   b. Balanced scorecard
   c. Bestshoring
   d. Product

5. In economics, and cost accounting, _____ describes the total economic cost of production and is made up of variable costs, which vary according to the quantity of a good produced and include inputs such as labor and raw materials, plus fixed costs, which are independent of the quantity of a good produced and include inputs (capital) that cannot be varied in the short term, such as buildings and machinery. _____ in economics includes the total opportunity cost of each factor of production as part of its fixed or variable costs.

The rate at which _____ changes as the amount produced changes is called marginal cost.

a. Total cost
b. Bliss point
c. Club good
d. Conjectural variation

1. c
2. c
3. c
4. d
5. a

You can take the complete Chapter Practice Test

for 17. Natural Resource and Energy Economics
on all key terms, persons, places, and concepts.

Online 99 Cents

http://www.JustTheFacts101.com

Use www.JustTheFacts101.com for all your study needs

including Facts101's online interactive problem solving labs in

chemistry, statistics, mathematics, and more.

18. Public Finance: Expenditures and Taxes

Public finance

Monopoly

Natural monopoly

Income

National income

Product

Tax Freedom Day

Transfer payment

Revenue

Deficit spending

OPEC

Production

Laffer curve

Personal income

Taxable income

Tax rate

Tax revenue

Average tax rate

Baby Boomers

Great Recession

Recession

CHAPTER OUTLINE: KEY TERMS, PEOPLE, PLACES, CONCEPTS

	Social security
	State bank
	Corporate tax
	Payroll
	Loan guarantee
	Lottery
	Lenovo
	Health care
	Elasticity
	Externality
	Income distribution
	Pricing
	Short run
	Public sector

18. Public Finance: Expenditures and Taxes

Public finance	Public finance is the study of the role of the government in the economy. It is the branch of economics which assesses the government revenue and government expenditure of the public authorities and the adjustment of one or the other to achieve desirable effects and avoid undesirable ones. The purview of public finance is considered to be threefold: governmental effects on (1) efficient allocation of resources, (2) distribution of income, and (3) macroeconomic stabilization.
Monopoly	A monopoly (from Greek monos μ???? + polein p??e?? (to sell)) exists when a specific person or enterprise is the only supplier of a particular commodity (this contrasts with a monopsony which relates to a single entity's control of a market to purchase a good or service, and with oligopoly which consists of a few entities dominating an industry). Monopolies are thus characterized by a lack of economic competition to produce the good or service and a lack of viable substitute goods. The verb 'monopolize' refers to the process by which a company gains the ability to raise prices or exclude competitors.
Natural monopoly	A monopoly is a firm which is the only one producing and selling a particular product. A natural monopoly is a monopoly in an industry in which it is most efficient (involving the lowest long-run average cost) for production to be concentrated in a single firm. This market situation gives the largest supplier in an industry, often the first supplier in a market, an overwhelming cost advantage over other actual and potential competitors, so a natural monopoly situation generally leads to an actual monopoly.
Income	Income is the consumption and savings opportunity gained by an entity within a specified timeframe, which is generally expressed in monetary terms. However, for households and individuals, 'income is the sum of all the wages, salaries, profits, interests payments, rents and other forms of earnings received... in a given period of time.' In the field of public economics, the term may refer to the accumulation of both monetary and non-monetary consumption ability, with the former (monetary) being used as a proxy for total income.
National income	A variety of measures of national income and output are used in economics to estimate total economic activity in a country or region, including gross domestic product, gross national product (GNP), net national income and adjusted national income. All are specially concerned with counting the total amount of goods and services produced within some 'boundary'. The boundary is usually defined by geography or citizenship, and may also restrict the goods and services that are counted.
Product	In marketing, a product is anything that can be offered to a market that might satisfy a want or need. In retailing, products are called merchandise. In manufacturing, products are bought as raw materials and sold as finished goods.

18. Public Finance: Expenditures and Taxes

Tax Freedom Day	Tax Freedom Day is the first day of the year in which a nation as a whole has theoretically earned enough income to fund its annual tax burden. It is annually calculated in the United States by the Tax Foundation--a Washington, D.C.-based tax research organization. Every dollar that is officially considered income by the government is counted, and every payment to the government that is officially considered a tax is counted.
Transfer payment	In economics, a transfer payment is a redistribution of income in the market system. These payments are considered to be non-exhaustive because they do not directly absorb resources or create output. In other words, the transfer is made without any exchange of goods or services.
Revenue	In business, revenue or turnover is income that a company receives from its normal business activities, usually from the sale of goods and services to customers. In many countries, revenue is referred to as turnover. Some companies receive revenue from interest, royalties, or other fees.
Deficit spending	Deficit spending is the amount by which spending exceeds revenue over a particular period of time, also called simply deficit, or budget deficit; the opposite of budget surplus. The term may be applied to the budget of a government, private company, or individual. Government deficit spending is a central point of controversy in economics, as discussed below.
OPEC	OPEC is an international organization whose mission is to coordinate the policies of the oil-producing countries. The goal is to secure a steady income to the member states and to secure supply of oil to consumers. OPEC is an intergovernmental organization that was created at the Baghdad Conference on 10-14 September 1960, by Iraq, Kuwait, Iran, Saudi Arabia and Venezuela.
Production	Production is a process of combining various material inputs and immaterial inputs in order to make something for consumption (the output). It is the act of creating output, a good or service which has value and contributes to the utility of individuals. Economic well-being is created in a production process, meaning all economic activities that aim directly or indirectly to satisfy human needs.
Laffer curve	In economics, the Laffer curve is a representation of the relationship between possible rates of taxation and the resulting levels of government revenue. It illustrates the concept of taxable income elasticity--i.e., taxable income will change in response to changes in the rate of taxation. It postulates that no tax revenue will be raised at the extreme tax rates of 0% and 100% and that there must be at least one rate where tax revenue would be a non-zero maximum.
Personal income	In economics, personal income refers to an individual's total earnings from wages, investment enterprises, and other ventures. It is the sum of all the incomes actually received by all the individuals or household during a given period.

18. Public Finance: Expenditures and Taxes

Taxable income	Taxable income refers to the base upon which an income tax system imposes tax. Generally, it includes some or all items of income and is reduced by expenses and other deductions. The amounts included as income, expenses, and other deductions vary by country or system.
Tax rate	In a tax system and in economics, the tax rate describes the burden ratio at which a business or person is taxed. There are several methods used to present a tax rate: statutory, average, marginal, and effective. These rates can also be presented using different definitions applied to a tax base: inclusive and exclusive.
Tax revenue	Tax revenue is the income that is gained by governments through taxation. Just as there are different types of tax, the form in which tax revenue is collected also differs; furthermore, the agency that collects the tax may not be part of central government, but may be an alternative third-party licenced to collect tax which they themselves will use. For example:•In the UK, the DVLA collects vehicle excise duty, which is then passed onto the treasury. Tax revenues on purchases can come from two forms: 'tax' itself is a percentage of the price added to the purchase (such as sales tax in US states, or VAT in the UK), while 'duty' is a fixed amount added to the purchase price (such as is commonly found on cigarettes).
Average tax rate	Average tax rate is the average percent you pay in taxes out of your taxable income, based upon the tax brackets you fall into. For example: John Doe files taxes as a single man, with a total of $65,000 in taxable income. The first $7,550 he made would be taxed at 10%, then income between $7,550 and $30,650 would be taxed at 15%, with the remainder taxed at 25%.
Baby Boomers	Baby boomers are people born during the demographic Post-World War II baby boom between the years 1946 and 1964. According to the U.S. Census Bureau, the term 'baby boomer' is also used in a cultural context. Therefore, it is impossible to achieve broad consensus of a precise date definition, even within a given territory. Different groups, organizations, individuals, and scholars may have widely varying opinions on what constitutes a baby boomer, both technically and culturally.
Great Recession	The Great Recession was a global economic decline in the late 2000s. According to aggregated national data, a worldwide recession began in Q3-2008 and ended in Q1-2009. It is related to a liquidity crisis, commonly being dated to have started when several central banks had to step in with liquidity lending to the interbank lending market on 9 August 2007. This was a response to a situation where BNP Paribas temporarily had to block money withdrawals from three hedge funds--citing a 'complete evaporation of liquidity'.
Recession	In economics, a recession is a business cycle contraction. It is a general slowdown in economic activity.

Social security	Social security is a concept enshrined in Article 22 of the Universal Declaration of Human Rights which states, Everyone, as a member of society, has the right to social security and is entitled to realization, through national effort and international co-operation and in accordance with the organization and resources of each State, of the economic, social and cultural rights indispensable for his dignity and the free development of his personality. In simple terms, the signatories agree that society in which a person lives should help them to develop and to make the most of all the advantages (culture, work, social welfare) which are offered to them in the country.
	Social security may also refer to the action programs of government intended to promote the welfare of the population through assistance measures guaranteeing access to sufficient resources for food and shelter and to promote health and well-being for the population at large and potentially vulnerable segments such as children, the elderly, the sick and the unemployed.
State bank	A state bank is generally a financial institution that is chartered by a state. It differs from a reserve bank in that it does not necessarily control monetary policy (indeed, the state in question may have no legal capacity to create monetary policy), but instead usually offers only retail and commercial services.
	A state bank that has been in operation for five years or less is called a de novo bank.
Corporate tax	Many countries impose corporate tax, also called corporation tax or company tax, on the income or capital of some types of legal entities. A similar tax may be imposed at state or lower levels. The taxes may also be referred to as income tax or capital tax.
Payroll	In a company, payroll is the sum of all financial records of salaries for an employee, wages, bonuses and deductions. In accounting, payroll refers to the amount paid to employees for services they provided during a certain period of time. Payroll plays a major role in a company for several reasons.
Loan guarantee	A loan guarantee, in finance, is a promise by one party to assume the debt obligation of a borrower if that borrower defaults. A guarantee can be limited or unlimited, making the guarantor liable for only a portion or all of the debt.
	Guarantor mortgages are popular with young borrowers who do not have a large deposit saved and need to borrow 100% of the property value to purchase a property.
Lottery	In expected utility theory, a lottery is a discrete distribution of probability on a set of states of nature. The elements of a lottery correspond to the probability that a certain outcome arises from a given state of nature. In economics, individuals are assumed to rank lotteries according to a rational system of preferences, although it is now accepted that people make irrational choices systematically.

18. Public Finance: Expenditures and Taxes

Lenovo	Lenovo Group Ltd. is a Chinese multinational technology company with headquarters in Beijing, China, and Morrisville, North Carolina, United States. It designs, develops, manufactures and sells personal computers, tablet computers, smartphones, workstations, servers, electronic storage devices, IT management software and smart televisions.
Health care	Health care is the diagnosis, treatment, and prevention of disease, illness, injury, and other physical and mental impairments in human beings. Health care is delivered by practitioners in allied health, dentistry, midwifery-obstetrics, medicine, nursing, optometry, pharmacy, psychology and other care providers. It refers to the work done in providing primary care, secondary care, and tertiary care, as well as in public health.
Elasticity	In economics, elasticity is the measurement of how responsive an economic variable is to a change in another. For example:•'If I lower the price of my product, how much more will I sell?'•'If I raise the price of one good, how will that affect sales of this other good?'•'If we learn that a resource is becoming scarce, will people scramble to acquire it?' An elastic variable (or elasticity value greater than 1) is one which responds more than proportionally to changes in other variables. In contrast, an inelastic variable (or elasticity value less than 1) is one which changes less than proportionally in response to changes in other variables.
Externality	In economics, an externality is the cost or benefit that affects a party who did not choose to incur that cost or benefit. For example, manufacturing activities that cause air pollution impose health and clean-up costs on the whole society, whereas the neighbors of an individual who chooses to fire-proof his home may benefit from a reduced risk of a fire spreading to their own houses. If external costs exist, such as pollution, the producer may choose to produce more of the product than would be produced if the producer were required to pay all associated environmental costs.
Income distribution	In economics, income distribution is how a nation's total GDP is distributed amongst its population. Income and distribution has always been a central concern of economic theory and economic policy. Classical economists such as Adam Smith, Thomas Malthus and David Ricardo were mainly concerned with factor income distribution, that is, the distribution of income between the main factors of production, land, labour and capital.
Pricing	Pricing is the process of determining what a company will receive in exchange for its product. Pricing factors are manufacturing cost, market place, competition, market condition, brand, and quality of product. Pricing is also a key variable in microeconomic price allocation theory.

18. Public Finance: Expenditures and Taxes

Short run	In microeconomics, the long run is the conceptual time period in which there are no fixed factors of production as to changing the output level by changing the capital stock or by entering or leaving an industry. The long run contrasts with the short run, in which some factors are variable and others are fixed, constraining entry or exit from an industry. In macroeconomics, the long run is the period when the general price level, contractual wage rates, and expectations adjust fully to the state of the economy, in contrast to the short run when these variables may not fully adjust.
Public sector	The public sector refers to the part of the economy concerned with providing various government services. The composition of the public sector varies by country, but in most countries the public sector includes such services as the military, police, public transit and care of public roads, public education, along with healthcare and those working for the government itself, such as elected officials. The public sector might provide services that a non-payer cannot be excluded from (such as street lighting), services which benefit all of society rather than just the individual who uses the service.

1. A monopoly is a firm which is the only one producing and selling a particular product. A _____ is a monopoly in an industry in which it is most efficient (involving the lowest long-run average cost) for production to be concentrated in a single firm. This market situation gives the largest supplier in an industry, often the first supplier in a market, an overwhelming cost advantage over other actual and potential competitors, so a _____ situation generally leads to an actual monopoly.

   a. Coercive monopoly
   b. Natural monopoly
   c. Free rider problem
   d. Global public good

2. _____ is the study of the role of the government in the economy. It is the branch of economics which assesses the government revenue and government expenditure of the public authorities and the adjustment of one or the other to achieve desirable effects and avoid undesirable ones.

   The purview of _____ is considered to be threefold: governmental effects on (1) efficient allocation of resources, (2) distribution of income, and (3) macroeconomic stabilization.

   a. Fuel protests in the United Kingdom
   b. Battle of Annaberg
   c. Freikorps Lichtschlag
   d. Public finance

3. A _____ (from Greek monos μ???? + polein p??e?? (to sell)) exists when a specific person or enterprise is the only supplier of a particular commodity (this contrasts with a monopsony which relates to a single entity's control of a market to purchase a good or service, and with oligopoly which consists of a few entities dominating an industry). _____(ies) are thus characterized by a lack of economic competition to produce the good or service and a lack of viable substitute goods. The verb 'monopolize' refers to the process by which a company gains the ability to raise prices or exclude competitors.

   a. Cellophane paradox
   b. Competition
   c. Monopoly
   d. Disequilibrium

4. _____ is an international organization whose mission is to coordinate the policies of the oil-producing countries. The goal is to secure a steady income to the member states and to secure supply of oil to consumers.

   _____ is an intergovernmental organization that was created at the Baghdad Conference on 10-14 September 1960, by Iraq, Kuwait, Iran, Saudi Arabia and Venezuela.

   a. OPEC
   b. Balassa index
   c. Banana Framework Agreement
   d. Bilateral trade

5. In economics, a _____ is a business cycle contraction. It is a general slowdown in economic activity. Macroeconomic indicators such as GDP (gross domestic product), investment spending, capacity utilization, household income, business profits, and inflation fall, while bankruptcies and the unemployment rate rise.

   a. Depression
   b. General glut
   c. Global recession
   d. Recession

ANSWER KEY
18. Public Finance: Expenditures and Taxes

1. b
2. d
3. c
4. a
5. d

You can take the complete Chapter Practice Test

for 18. Public Finance: Expenditures and Taxes
on all key terms, persons, places, and concepts.

Online 99 Cents

http://www.JustTheFacts101.com

Use www.JustTheFacts101.com for all your study needs

including Facts101's online interactive problem solving labs in

chemistry, statistics, mathematics, and more.

CHAPTER OUTLINE: KEY TERMS, PEOPLE, PLACES, CONCEPTS

Allocative efficiency

Antitrust

Income

Monopolistic competition

National income

Natural monopoly

Oligopoly

Product

Federal Trade Commission

Interlocking directorate

Justice

Price discrimination

Occupational segregation

Behavioral economics

Relevant market

Creative destruction

Menu cost

Monopoly

Conglomerate merger

Herfindahl index

Present value

19. Antitrust Policy and Regulation

CHAPTER OUTLINE: KEY TERMS, PEOPLE, PLACES, CONCEPTS

_____ | Inflation

_____ | Federal Communications Commission

_____ | X-inefficiency

_____ | Interest rate

_____ | Transfer payment

_____ | Deregulation

_____ | Enron

_____ | Gateway

CHAPTER HIGHLIGHTS & NOTES: KEY TERMS, PEOPLE, PLACES, CONCEPTS

Allocative efficiency	Allocative efficiency is a type of economic efficiency in which economy/producers produce only those types of goods and services that are more desirable in the society and also in high demand. According to the formula the point of allocative efficiency is a point where price is equal to marginal cost (P=MC)or (MC=MR). At this point the social surplus is maximized with no deadweight loss, or the value society puts on that level of output produced minus the value of resources used to achieve that level, yet can be applied to other things such as level of pollution.
Antitrust	Competition law is law that promotes or seeks to maintain market competition by regulating anti-competitive conduct by companies. Competition law is known as antitrust law in the United States and anti-monopoly law in China and Russia. In previous years it has been known as trade practices law in the United Kingdom and Australia.
Income	Income is the consumption and savings opportunity gained by an entity within a specified timeframe, which is generally expressed in monetary terms. However, for households and individuals, 'income is the sum of all the wages, salaries, profits, interests payments, rents and other forms of earnings received... in a given period of time.'

	In the field of public economics, the term may refer to the accumulation of both monetary and non-monetary consumption ability, with the former (monetary) being used as a proxy for total income.
Monopolistic competition	Monopolistic competition is a type of imperfect competition such that many producers sell products that are differentiated from one another and hence are not perfect substitutes. In monopolistic competition, a firm takes the prices charged by its rivals as given and ignores the impact of its own prices on the prices of other firms. In the presence of coercive government, monopolistic competition will fall into government-granted monopoly.
National income	A variety of measures of national income and output are used in economics to estimate total economic activity in a country or region, including gross domestic product, gross national product (GNP), net national income and adjusted national income. All are specially concerned with counting the total amount of goods and services produced within some 'boundary'. The boundary is usually defined by geography or citizenship, and may also restrict the goods and services that are counted.
Natural monopoly	A monopoly is a firm which is the only one producing and selling a particular product. A natural monopoly is a monopoly in an industry in which it is most efficient (involving the lowest long-run average cost) for production to be concentrated in a single firm. This market situation gives the largest supplier in an industry, often the first supplier in a market, an overwhelming cost advantage over other actual and potential competitors, so a natural monopoly situation generally leads to an actual monopoly.
Oligopoly	An oligopoly is a market form in which a market or industry is dominated by a small number of sellers . Oligopolies can result from various forms of collusion which reduce competition and lead to higher prices for consumers. With few sellers, each oligopolist is likely to be aware of the actions of the others.
Product	In marketing, a product is anything that can be offered to a market that might satisfy a want or need. In retailing, products are called merchandise. In manufacturing, products are bought as raw materials and sold as finished goods.
Federal Trade Commission	The Federal Trade Commission is an independent agency of the United States government, established in 1914 by the Federal Trade Commission Act. Its principal mission is the promotion of consumer protection and the elimination and prevention of anticompetitive business practices, such as coercive monopoly. The Federal Trade Commission Act was one of President Woodrow Wilson's major acts against trusts.
Interlocking directorate	Interlocking directorate refers to the practice of members of a corporate board of directors serving on the boards of multiple corporations. A person that sits on multiple boards is known as a multiple director.

19. Antitrust Policy and Regulation

Justice	Justice in economics is a subcategory of welfare economics with models frequently representing the ethical-social requirements of a given theory, whether 'in the large,' as of a just social order, or 'in the small,' as in the equity of 'how institutions distribute specific benefits and burdens.' That theory may or may not elicit acceptance. In the Journal of Economic Literature classification codes 'justice' is scrolled to at JEL: D63, wedged on the same line between 'Equity' and 'Inequality' along with 'Other Normative Criteria and Measurement'. Categories above and below the line are Externalities and Altruism.
Price discrimination	Price discrimination or price differentiation is a pricing strategy where identical or largely similar goods or services are transacted at different prices by the same provider in different markets or territories. Price differentiation is distinguished from product differentiation by the more substantial difference in production cost for the differently priced products involved in the latter strategy. Price differentiation essentially relies on the variation in the customers' willingness to pay.
Occupational segregation	Occupational segregation is the distribution of people based upon demographic characteristics, most often gender, both across and within occupations and jobs. Occupational segregation levels differ on a basis of perfect segregation and integration. Perfect segregation occurs where any given occupation employs only one group.
Behavioral economics	Behavioral economics and the related field, behavioral finance, study the effects of social, cognitive, and emotional factors on the economic decisions of individuals and institutions and the consequences for market prices, returns, and the resource allocation. The fields are primarily concerned with the bounds of rationality of economic agents. Behavioral models typically integrate insights from psychology with microeconomic theory; in so doing, these behavioral models cover a range of concepts, methods, and fields.
Relevant market	In competition law, a relevant market is a market in which a particular product or service is sold. It is the intersection of a relevant product market and a relevant geographic market. The European Commission defines a relevant market and its product and geographic components as follows:•A relevant product market comprises all those products and/or services which are regarded as interchangeable or substitutable by the consumer by reason of the products' characteristics, their prices and their intended use;•A relevant geographic market comprises the area in which the firms concerned are involved in the supply of products or services and in which the conditions of competition are sufficiently homogeneous.
Creative destruction	Creative destruction, sometimes known as Schumpeter's gale, is a term in economics which has since the 1950s become most readily identified with the Austrian American economist Joseph Schumpeter's theory of economic innovation and business cycle. Creative destruction describes the 'process of industrial mutation that incessantly revolutionizes the economic structure from within, incessantly destroying the old one, incessantly creating a new one.'

	The German Marxist sociologist Werner Sombart who has been credited with the first use of these terms in his work Krieg und Kapitalismus ('War and Capitalism', 1913). In the earlier work of Marx, however, the idea of creative destruction or annihilation (German: Vernichtung) implies not only that capitalism destroys and reconfigures previous economic orders, but also that it must ceaselessly devalue existing wealth (whether through war, dereliction, or regular and periodic economic crises) in order to clear the ground for the creation of new wealth.
Menu cost	In economics, a menu cost is the cost to a firm resulting from changing its prices. The name stems from the cost of restaurants literally printing new menus, but economists use it to refer to the costs of changing nominal prices in general. In this broader definition, menu costs might include updating computer systems, re-tagging items, and hiring consultants to develop new pricing strategies as well as the literal costs of printing menus.
Monopoly	A monopoly (from Greek monos μ???? + polein p??e?? (to sell)) exists when a specific person or enterprise is the only supplier of a particular commodity (this contrasts with a monopsony which relates to a single entity's control of a market to purchase a good or service, and with oligopoly which consists of a few entities dominating an industry). Monopolies are thus characterized by a lack of economic competition to produce the good or service and a lack of viable substitute goods. The verb 'monopolize' refers to the process by which a company gains the ability to raise prices or exclude competitors.
Conglomerate merger	A conglomerate merger is officially defined as being 'any merger that is not horizontal or vertical; in general, it is the combination of firms in different industries or firms operating in different geographic areas'. Conglomerate mergers can serve various purposes, including extending corporate territories and extending a product range. One example of a conglomerate merger was the merger between the Walt Disney Company and the American Broadcasting Company.
Herfindahl index	The Herfindahl index is a measure of the size of firms in relation to the industry and an indicator of the amount of competition among them. Named after economists Orris C. Herfindahl and Albert O. Hirschman, it is an economic concept widely applied in competition law, antitrust and also technology management. It is defined as the sum of the squares of the market shares of the 50 largest firms (or summed over all the firms if there are fewer than 50) within the industry, where the market shares are expressed as fractions.
Present value	Present value, also known as present discounted value, is a future amount of money that has been discounted to reflect its current value, as if it existed today. The present value is always less than or equal to the future value because money has interest-earning potential, a characteristic referred to as the time value of money. Time value can be described with the simplified phrase, "A dollar today is worth more than a dollar tomorrow".

19. Antitrust Policy and Regulation

Inflation	In economics, inflation is a sustained increase in the general price level of goods and services in an economy over a period of time. When the general price level rises, each unit of currency buys fewer goods and services. Consequently, inflation reflects a reduction in the purchasing power per unit of money - a loss of real value in the medium of exchange and unit of account within the economy.
Federal Communications Commission	The Federal Communications Commission is an independent agency of the United States government, created by Congressional statute to regulate interstate and international communications by radio, television, wire, satellite, and cable in all 50 states, the District of Columbia and U.S. territories. The Federal Communications Commission works towards six goals in the areas of broadband, competition, the spectrum, the media, public safety and homeland security. The Commission is also in the process of modernizing itself.
X-inefficiency	X-inefficiency is the difference between efficient behavior of businesses assumed or implied by economic theory and their observed behavior in practice. It occurs when technical-efficiency is not being achieved due to a lack of competitive pressure. The concepts of x-inefficiency were introduced by Harvey Leibenstein.
Interest rate	An interest rate is the rate at which interest is paid by a borrower for the use of money that they borrow from a lender (creditor). Specifically, the interest rate is a percent of principal (P) paid a certain amount of times (m) per period (usually quoted per annum). For example, a small company borrows capital from a bank to buy new assets for its business, and in return the lender receives interest at a predetermined interest rate for deferring the use of funds and instead lending it to the borrower.
Transfer payment	In economics, a transfer payment is a redistribution of income in the market system. These payments are considered to be non-exhaustive because they do not directly absorb resources or create output. In other words, the transfer is made without any exchange of goods or services.
Deregulation	Deregulation is the process of removing or reducing state regulations. It is therefore opposite of regulation, which refers to the process of the government regulating certain activities.
Enron	Enron Corporation was an American energy, commodities, and services company based in Houston, Texas. Before its bankruptcy on December 2, 2001, Enron employed approximately 20,000 staff and was one of the world's major electricity, natural gas, communications, and pulp and paper companies, with claimed revenues of nearly $101 billion during 2000. Fortune named Enron 'America's Most Innovative Company' for six consecutive years. At the end of 2001, it was revealed that its reported financial condition was sustained substantially by an institutionalized, systematic, and creatively planned accounting fraud, known since as the Enron scandal.

Gateway	Gateway is a phrase used by webmasters and search engine optimizers to describe a webpage designed to attract visitors and search engines to a particular website. A typical gateway page is small, simple and highly optimized. Its primary goal is to attract visitors searching for relevant key words or phrases, and provide hyperlinks to pages within the website.

CHAPTER QUIZ: KEY TERMS, PEOPLE, PLACES, CONCEPTS

1. _____ is the difference between efficient behavior of businesses assumed or implied by economic theory and their observed behavior in practice. It occurs when technical-efficiency is not being achieved due to a lack of competitive pressure. The concepts of _____ were introduced by Harvey Leibenstein.

   a. X-inefficiency
   b. Cluster theory
   c. Distortion
   d. Distributive efficiency

2. A _____ is officially defined as being 'any merger that is not horizontal or vertical; in general, it is the combination of firms in different industries or firms operating in different geographic areas'. _____s can serve various purposes, including extending corporate territories and extending a product range. One example of a _____ was the merger between the Walt Disney Company and the American Broadcasting Company.

   a. Business ecosystem
   b. Center for Business and Economic Research
   c. Fuel protests in the United Kingdom
   d. Conglomerate merger

3. An _____ is the rate at which interest is paid by a borrower for the use of money that they borrow from a lender (creditor). Specifically, the _____ is a percent of principal (P) paid a certain amount of times (m) per period (usually quoted per annum). For example, a small company borrows capital from a bank to buy new assets for its business, and in return the lender receives interest at a predetermined _____ for deferring the use of funds and instead lending it to the borrower.

   a. Bernanke doctrine
   b. Discretionary policy
   c. Interest rate
   d. Battle of Annaberg

19. Antitrust Policy and Regulation

4. A variety of measures of _____ and output are used in economics to estimate total economic activity in a country or region, including gross domestic product, gross national product (GNP), net _____ and adjusted _____. All are specially concerned with counting the total amount of goods and services produced within some 'boundary'. The boundary is usually defined by geography or citizenship, and may also restrict the goods and services that are counted.

    a. Fuel protests in the United Kingdom
    b. Competition
    c. National income
    d. Disequilibrium

5. In marketing, a _____ is anything that can be offered to a market that might satisfy a want or need. In retailing, _____s are called merchandise. In manufacturing, _____s are bought as raw materials and sold as finished goods.

    a. Back office
    b. Balanced scorecard
    c. Bestshoring
    d. Product

1. a
2. d
3. c
4. c
5. d

You can take the complete Chapter Practice Test

for 19. Antitrust Policy and Regulation
on all key terms, persons, places, and concepts.

Online 99 Cents

http://www.JustTheFacts101.com

Use www.JustTheFacts101.com for all your study needs

including Facts101's online interactive problem solving labs in

chemistry, statistics, mathematics, and more.

20. Agriculture: Economics and Policy

CHAPTER OUTLINE: KEY TERMS, PEOPLE, PLACES, CONCEPTS

Short run

Tying

Aggregate supply

Income

Instability

Great Recession

International trade

Recession

Commodity

Expression

Labor force

Subsidy

Price support

Production

Acreage allotments

Logrolling

Public choice

Corruption

Freedom

World Trade Organization

Import quota

	Residual claimant

Short run	In microeconomics, the long run is the conceptual time period in which there are no fixed factors of production as to changing the output level by changing the capital stock or by entering or leaving an industry. The long run contrasts with the short run, in which some factors are variable and others are fixed, constraining entry or exit from an industry. In macroeconomics, the long run is the period when the general price level, contractual wage rates, and expectations adjust fully to the state of the economy, in contrast to the short run when these variables may not fully adjust.
Tying	Tying is the practice of selling one product or service as a mandatory addition to the purchase of a different product or service. In legal terms, a tying sale makes the sale of one good (the tying good) to the de facto customer (or de jure customer) conditional on the purchase of a second distinctive good (the tied good). Tying is often illegal when the products are not naturally related.
Aggregate supply	In economics, aggregate supply is the total supply of goods and services that firms in a national economy plan on selling during a specific time period. It is the total amount of goods and services that firms are willing to sell at a given price level in an economy.
Income	Income is the consumption and savings opportunity gained by an entity within a specified timeframe, which is generally expressed in monetary terms. However, for households and individuals, 'income is the sum of all the wages, salaries, profits, interests payments, rents and other forms of earnings received... in a given period of time.' In the field of public economics, the term may refer to the accumulation of both monetary and non-monetary consumption ability, with the former (monetary) being used as a proxy for total income.
Instability	In numerous fields of study, the component of instability within a system is generally characterized by some of the outputs or internal states growing without bounds. Not all systems that are not stable are unstable; systems can also be marginally stable or exhibit limit cycle behavior. In control theory, a system is unstable if any of the roots of its characteristic equation has real part greater than zero (or if zero is a repeated root).
Great Recession	The Great Recession was a global economic decline in the late 2000s. According to aggregated national data, a worldwide recession began in Q3-2008 and ended in Q1-2009.

It is related to a liquidity crisis, commonly being dated to have started when several central banks had to step in with liquidity lending to the interbank lending market on 9 August 2007. This was a response to a situation where BNP Paribas temporarily had to block money withdrawals from three hedge funds--citing a 'complete evaporation of liquidity'.

International trade	International trade is the exchange of capital, goods, and services across international borders or territories. In most countries, such trade represents a significant share of gross domestic product (GDP). While international trade has been present throughout much of history, its economic, social, and political importance has been on the rise in recent centuries.
Recession	In economics, a recession is a business cycle contraction. It is a general slowdown in economic activity. Macroeconomic indicators such as GDP (gross domestic product), investment spending, capacity utilization, household income, business profits, and inflation fall, while bankruptcies and the unemployment rate rise.
Commodity	In classical political economy and especially Karl Marx's critique of political economy, a commodity is any good or service produced by human labour and offered as a product for general sale on the market. Some other priced goods are also treated as commodities, e.g. human labor-power, works of art and natural resources, even though they may not be produced specifically for the market, or be non-reproducible goods. Marx's analysis of the commodity is intended to help solve the problem of what establishes the economic value of goods, using the labor theory of value.
Expression	In mathematics, an expression is a finite combination of symbols that is well-formed according to rules that depend on the context. Symbols can designate numbers (constants), variables, operations, functions, and other mathematical symbols, as well as punctuation, symbols of grouping, and other syntactic symbols. The use of expressions can range from the simple: $0 + 0$ to the complex: $$f(a) + \sum_{k=1}^{n} \frac{1}{k!} \frac{d^k}{dt^k} \Big|_{t=0} f(u(t)) + \int_0^1 \frac{(1-t)^n}{n!} \frac{d^{n+1}}{dt^{n+1}} f(u(t))\, dt.$$ We can think of algebraic expressions as generalizations of common arithmetic operations that are formed by combining numbers, variables, and mathematical operations.
Labor force	The labor force is the actual number of people available for work. The labor force of a country includes both the employed and the unemployed.

20. Agriculture: Economics and Policy

Subsidy	A subsidy is a form of financial or in kind support extended to an economic sector generally with the aim of promoting economic and social policy. Although commonly extended from Government, the term subsidy can relate to any type of support - for example from NGOs or implicit subsidies. Subsidies come in various forms including: direct (cash grants, interest-free loans) and indirect (tax breaks, insurance, low-interest loans, depreciation write-offs, rent rebates).
Price support	In economics, a price support may be either a subsidy or a price control, both with the intended effect of keeping the market price of a good higher than the competitive equilibrium level. In the case of a price control, a price support is the minimum legal price a seller may charge, typically placed above equilibrium. It is the support of certain price levels at or above market values by the government.
Production	Production is a process of combining various material inputs and immaterial inputs in order to make something for consumption (the output). It is the act of creating output, a good or service which has value and contributes to the utility of individuals. Economic well-being is created in a production process, meaning all economic activities that aim directly or indirectly to satisfy human needs.
Acreage allotments	A farm's acreage allotment, under provisions of permanent commodity price support law, is its share, based on its previous production, of the national acreage needed to produce sufficient supplies of a particular crop. Under the 2002 farm bill (P.L. 101-171, Title I), acreage allotments are not applicable to the covered commodities, peanuts, or sugar. Subsequently, allotments and quotas and price support for tobacco were eliminated beginning in 2005 (P.L. 108-357, Title VI).
Logrolling	Logrolling is the trading of favors, or quid pro quo, such as vote trading by legislative members to obtain passage of actions of interest to each legislative member. In an academic context, the Nuttall Encyclopedia describes logrolling as 'mutual praise by authors of each other's work.' In organizational analysis, it refers to a practice in which different organizations promote each other's agendas, each in the expectation that the other will reciprocate.
Public choice	Public choice theory has been described as 'the use of economic tools to deal with traditional problems of political science'. Its content includes the study of political behavior. In political science, it is the subset of positive political theory that models voters, politicians, and bureaucrats as mainly self-interested.
Corruption	In philosophical, theological, or moral discussions, corruption is spiritual or moral impurity or deviation from an ideal. Corruption may include many activities including bribery and embezzlement. Government, or 'political', corruption occurs when an office-holder or other governmental employee acts in an official capacity for personal gain.
Freedom	Freedom is a London-based anarchist newspaper published monthly by Freedom Press ceasing print publication in 2014.

	The paper was started in 1886 by volunteers including Peter Kropotkin and Charlotte Wilson and continues to 2014 as an unpaid project. Originally, the subtitle was 'A Journal of Anarchist Socialism.' The title was changed to 'A Journal of Anarchist Communism' in June 1889. Today it is unlabelled.
World Trade Organization	The World Trade Organization is an organization that intends to supervise and liberalize international trade. The organization officially commenced on 1 January 1995 under the Marrakech Agreement, replacing the General Agreement on Tariffs and Trade (GATT), which commenced in 1948. The organization deals with regulation of trade between participating countries; it provides a framework for negotiating and formalizing trade agreements, and a dispute resolution process aimed at enforcing participant's adherence to World Trade Organization agreements, which are signed by representatives of member governments and ratified by their parliaments. Most of the issues that the World Trade Organization focuses on derive from previous trade negotiations, especially from the Uruguay Round (1986-1994).
Import quota	An import quota is a limit on the quantity of a good that can be produced abroad and sold domestically. It is a type of protectionist trade restriction that sets a physical limit on the quantity of a good that can be imported into a country in a given period of time. If a quota is put on a good, less of it is imported.
Residual claimant	In economics, the residual claimant is the agent who receives the net income . Residual claimancy is generally required in order for there to be moral hazard, which is a problem typical of information asymmetry. This is specifically the case for the principal-agent problem.

CHAPTER QUIZ: KEY TERMS, PEOPLE, PLACES, CONCEPTS

1. A farm's _____(s), under provisions of permanent commodity price support law, is its share, based on its previous production, of the national acreage needed to produce sufficient supplies of a particular crop. Under the 2002 farm bill (P.L. 101-171, Title I), _____ are not applicable to the covered commodities, peanuts, or sugar. Subsequently, allotments and quotas and price support for tobacco were eliminated beginning in 2005 (P.L. 108-357, Title VI).

   a. 2008 Central Asia energy crisis
   b. Acreage allotments
   c. Cost driver
   d. Diseconomies of scale

2. . In microeconomics, the long run is the conceptual time period in which there are no fixed factors of production as to changing the output level by changing the capital stock or by entering or leaving an industry.

20. Agriculture: Economics and Policy

The long run contrasts with the _____, in which some factors are variable and others are fixed, constraining entry or exit from an industry. In macroeconomics, the long run is the period when the general price level, contractual wage rates, and expectations adjust fully to the state of the economy, in contrast to the _____ when these variables may not fully adjust.

a. Fuel protests in the United Kingdom
b. Short run
c. Freikorps Lichtschlag
d. Freikorps Oberland

3. In economics, _____ is the total supply of goods and services that firms in a national economy plan on selling during a specific time period. It is the total amount of goods and services that firms are willing to sell at a given price level in an economy.

a. Fuel protests in the United Kingdom
b. Battle of Annaberg
c. Freikorps Lichtschlag
d. Aggregate supply

4. In numerous fields of study, the component of _____ within a system is generally characterized by some of the outputs or internal states growing without bounds. Not all systems that are not stable are unstable; systems can also be marginally stable or exhibit limit cycle behavior.

In control theory, a system is unstable if any of the roots of its characteristic equation has real part greater than zero (or if zero is a repeated root).

a. Energy Task Force
b. Instability
c. Freikorps Lichtschlag
d. Freikorps Oberland

5. _____ is the exchange of capital, goods, and services across international borders or territories. In most countries, such trade represents a significant share of gross domestic product (GDP). While _____ has been present throughout much of history, its economic, social, and political importance has been on the rise in recent centuries.

a. 2008 G-20 Washington summit
b. Backsourcing
c. International trade
d. Bureau de change

ANSWER KEY
20. Agriculture: Economics and Policy

1. b
2. b
3. d
4. b
5. c

You can take the complete Chapter Practice Test

for 20. Agriculture: Economics and Policy
on all key terms, persons, places, and concepts.

Online 99 Cents

http://www.JustTheFacts101.com

Use www.JustTheFacts101.com for all your study needs

including Facts101's online interactive problem solving labs in

chemistry, statistics, mathematics, and more.

21. Income Inequality, Poverty, and Discrimination

CHAPTER OUTLINE: KEY TERMS, PEOPLE, PLACES, CONCEPTS

	Income
	Income inequality
	Pricing
	Lorenz curve
	Great Recession
	Recession
	Transfer payment
	Income distribution
	Monopoly
	Natural monopoly
	Health insurance
	Inflation
	Skilled worker
	Baby Boomers
	Interest rate
	Incentive
	Poverty
	Wage ratio
	Fiscal policy
	Medicaid
	Medicare

21. Income Inequality, Poverty, and Discrimination

	Social insurance
	Supplemental Security Income
	Health care
	Social security
	Electronic Benefit Transfer
	Means test
	Occupational segregation
	Survey of Consumer Finances

CHAPTER HIGHLIGHTS & NOTES: KEY TERMS, PEOPLE, PLACES, CONCEPTS

Income	Income is the consumption and savings opportunity gained by an entity within a specified timeframe, which is generally expressed in monetary terms. However, for households and individuals, 'income is the sum of all the wages, salaries, profits, interests payments, rents and other forms of earnings received... in a given period of time.' In the field of public economics, the term may refer to the accumulation of both monetary and non-monetary consumption ability, with the former (monetary) being used as a proxy for total income.
Income inequality	Economic inequality (also described as the gap between rich and poor, income inequality, wealth disparity, wealth and income differences or wealth gap) is the state of affairs in which assets, wealth, or income are distributed unequally among individuals in a group, among groups in a population, or among countries. The issue of economic inequality can implicate notions of equity, equality of outcome, equality of opportunity, and even life expectancy. Although the phrase uses the term income, the discussion often includes inequality in wealth or assets, which are different concepts.
Pricing	Pricing is the process of determining what a company will receive in exchange for its product. Pricing factors are manufacturing cost, market place, competition, market condition, brand, and quality of product.

Lorenz curve	In economics, the Lorenz curve is a graphical representation of the cumulative distribution function of the empirical probability distribution of wealth, and was developed by Max O. Lorenz in 1905 for representing inequality of the wealth distribution.
	The curve is a graph showing the proportion of the distribution assumed by the bottom y% of the values, although this is not rigorously true for a finite population . It is often used to represent income distribution, where it shows for the bottom x% of households, what percentage y% of the total income they have.
Great Recession	The Great Recession was a global economic decline in the late 2000s. According to aggregated national data, a worldwide recession began in Q3-2008 and ended in Q1-2009.
	It is related to a liquidity crisis, commonly being dated to have started when several central banks had to step in with liquidity lending to the interbank lending market on 9 August 2007. This was a response to a situation where BNP Paribas temporarily had to block money withdrawals from three hedge funds--citing a 'complete evaporation of liquidity'.
Recession	In economics, a recession is a business cycle contraction. It is a general slowdown in economic activity. Macroeconomic indicators such as GDP (gross domestic product), investment spending, capacity utilization, household income, business profits, and inflation fall, while bankruptcies and the unemployment rate rise.
Transfer payment	In economics, a transfer payment is a redistribution of income in the market system. These payments are considered to be non-exhaustive because they do not directly absorb resources or create output. In other words, the transfer is made without any exchange of goods or services.
Income distribution	In economics, income distribution is how a nation's total GDP is distributed amongst its population.
	Income and distribution has always been a central concern of economic theory and economic policy. Classical economists such as Adam Smith, Thomas Malthus and David Ricardo were mainly concerned with factor income distribution, that is, the distribution of income between the main factors of production, land, labour and capital.
Monopoly	A monopoly (from Greek monos μ???? + polein p??e?? (to sell)) exists when a specific person or enterprise is the only supplier of a particular commodity (this contrasts with a monopsony which relates to a single entity's control of a market to purchase a good or service, and with oligopoly which consists of a few entities dominating an industry). Monopolies are thus characterized by a lack of economic competition to produce the good or service and a lack of viable substitute goods. The verb 'monopolize' refers to the process by which a company gains the ability to raise prices or exclude competitors.
Natural monopoly	A monopoly is a firm which is the only one producing and selling a particular product.

21. Income Inequality, Poverty, and Discrimination

	A natural monopoly is a monopoly in an industry in which it is most efficient (involving the lowest long-run average cost) for production to be concentrated in a single firm. This market situation gives the largest supplier in an industry, often the first supplier in a market, an overwhelming cost advantage over other actual and potential competitors, so a natural monopoly situation generally leads to an actual monopoly.
Health insurance	Health insurance is insurance against the risk of incurring medical expenses among individuals. By estimating the overall risk of health care and health system expenses, among a targeted group, an insurer can develop a routine finance structure, such as a monthly premium or payroll tax, to ensure that money is available to pay for the health care benefits specified in the insurance agreement. The benefit is administered by a central organization such as a government agency, private business, or not-for-profit entity.
Inflation	In economics, inflation is a sustained increase in the general price level of goods and services in an economy over a period of time. When the general price level rises, each unit of currency buys fewer goods and services. Consequently, inflation reflects a reduction in the purchasing power per unit of money - a loss of real value in the medium of exchange and unit of account within the economy.
Skilled worker	A skilled worker is any worker who has some special skill, knowledge, or ability in their work. A skilled worker may have attended a college, university or technical school. Or, a skilled worker may have learned their skills on the job.
Baby Boomers	Baby boomers are people born during the demographic Post-World War II baby boom between the years 1946 and 1964. According to the U.S. Census Bureau, the term 'baby boomer' is also used in a cultural context. Therefore, it is impossible to achieve broad consensus of a precise date definition, even within a given territory. Different groups, organizations, individuals, and scholars may have widely varying opinions on what constitutes a baby boomer, both technically and culturally.
Interest rate	An interest rate is the rate at which interest is paid by a borrower for the use of money that they borrow from a lender (creditor). Specifically, the interest rate is a percent of principal (P) paid a certain amount of times (m) per period (usually quoted per annum). For example, a small company borrows capital from a bank to buy new assets for its business, and in return the lender receives interest at a predetermined interest rate for deferring the use of funds and instead lending it to the borrower.
Incentive	An incentive is something that motivates an individual to perform an action. The study of incentive structures is central to the study of all economic activities (both in terms of individual decision-making and in terms of co-operation and competition within a larger institutional structure).

Poverty	Poverty is general scarcity or dearth, or the state of one who lacks a certain amount of material possessions or money. Absolute poverty or destitution refers to the deprivation of basic human needs, which commonly includes food, water, sanitation, clothing, shelter, health care and education. Relative poverty is defined contextually as economic inequality in the location or society in which people live.
Wage ratio	In economics, the wage ratio refers to the ratio of the top salaries in a group to the bottom salaries. It is a measure of wage dispersion.
Fiscal policy	In economics and political science, fiscal policy is the use of government revenue collection and expenditure (spending) to influence the economy, or else it involves the government changing the levels of taxation and government spending in order to influence Aggregate Demand and the level of economic activity. The two main instruments of fiscal policy are changes in the level and composition of taxation and government spending in various sectors. These changes can affect the following macroeconomic variables in an economy:•Aggregate demand and the level of economic activity;•The distribution of income;•The pattern of resource allocation within the government sector and relative to the private sector. Fiscal policy refers to the use of the government budget to influence economic activity.
Medicaid	Medicaid in the United States is a social health care program for families and individuals with low income and resources. The Health Insurance Association of America describes Medicaid as a 'government insurance program for persons of all ages whose income and resources are insufficient to pay for health care.' (America's Health Insurance Plans (HIAA), pg. 232). Medicaid is the largest source of funding for medical and health-related services for people with low income in the United States.
Medicare	In the United States, Medicare is a national social insurance program, administered by the U.S. federal government since 1966, that guarantees access to health insurance for Americans aged 65 and older who have worked and paid into the system, and younger people with disabilities as well as people with end stage renal disease (Medicare.gov, 2012) and persons with amyotrophic lateral sclerosis. As a social insurance program, Medicare spreads the financial risk associated with illness across society to protect everyone, and thus has a somewhat different social role from for-profit private insurers, which manage their risk portfolio by adjusting their pricing according to perceived risk. In 2010, Medicare provided health insurance to 48 million Americans--40 million people age 65 and older and eight million younger people with disabilities.
Social insurance	Social insurance is any government-sponsored program with the following four characteristics:

Social insurance has also been defined as a program where risks are transferred to and pooled by an organization, often governmental, that is legally required to provide certain benefits.

In the U.S., programs that meet these definitions include Social Security, Medicare, the PBGC program, the railroad retirement program and state-sponsored unemployment insurance programs. The Canada Pension Plan (CPP) is also a social insurance program.

Supplemental Security Income	Supplemental Security Income is a United States government program that provides stipends to low-income people who are either aged (65 or older), blind, or disabled. Although administered by the Social Security Administration, Supplemental Security Income is funded from the U.S. Treasury general funds, not the Social Security trust fund. Supplemental Security Income was created in 1974 to replace federal-state adult assistance programs that served the same purpose.
Health care	Health care is the diagnosis, treatment, and prevention of disease, illness, injury, and other physical and mental impairments in human beings. Health care is delivered by practitioners in allied health, dentistry, midwifery-obstetrics, medicine, nursing, optometry, pharmacy, psychology and other care providers. It refers to the work done in providing primary care, secondary care, and tertiary care, as well as in public health.
Social security	Social security is a concept enshrined in Article 22 of the Universal Declaration of Human Rights which states, Everyone, as a member of society, has the right to social security and is entitled to realization, through national effort and international co-operation and in accordance with the organization and resources of each State, of the economic, social and cultural rights indispensable for his dignity and the free development of his personality. In simple terms, the signatories agree that society in which a person lives should help them to develop and to make the most of all the advantages (culture, work, social welfare) which are offered to them in the country.

Social security may also refer to the action programs of government intended to promote the welfare of the population through assistance measures guaranteeing access to sufficient resources for food and shelter and to promote health and well-being for the population at large and potentially vulnerable segments such as children, the elderly, the sick and the unemployed. |
| Electronic Benefit Transfer | Electronic Benefit Transfer is an electronic system that allows state welfare departments to issue benefits via a magnetically encoded payment card, used in the United States and the United Kingdom.

Common benefits provided (in the United States) via Electronic Benefit Transfer are typically of two general categories: food and cash benefits. Food benefits are federally authorized benefits that can be used only to purchase food and non-alcoholic beverages. |

Means test	A means test is a determination of whether an individual or family is eligible for government assistance, based upon whether the individual or family possesses the means to do without that help.
Occupational segregation	Occupational segregation is the distribution of people based upon demographic characteristics, most often gender, both across and within occupations and jobs. Occupational segregation levels differ on a basis of perfect segregation and integration. Perfect segregation occurs where any given occupation employs only one group.
Survey of Consumer Finances	The Survey of Consumer Finances is a triennial statistical survey of the balance sheet, pension, income and other demographic characteristics of families in the United States; the survey also gathers information on the use of financial institutions.
	It is sponsored by the United States Federal Reserve Board in cooperation with the U.S. Treasury Department. Since 1992, data have been collected by the National Opinion Research Center at the University of Chicago, located in Chicago, Illinois.

CHAPTER QUIZ: KEY TERMS, PEOPLE, PLACES, CONCEPTS

1. In economics, the _____ is a graphical representation of the cumulative distribution function of the empirical probability distribution of wealth, and was developed by Max O. Lorenz in 1905 for representing inequality of the wealth distribution.

    The curve is a graph showing the proportion of the distribution assumed by the bottom y% of the values, although this is not rigorously true for a finite population . It is often used to represent income distribution, where it shows for the bottom x% of households, what percentage y% of the total income they have.

    a. Lorenz curve
    b. Bereavement benefit
    c. Biological standard of living
    d. Bodily integrity

2. . _____ is a United States government program that provides stipends to low-income people who are either aged (65 or older), blind, or disabled. Although administered by the Social Security Administration, _____ is funded from the U.S. Treasury general funds, not the Social Security trust fund. _____ was created in 1974 to replace federal-state adult assistance programs that served the same purpose.

    a. Bituah Leumi
    b. Supplemental Security Income
    c. Children in Scotland

21. Income Inequality, Poverty, and Discrimination

3. _____ is the consumption and savings opportunity gained by an entity within a specified timeframe, which is generally expressed in monetary terms. However, for households and individuals, '_____ is the sum of all the wages, salaries, profits, interests payments, rents and other forms of earnings received... in a given period of time.'

   In the field of public economics, the term may refer to the accumulation of both monetary and non-monetary consumption ability, with the former (monetary) being used as a proxy for total _____.

   a. Fuel protests in the United Kingdom
   b. Battle of Annaberg
   c. Income
   d. Freikorps Oberland

4. Economic inequality (also described as the gap between rich and poor, _____, wealth disparity, wealth and income differences or wealth gap) is the state of affairs in which assets, wealth, or income are distributed unequally among individuals in a group, among groups in a population, or among countries. The issue of economic inequality can implicate notions of equity, equality of outcome, equality of opportunity, and even life expectancy. Although the phrase uses the term income, the discussion often includes inequality in wealth or assets, which are different concepts.

   a. Energy Task Force
   b. Battle of Annaberg
   c. Freikorps Lichtschlag
   d. Income inequality

5. _____ is the process of determining what a company will receive in exchange for its product. _____ factors are manufacturing cost, market place, competition, market condition, brand, and quality of product. _____ is also a key variable in microeconomic price allocation theory.

   a. Fuel protests in the United Kingdom
   b. Battle of Annaberg
   c. Pricing
   d. Freikorps Oberland

1. a
2. b
3. c
4. d
5. c

22. Health Care

CHAPTER OUTLINE: KEY TERMS, PEOPLE, PLACES, CONCEPTS

	Great Recession
	Recession
	Health care
	National health insurance
	Health care industry
	Health insurance
	Poverty
	Copayment
	Deductible
	Medicaid
	Supplemental Security Income
	Quality
	Agricultural Adjustment Act
	Comparative advantage
	Medicare
	Offshoring
	State bank
	Market failure
	Price elasticity
	Elasticity
	Baby Boomers

22. Health Care
CHAPTER OUTLINE: KEY TERMS, PEOPLE, PLACES, CONCEPTS

	Phillips curve

	Moral hazard

	Subsidy

	Allocative efficiency

	Managed care

	Preferred provider organization

	World Health Organization

CHAPTER HIGHLIGHTS & NOTES: KEY TERMS, PEOPLE, PLACES, CONCEPTS

Great Recession	The Great Recession was a global economic decline in the late 2000s. According to aggregated national data, a worldwide recession began in Q3-2008 and ended in Q1-2009. It is related to a liquidity crisis, commonly being dated to have started when several central banks had to step in with liquidity lending to the interbank lending market on 9 August 2007. This was a response to a situation where BNP Paribas temporarily had to block money withdrawals from three hedge funds--citing a 'complete evaporation of liquidity'.
Recession	In economics, a recession is a business cycle contraction. It is a general slowdown in economic activity. Macroeconomic indicators such as GDP (gross domestic product), investment spending, capacity utilization, household income, business profits, and inflation fall, while bankruptcies and the unemployment rate rise.
Health care	Health care is the diagnosis, treatment, and prevention of disease, illness, injury, and other physical and mental impairments in human beings. Health care is delivered by practitioners in allied health, dentistry, midwifery-obstetrics, medicine, nursing, optometry, pharmacy, psychology and other care providers. It refers to the work done in providing primary care, secondary care, and tertiary care, as well as in public health.
National health insurance	National health insurance is health insurance that insures a national population for the costs of health care and usually is instituted as a program of healthcare reform. It is enforced by law.

22. Health Care

Health care industry	The health care industry, or medical industry, is an aggregation of sectors within the economic system that provides goods and services to treat patients with curative, preventive, rehabilitative, and palliative care. The modern health care industry is divided into many sectors and depends on interdisciplinary teams of trained professionals and paraprofessionals to meet health needs of individuals and populations. The health care industry is one of the world's largest and fastest-growing industries.
Health insurance	Health insurance is insurance against the risk of incurring medical expenses among individuals. By estimating the overall risk of health care and health system expenses, among a targeted group, an insurer can develop a routine finance structure, such as a monthly premium or payroll tax, to ensure that money is available to pay for the health care benefits specified in the insurance agreement. The benefit is administered by a central organization such as a government agency, private business, or not-for-profit entity.
Poverty	Poverty is general scarcity or dearth, or the state of one who lacks a certain amount of material possessions or money. Absolute poverty or destitution refers to the deprivation of basic human needs, which commonly includes food, water, sanitation, clothing, shelter, health care and education. Relative poverty is defined contextually as economic inequality in the location or society in which people live.
Copayment	In the United States, copayment or copay is a payment defined in the insurance policy and paid by the insured person each time a medical service is accessed. It is technically a form of coinsurance, but is defined differently in health insurance where a coinsurance is a percentage payment after the deductible up to a certain limit. It must be paid before any policy benefit is payable by an insurance company.
Deductible	In an insurance policy, the deductible is the amount of expenses that must be paid out of pocket before an insurer will pay any expenses. Example: if you have a $5000 deductible per year and you happen to spend $6000 this year, you will get your reimbursement for $1000 this year. In general usage, the term deductible may be used to describe one of several types of clauses that are used by insurance companies as a threshold for policy payments.
Medicaid	Medicaid in the United States is a social health care program for families and individuals with low income and resources. The Health Insurance Association of America describes Medicaid as a 'government insurance program for persons of all ages whose income and resources are insufficient to pay for health care.' (America's Health Insurance Plans (HIAA), pg. 232). Medicaid is the largest source of funding for medical and health-related services for people with low income in the United States.
Supplemental Security Income	Supplemental Security Income is a United States government program that provides stipends to low-income people who are either aged (65 or older), blind, or disabled.

22. Health Care

	Although administered by the Social Security Administration, Supplemental Security Income is funded from the U.S. Treasury general funds, not the Social Security trust fund. Supplemental Security Income was created in 1974 to replace federal-state adult assistance programs that served the same purpose.
Quality	Quality in business, engineering and manufacturing has a pragmatic interpretation as the non-inferiority or superiority of something; it is also defined as fitness for purpose. Quality is a perceptual, conditional, and somewhat subjective attribute and may be understood differently by different people. Consumers may focus on the specification quality of a product/service, or how it compares to competitors in the marketplace.
Agricultural Adjustment Act	The Agricultural Adjustment Act was a United States federal law of the New Deal era which reduced agricultural production by paying farmers subsidies not to plant on part of their land and to kill off excess livestock. Its purpose was to reduce crop surplus and therefore effectively raise the value of crops. The money for these subsidies was generated through an exclusive tax on companies which processed farm products.
Comparative advantage	In economics, comparative advantage refers to the ability of a party to produce a particular good or service at a lower marginal and opportunity cost over another. Even if one country is more efficient in the production of all goods (absolute advantage in all goods) than the other, both countries will still gain by trading with each other, as long as they have different relative efficiencies.
	For example, if, using machinery, a worker in one country can produce both shoes and shirts at 6 per hour, and a worker in a country with less machinery can produce either 2 shoes or 4 shirts in an hour, each country can gain from trade because their internal trade-offs between shoes and shirts are different.
Medicare	In the United States, Medicare is a national social insurance program, administered by the U.S. federal government since 1966, that guarantees access to health insurance for Americans aged 65 and older who have worked and paid into the system, and younger people with disabilities as well as people with end stage renal disease (Medicare.gov, 2012) and persons with amyotrophic lateral sclerosis. As a social insurance program, Medicare spreads the financial risk associated with illness across society to protect everyone, and thus has a somewhat different social role from for-profit private insurers, which manage their risk portfolio by adjusting their pricing according to perceived risk.
	In 2010, Medicare provided health insurance to 48 million Americans--40 million people age 65 and older and eight million younger people with disabilities.
Offshoring	Offshoring is the relocation by a company of a business process from one country to another--typically an operational process, such as manufacturing, or supporting processes, such as accounting. Even state governments employ offshoring.

State bank	A state bank is generally a financial institution that is chartered by a state. It differs from a reserve bank in that it does not necessarily control monetary policy (indeed, the state in question may have no legal capacity to create monetary policy), but instead usually offers only retail and commercial services.
	A state bank that has been in operation for five years or less is called a de novo bank.
Market failure	Market failure is a concept within economic theory describing when the allocation of goods and services by a free market is not efficient. That is, there exists another conceivable outcome where a market participant may be made better-off without making someone else worse-off. (The outcome is not Pareto optimal).
Price elasticity	Price elasticity of demand is a measure used in economics to show the responsiveness, or elasticity, of the quantity demanded of a good or service to a change in its price. More precisely, it gives the percentage change in quantity demanded in response to a one percent change in price (ceteris paribus, i.e. holding constant all the other determinants of demand, such as income).
	Price elasticities are almost always negative, although analysts tend to ignore the sign even though this can lead to ambiguity.
Elasticity	In economics, elasticity is the measurement of how responsive an economic variable is to a change in another. For example:•'If I lower the price of my product, how much more will I sell?'•'If I raise the price of one good, how will that affect sales of this other good?'•'If we learn that a resource is becoming scarce, will people scramble to acquire it?'
	An elastic variable (or elasticity value greater than 1) is one which responds more than proportionally to changes in other variables. In contrast, an inelastic variable (or elasticity value less than 1) is one which changes less than proportionally in response to changes in other variables.
Baby Boomers	Baby boomers are people born during the demographic Post-World War II baby boom between the years 1946 and 1964. According to the U.S. Census Bureau, the term 'baby boomer' is also used in a cultural context. Therefore, it is impossible to achieve broad consensus of a precise date definition, even within a given territory. Different groups, organizations, individuals, and scholars may have widely varying opinions on what constitutes a baby boomer, both technically and culturally.
Phillips curve	In economics, the Phillips curve is a historical inverse relationship between rates of unemployment and corresponding rates of inflation that result in an economy. Stated simply, decreased unemployment, (i.e., increased levels of employment) in an economy will correlate with higher rates of inflation.

22. Health Care

Moral hazard	In economic theory, a moral hazard is a situation where a party will have a tendency to take risks because the costs that could result will not be felt by the party taking the risk. In other words, it is a tendency to be more willing to take a risk, knowing that the potential costs or burdens of taking such risk will be borne, in whole or in part, by others. A moral hazard may occur where the actions of one party may change to the detriment of another after a financial transaction has taken place.
Subsidy	A subsidy is a form of financial or in kind support extended to an economic sector generally with the aim of promoting economic and social policy. Although commonly extended from Government, the term subsidy can relate to any type of support - for example from NGOs or implicit subsidies. Subsidies come in various forms including: direct (cash grants, interest-free loans) and indirect (tax breaks, insurance, low-interest loans, depreciation write-offs, rent rebates).
Allocative efficiency	Allocative efficiency is a type of economic efficiency in which economy/producers produce only those types of goods and services that are more desirable in the society and also in high demand. According to the formula the point of allocative efficiency is a point where price is equal to marginal cost (P=MC)or (MC=MR). At this point the social surplus is maximized with no deadweight loss, or the value society puts on that level of output produced minus the value of resources used to achieve that level, yet can be applied to other things such as level of pollution.
Managed care	The term managed care or managed health care is used in the United States to describe a variety of techniques intended to reduce the cost of providing health benefits and improve the quality of care ('managed care techniques'), for organizations that use those techniques or provide them as services to other organizations ('managed care organization' or 'MCO'), or to describe systems of financing and delivering health care to enrollees organized around managed care techniques and concepts ('managed care delivery systems'). '

...intended to reduce unnecessary health care costs through a variety of mechanisms, including: economic incentives for physicians and patients to select less costly forms of care; programs for reviewing the medical necessity of specific services; increased beneficiary cost sharing; controls on inpatient admissions and lengths of stay; the establishment of cost-sharing incentives for outpatient surgery; selective contracting with health care providers; and the intensive management of high-cost health care cases. The programs may be provided in a variety of settings, such as Health Maintenance Organizations and Preferred Provider Organizations.' |
| Preferred provider organization | In health insurance in the United States, a preferred provider organization is a managed care organization of medical doctors, hospitals, and other health care providers who have agreed with an insurer or a third-party administrator to provide health care at reduced rates to the insurer's or administrator's clients. |
| World Health Organization | The World Health Organization is a specialized agency of the United Nations (UN) that is concerned with international public health. It was established on 7 April 1948, with its headquarters in Geneva, Switzerland. |

22. Health Care

1. _____ of demand is a measure used in economics to show the responsiveness, or elasticity, of the quantity demanded of a good or service to a change in its price. More precisely, it gives the percentage change in quantity demanded in response to a one percent change in price (ceteris paribus, i.e. holding constant all the other determinants of demand, such as income).

   _____(ies) are almost always negative, although analysts tend to ignore the sign even though this can lead to ambiguity.

   a. Fuel protests in the United Kingdom
   b. Price elasticity
   c. Base effect
   d. Benefit shortfall

2. _____ is the relocation by a company of a business process from one country to another--typically an operational process, such as manufacturing, or supporting processes, such as accounting. Even state governments employ _____. More recently, _____ has been associated primarily with the outsourcing of technical and administrative services supporting domestic and global operations from outside the home country, by means of internal (captive) or external (outsourcing) delivery models.

   a. 2008 G-20 Washington summit
   b. Backsourcing
   c. Bimetallism
   d. Offshoring

3. The _____ was a global economic decline in the late 2000s. According to aggregated national data, a worldwide recession began in Q3-2008 and ended in Q1-2009.

   It is related to a liquidity crisis, commonly being dated to have started when several central banks had to step in with liquidity lending to the interbank lending market on 9 August 2007. This was a response to a situation where BNP Paribas temporarily had to block money withdrawals from three hedge funds--citing a 'complete evaporation of liquidity'.

   a. Commercial Revolution
   b. Mercantilism
   c. Great Recession
   d. 1 kroon coin

4. In health insurance in the United States, a _____ is a managed care organization of medical doctors, hospitals, and other health care providers who have agreed with an insurer or a third-party administrator to provide health care at reduced rates to the insurer's or administrator's clients.

   a. Bundled payment
   b. Preferred provider organization
   c. Case mix group
   d. Centre for Reviews and Dissemination

22. Health Care

5. _____ in the United States is a social health care program for families and individuals with low income and resources. The Health Insurance Association of America describes _____ as a 'government insurance program for persons of all ages whose income and resources are insufficient to pay for health care.' (America's Health Insurance Plans (HIAA), pg. 232). _____ is the largest source of funding for medical and health-related services for people with low income in the United States.

   a. Medicaid
   b. Child Poverty Act 2010
   c. Child Poverty Action Group
   d. Compassion International

ANSWER KEY
22. Health Care

1. b
2. d
3. c
4. b
5. a

You can take the complete Chapter Practice Test

for 22. Health Care
on all key terms, persons, places, and concepts.

Online 99 Cents

http://www.JustTheFacts101.com

Use www.JustTheFacts101.com for all your study needs

including Facts101's online interactive problem solving labs in

chemistry, statistics, mathematics, and more.

23. Immigration

CHAPTER OUTLINE: KEY TERMS, PEOPLE, PLACES, CONCEPTS

Great Recession

Recession

Illegal immigration

Skilled worker

Earnings

Human capital

Lorenz curve

Income inequality

Labor force

Wage ratio

Council of Economic Advisers

Interest rate

Brain drain

Income

Income distribution

Pricing

Remittance

Full employment

Supplemental Security Income

Insurance fraud

Loan guarantee

23. Immigration

	State bank
	Free trade
	North American Free Trade Agreement
	Slowdown

CHAPTER HIGHLIGHTS & NOTES: KEY TERMS, PEOPLE, PLACES, CONCEPTS

Great Recession	The Great Recession was a global economic decline in the late 2000s. According to aggregated national data, a worldwide recession began in Q3-2008 and ended in Q1-2009. It is related to a liquidity crisis, commonly being dated to have started when several central banks had to step in with liquidity lending to the interbank lending market on 9 August 2007. This was a response to a situation where BNP Paribas temporarily had to block money withdrawals from three hedge funds--citing a 'complete evaporation of liquidity'.
Recession	In economics, a recession is a business cycle contraction. It is a general slowdown in economic activity. Macroeconomic indicators such as GDP (gross domestic product), investment spending, capacity utilization, household income, business profits, and inflation fall, while bankruptcies and the unemployment rate rise.
Illegal immigration	Illegal immigration refers to the migration of people across national borders, or the residence of foreign nationals in a country, in a way that violates the immigration laws of the destination country. Illegal immigration is overwhelmingly upward, from a poorer to a richer country. One measurable factor is the 'push-pull' incentive - the quality of life in the host country against the home country.
Skilled worker	A skilled worker is any worker who has some special skill, knowledge, or ability in their work. A skilled worker may have attended a college, university or technical school. Or, a skilled worker may have learned their skills on the job.
Earnings	Earnings are the net benefits of a corporation's operation. Earnings is also the amount on which corporate tax is due.

Human capital	Human capital is the stock of competencies, knowledge, habits, social and personality attributes, including creativity, cognitive abilities, embodied in the ability to perform labor so as to produce economic value. It is an aggregate economic view of the human being acting within economies, which is an attempt to capture the social, biological, cultural and psychological complexity as they interact in explicit and/or economic transactions. Many theories explicitly connect investment in human capital development to education, and the role of human capital in economic development, productivity growth, and innovation has frequently been cited as a justification for government subsidies for education and job skills training.
Lorenz curve	In economics, the Lorenz curve is a graphical representation of the cumulative distribution function of the empirical probability distribution of wealth, and was developed by Max O. Lorenz in 1905 for representing inequality of the wealth distribution.
	The curve is a graph showing the proportion of the distribution assumed by the bottom y% of the values, although this is not rigorously true for a finite population . It is often used to represent income distribution, where it shows for the bottom x% of households, what percentage y% of the total income they have.
Income inequality	Economic inequality (also described as the gap between rich and poor, income inequality, wealth disparity, wealth and income differences or wealth gap) is the state of affairs in which assets, wealth, or income are distributed unequally among individuals in a group, among groups in a population, or among countries. The issue of economic inequality can implicate notions of equity, equality of outcome, equality of opportunity, and even life expectancy. Although the phrase uses the term income, the discussion often includes inequality in wealth or assets, which are different concepts.
Labor force	The labor force is the actual number of people available for work. The labor force of a country includes both the employed and the unemployed. The labor force participation rate, LFPR (or economic activity rate, EAR), is the ratio between the labor force and the overall size of their cohort (national population of the same age range).
Wage ratio	In economics, the wage ratio refers to the ratio of the top salaries in a group to the bottom salaries. It is a measure of wage dispersion.
Council of Economic Advisers	The Council of Economic Advisers is a group of economists and captains of industry who advise the Scottish Government. It was established in 2007, meeting for the first time on 21 September.
	Minutes of its quarterly meetings will be published a fortnight after each meeting.
Interest rate	An interest rate is the rate at which interest is paid by a borrower for the use of money that they borrow from a lender (creditor). Specifically, the interest rate is a percent of principal (P) paid a certain amount of times (m) per period (usually quoted per annum).

23. Immigration

Brain drain	Brain drain, or human capital flight, is a buzzword that describes the departure or emigration of individuals with technical skills or knowledge from organizations, industries, or geographical regions. Brain drain is common among developing nations, such as many former African colonies, the island nations of the Caribbean, and in centralized economies such as former East Germany and the Soviet Union. China and India have recently been documented as the world leaders in brain drain.
Income	Income is the consumption and savings opportunity gained by an entity within a specified timeframe, which is generally expressed in monetary terms. However, for households and individuals, 'income is the sum of all the wages, salaries, profits, interests payments, rents and other forms of earnings received... in a given period of time.' In the field of public economics, the term may refer to the accumulation of both monetary and non-monetary consumption ability, with the former (monetary) being used as a proxy for total income.
Income distribution	In economics, income distribution is how a nation's total GDP is distributed amongst its population. Income and distribution has always been a central concern of economic theory and economic policy. Classical economists such as Adam Smith, Thomas Malthus and David Ricardo were mainly concerned with factor income distribution, that is, the distribution of income between the main factors of production, land, labour and capital.
Pricing	Pricing is the process of determining what a company will receive in exchange for its product. Pricing factors are manufacturing cost, market place, competition, market condition, brand, and quality of product. Pricing is also a key variable in microeconomic price allocation theory.
Remittance	A remittance is a transfer of money by a foreign worker to an individual in his or her home country. Money sent home by migrants competes with international aid as some of the largest financial inflows to developing countries. In 2012, according to the World Bank Report, $401 billion went to developing countries (a new record) with overall global remittances at $514 billion.
Full employment	Full employment, in macroeconomics, is the level of employment rates where there is no cyclical or deficient-demand unemployment. It is defined by the majority of mainstream economists as being an acceptable level of unemployment somewhere above 0%. The discrepancy from 0% arises due to non-cyclical types of unemployment.
Supplemental Security Income	Supplemental Security Income is a United States government program that provides stipends to low-income people who are either aged (65 or older), blind, or disabled. Although administered by the Social Security Administration, Supplemental Security Income is funded from the U.S. Treasury general funds, not the Social Security trust fund. Supplemental Security Income was created in 1974 to replace federal-state adult assistance programs that served the same purpose.

23. Immigration

Insurance fraud	Insurance fraud occurs when any act is committed with the intent to fraudulently obtain some benefit or advantage to which they are not otherwise entitled or someone knowingly denies some benefit that is due and to which someone is entitled. According to the United States Federal Bureau of Investigation the most common schemes include: Premium Diversion, Fee Churning, Asset Diversion and Workers Compensation Fraud. The perpetrators in these schemes can be both insurance company employees and claimants.
Loan guarantee	A loan guarantee, in finance, is a promise by one party to assume the debt obligation of a borrower if that borrower defaults. A guarantee can be limited or unlimited, making the guarantor liable for only a portion or all of the debt. Guarantor mortgages are popular with young borrowers who do not have a large deposit saved and need to borrow 100% of the property value to purchase a property.
State bank	A state bank is generally a financial institution that is chartered by a state. It differs from a reserve bank in that it does not necessarily control monetary policy (indeed, the state in question may have no legal capacity to create monetary policy), but instead usually offers only retail and commercial services. A state bank that has been in operation for five years or less is called a de novo bank.
Free trade	Free trade is a policy in international markets in which governments do not restrict imports or exports. Free trade is exemplified by the European Union / European Economic Area and the North American Free Trade Agreement, which have established open markets. Most nations are today members of the World Trade Organization (WTO) multilateral trade agreements.
North American Free Trade Agreement	The North American Free Trade Agreement is an agreement signed by Canada, Mexico, and the United States, creating a trilateral rules-based trade bloc in North America. The agreement came into force on January 1, 1994. It superseded the Canada-United States Free Trade Agreement between the U.S. and Canada. North American Free Trade Agreement has two supplements: the North American Agreement on Environmental Cooperation (NAAEC) and the North American Agreement on Labor Cooperation (NAALC). In terms of combined purchasing power parity GDP of its members, as of 2007 the trade bloc is the largest in the world and second largest by nominal GDP comparison.
Slowdown	A slowdown is an industrial action in which employees perform their duties but seek to reduce productivity or efficiency in their performance of these duties. A slowdown may be used as either a prelude or an alternative to a strike, as it is seen as less disruptive as well as less risky and costly for workers and their union.

23. Immigration

1. In economics, the _____ refers to the ratio of the top salaries in a group to the bottom salaries. It is a measure of wage dispersion.

   a. Wage ratio
   b. Care work
   c. Cash collection
   d. Commercial location development

2. _____, in macroeconomics, is the level of employment rates where there is no cyclical or deficient-demand unemployment. It is defined by the majority of mainstream economists as being an acceptable level of unemployment somewhere above 0%. The discrepancy from 0% arises due to non-cyclical types of unemployment.

   a. Fuel protests in the United Kingdom
   b. Full employment
   c. Freikorps Lichtschlag
   d. Freikorps Oberland

3. The _____ was a global economic decline in the late 2000s. According to aggregated national data, a worldwide recession began in Q3-2008 and ended in Q1-2009.

   It is related to a liquidity crisis, commonly being dated to have started when several central banks had to step in with liquidity lending to the interbank lending market on 9 August 2007. This was a response to a situation where BNP Paribas temporarily had to block money withdrawals from three hedge funds--citing a 'complete evaporation of liquidity'.

   a. Commercial Revolution
   b. Mercantilism
   c. Via Argentaria
   d. Great Recession

4. In economics, a _____ is a business cycle contraction. It is a general slowdown in economic activity. Macroeconomic indicators such as GDP (gross domestic product), investment spending, capacity utilization, household income, business profits, and inflation fall, while bankruptcies and the unemployment rate rise.

   a. Depression
   b. General glut
   c. Recession
   d. Great Recession in South America

5. . In economics, the _____ is a graphical representation of the cumulative distribution function of the empirical probability distribution of wealth, and was developed by Max O. Lorenz in 1905 for representing inequality of the wealth distribution.

   The curve is a graph showing the proportion of the distribution assumed by the bottom y% of the values, although this is not rigorously true for a finite population .

It is often used to represent income distribution, where it shows for the bottom x% of households, what percentage y% of the total income they have.

a. Baker cube
b. Bereavement benefit
c. Lorenz curve
d. Bodily integrity

1. a
2. b
3. d
4. c
5. c

You can take the complete Chapter Practice Test

for 23. Immigration
on all key terms, persons, places, and concepts.

Online 99 Cents

http://www.JustTheFacts101.com

Use www.JustTheFacts101.com for all your study needs

including Facts101's online interactive problem solving labs in

chemistry, statistics, mathematics, and more.

24. An Introduction to Macroeconomics

CHAPTER OUTLINE: KEY TERMS, PEOPLE, PLACES, CONCEPTS

	Macroeconomics
	Business cycle
	Great Recession
	Inflation
	Recession
	Gross domestic product
	Product
	Economic growth
	Industrial Revolution
	Macroeconomic model
	Financial economics
	Income
	National income
	Demand shock
	Supply shock
	Great Depression
	Austrian School
	Structural adjustment

24. An Introduction to Macroeconomics

Macroeconomics	Macroeconomics is the study of the macroeconomy. It is a branch of economics dealing with the performance, structure, behavior, and decision-making of an economy as a whole, rather than individual markets. This includes national, regional, and global economies.
Business cycle	The term business cycle refers fluctuations in aggregate production, trade and activity over several months or years in a market economy. The business cycle is the upward and downward movements of levels of gross domestic product (GDP) and refers to the period of expansions and contractions in the level of economic activities (business fluctuations) around its long-term growth trend. These fluctuations occur around a long-term growth trend, and typically involve shifts over time between periods of relatively rapid economic growth (an expansion or boom), and periods of relative stagnation or decline (a contraction or recession).
Great Recession	The Great Recession was a global economic decline in the late 2000s. According to aggregated national data, a worldwide recession began in Q3-2008 and ended in Q1-2009. It is related to a liquidity crisis, commonly being dated to have started when several central banks had to step in with liquidity lending to the interbank lending market on 9 August 2007. This was a response to a situation where BNP Paribas temporarily had to block money withdrawals from three hedge funds--citing a 'complete evaporation of liquidity'.
Inflation	In economics, inflation is a sustained increase in the general price level of goods and services in an economy over a period of time. When the general price level rises, each unit of currency buys fewer goods and services. Consequently, inflation reflects a reduction in the purchasing power per unit of money - a loss of real value in the medium of exchange and unit of account within the economy.
Recession	In economics, a recession is a business cycle contraction. It is a general slowdown in economic activity. Macroeconomic indicators such as GDP (gross domestic product), investment spending, capacity utilization, household income, business profits, and inflation fall, while bankruptcies and the unemployment rate rise.
Gross domestic product	Gross domestic product is the market value of all officially recognized final goods and services produced within a country in a year, or other given period of time. Gross domestic product per capita is often considered an indicator of a country's standard of living. Gross domestic product per capita is not a measure of personal income .
Product	In marketing, a product is anything that can be offered to a market that might satisfy a want or need. In retailing, products are called merchandise.

Economic growth	Economic growth is the increase in the market value of the goods and services produced by an economy over time. It is conventionally measured as the percent rate of increase in real gross domestic product, or real GDP. Of more importance is the growth of the ratio of GDP to population (GDP per capita), which is also called per capita income. An increase in per capita income is referred to as intensive growth.
Industrial Revolution	The Industrial Revolution was the transition to new manufacturing processes in the period from about 1760 to sometime between 1820 and 1840. This transition included going from hand production methods to machines, new chemical manufacturing and iron production processes, improved efficiency of water power, the increasing use of steam power and the development of machine tools. It also included the change from wood and other bio-fuels to coal. Textiles were the dominant industry of the Industrial Revolution in terms of employment, value of output and capital invested.
Macroeconomic model	A macroeconomic model is an analytical tool designed to describe the operation of the economy of a country or a region. These models are usually designed to examine the dynamics of aggregate quantities such as the total amount of goods and services produced, total income earned, the level of employment of productive resources, and the level of prices. Macroeconomic models may be logical, mathematical, and/or computational; the different types of macroeconomic models serve different purposes and have different advantages and disadvantages.
Financial economics	Financial economics is the branch of economics characterized by a 'concentration on monetary activities', in which 'money of one type or another is likely to appear on both sides of a trade'. It is concerned with 'the allocation and deployment of economic resources, both spatially and across time, in an uncertain environment'. It is built on the foundations of microeconomics and decision theory.
Income	Income is the consumption and savings opportunity gained by an entity within a specified timeframe, which is generally expressed in monetary terms. However, for households and individuals, 'income is the sum of all the wages, salaries, profits, interests payments, rents and other forms of earnings received... in a given period of time.' In the field of public economics, the term may refer to the accumulation of both monetary and non-monetary consumption ability, with the former (monetary) being used as a proxy for total income.
National income	A variety of measures of national income and output are used in economics to estimate total economic activity in a country or region, including gross domestic product, gross national product (GNP), net national income and adjusted national income. All are specially concerned with counting the total amount of goods and services produced within some 'boundary'.

24. An Introduction to Macroeconomics

Demand shock	In economics, a demand shock is a sudden event that increases or decreases demand for goods or services temporarily.
Supply shock	A supply shock is an event that suddenly changes the price of a commodity or service. It may be caused by a sudden increase or decrease in the supply of a particular good. This sudden change affects the equilibrium price.
Great Depression	The Great Depression was a severe worldwide economic depression in the decade preceding World War II. The timing of the Great Depression varied across nations, but in most countries it started in 1930 and lasted until the late 1930s or middle 1940s. It was the longest, deepest, and most widespread depression of the 20th century. In the 21st century, the Great Depression is commonly used as an example of how far the world's economy can decline.
Austrian School	The Austrian School is a school of economic thought that is based on the analysis of the purposeful actions of individuals . It originated in late-19th and early-20th century Vienna with the work of Carl Menger, Eugen von Böhm-Bawerk, Friedrich von Wieser, and others. Current-day economists working in this tradition are located in many different countries, but their work is referred to as Austrian economics.
Structural adjustment	Structural adjustments are the policies implemented by the International Monetary Fund and the World Bank (the Bretton Woods Institutions) in developing countries. These policy changes are conditions for receiving new loans from the IMF or World Bank or for obtaining lower interest rates on existing loans. Conditions are implemented to ensure that the money lent will be spent in accordance with the overall goals of the loan.

24. An Introduction to Macroeconomics

1. _____ is the market value of all officially recognized final goods and services produced within a country in a year, or other given period of time. _____ per capita is often considered an indicator of a country's standard of living.

   _____ per capita is not a measure of personal income .

   a. Fuel protests in the United Kingdom
   b. Gross domestic product
   c. Freikorps Lichtschlag
   d. Freikorps Oberland

2. The _____ was a global economic decline in the late 2000s. According to aggregated national data, a worldwide recession began in Q3-2008 and ended in Q1-2009.

   It is related to a liquidity crisis, commonly being dated to have started when several central banks had to step in with liquidity lending to the interbank lending market on 9 August 2007. This was a response to a situation where BNP Paribas temporarily had to block money withdrawals from three hedge funds--citing a 'complete evaporation of liquidity'.

   a. Commercial Revolution
   b. Great Recession
   c. Via Argentaria
   d. 1 kroon coin

3. The _____ was the transition to new manufacturing processes in the period from about 1760 to sometime between 1820 and 1840. This transition included going from hand production methods to machines, new chemical manufacturing and iron production processes, improved efficiency of water power, the increasing use of steam power and the development of machine tools. It also included the change from wood and other bio-fuels to coal.

   Textiles were the dominant industry of the _____ in terms of employment, value of output and capital invested.

   a. Bendigo Petition
   b. Industrial Revolution
   c. Charcuterie
   d. Commercial Revolution

4. . A _____ is an analytical tool designed to describe the operation of the economy of a country or a region. These models are usually designed to examine the dynamics of aggregate quantities such as the total amount of goods and services produced, total income earned, the level of employment of productive resources, and the level of prices.

   _____s may be logical, mathematical, and/or computational; the different types of _____s serve different purposes and have different advantages and disadvantages.

   a. Beer distribution game
   b. Macroeconomic model

    c. Big push model
    d. Cass criterion

5. In economics, _____ is a sustained increase in the general price level of goods and services in an economy over a period of time. When the general price level rises, each unit of currency buys fewer goods and services. Consequently, _____ reflects a reduction in the purchasing power per unit of money - a loss of real value in the medium of exchange and unit of account within the economy.

    a. Bank Transfer Day
    b. Bankruptcy
    c. Base effect
    d. Inflation

ANSWER KEY
24. An Introduction to Macroeconomics

1. b
2. b
3. b
4. b
5. d

You can take the complete Chapter Practice Test

for 24. An Introduction to Macroeconomics
on all key terms, persons, places, and concepts.

Online 99 Cents

http://www.JustTheFacts101.com

Use www.JustTheFacts101.com for all your study needs

including Facts101's online interactive problem solving labs in

chemistry, statistics, mathematics, and more.

25. Measuring Domestic Output and National Income

CHAPTER OUTLINE: KEY TERMS, PEOPLE, PLACES, CONCEPTS

National income

Gross domestic product

Income

National Income and Product Accounts

Product

Final good

Intermediate good

Value added

Financial transaction

Stock exchange

Transfer payment

Durable good

Gross private domestic investment

International trade

Net export

Monopoly

Natural monopoly

Depreciation

Economic growth

Fixed capital

Dividend

25. Measuring Domestic Output and National Income

Laffer curve

Corporate tax

Production

Consumption

Consumption of fixed capital

Net domestic product

Personal income

Price index

Lehman Brothers

OPEC

Well-being

Quality

CHAPTER HIGHLIGHTS & NOTES: KEY TERMS, PEOPLE, PLACES, CONCEPTS

National income	A variety of measures of national income and output are used in economics to estimate total economic activity in a country or region, including gross domestic product, gross national product (GNP), net national income and adjusted national income. All are specially concerned with counting the total amount of goods and services produced within some 'boundary'. The boundary is usually defined by geography or citizenship, and may also restrict the goods and services that are counted.
Gross domestic product	Gross domestic product is the market value of all officially recognized final goods and services produced within a country in a year, or other given period of time. Gross domestic product per capita is often considered an indicator of a country's standard of living.

Income	Income is the consumption and savings opportunity gained by an entity within a specified timeframe, which is generally expressed in monetary terms. However, for households and individuals, 'income is the sum of all the wages, salaries, profits, interests payments, rents and other forms of earnings received... in a given period of time.' In the field of public economics, the term may refer to the accumulation of both monetary and non-monetary consumption ability, with the former (monetary) being used as a proxy for total income.
National Income and Product Accounts	The national income and product accounts are part of the national accounts of the United States. They are produced by the Bureau of Economic Analysis of the Department of Commerce. They are one of the main sources of data on general economic activity in the United States.
Product	In marketing, a product is anything that can be offered to a market that might satisfy a want or need. In retailing, products are called merchandise. In manufacturing, products are bought as raw materials and sold as finished goods.
Final good	In economics, any commodity which is produced and subsequently consumed by the consumer, to satisfy its current wants or needs, is a consumer good or final good. Consumer goods are goods that are ultimately consumed rather than used in the production of another good. For example, a microwave oven or a bicycle which is sold to a consumer is a final good or consumer good, whereas the components which are sold to be used in those goods are called intermediate goods.
Intermediate good	Intermediate goods or producer goods or semi-finished products are goods used as inputs in the production of other goods, such as partly finished goods. Also, they are goods used in production of final goods. A firm may make and then use intermediate goods, or make and then sell, or buy then use them.
Value added	In business, the difference between the sale price and the production cost of a product is the unit profit. In economics, the sum of the unit profit, the unit depreciation cost, and the unit labor cost is the unit value added. Summing value added per unit over all units sold is total value added.
Financial transaction	A financial transaction is an agreement, communication, or movement carried out between a buyer and a seller to exchange an asset for payment. It involves a change in the status of the finances of two or more businesses or individuals. The buyer and seller are separate entities or objects, often involving the exchange of items of value, such as information, goods, services, and money.
Stock exchange	A stock exchange is a form of exchange which provides services for stock brokers and traders to trade stocks, bonds, and other securities. Stock exchanges also provide facilities for issue and redemption of securities and other financial instruments, and capital events including the payment of income and dividends. Securities traded on a stock exchange include stock issued by companies, unit trusts, derivatives, pooled investment products and bonds.
Transfer payment	In economics, a transfer payment is a redistribution of income in the market system.

25. Measuring Domestic Output and National Income

	These payments are considered to be non-exhaustive because they do not directly absorb resources or create output. In other words, the transfer is made without any exchange of goods or services.
Durable good	In economics, a durable good or a hard good is a good that does not quickly wear out, or more specifically, one that yields utility over time rather than being completely consumed in one use. Items like bricks could be considered perfectly durable goods, because they should theoretically never wear out. Highly durable goods such as refrigerators, cars, or mobile phones usually continue to be useful for three or more years of use, so durable goods are typically characterized by long periods between successive purchases.
Gross private domestic investment	Gross private domestic investment is the measure of investment used to compute GDP in economic measurement of nations. This is an important component of GDP because it provides an indicator of the future productive capacity of the economy. It includes replacement purchases plus net additions to capital assets plus investments in inventories.
International trade	International trade is the exchange of capital, goods, and services across international borders or territories. In most countries, such trade represents a significant share of gross domestic product (GDP). While international trade has been present throughout much of history, its economic, social, and political importance has been on the rise in recent centuries.
Net export	The commercial balance or net exports, is the difference between the monetary value of exports and imports of output in an economy over a certain period, measured in the currency of that economy. It is the relationship between a nation's imports and exports. A positive balance is known as a trade surplus if it consists of exporting more than is imported; a negative balance is referred to as a trade deficit or, informally, a trade gap.
Monopoly	A monopoly (from Greek monos μ???? + polein p??e?? (to sell)) exists when a specific person or enterprise is the only supplier of a particular commodity (this contrasts with a monopsony which relates to a single entity's control of a market to purchase a good or service, and with oligopoly which consists of a few entities dominating an industry). Monopolies are thus characterized by a lack of economic competition to produce the good or service and a lack of viable substitute goods. The verb 'monopolize' refers to the process by which a company gains the ability to raise prices or exclude competitors.
Natural monopoly	A monopoly is a firm which is the only one producing and selling a particular product. A natural monopoly is a monopoly in an industry in which it is most efficient (involving the lowest long-run average cost) for production to be concentrated in a single firm. This market situation gives the largest supplier in an industry, often the first supplier in a market, an overwhelming cost advantage over other actual and potential competitors, so a natural monopoly situation generally leads to an actual monopoly.

Depreciation	In accountancy, depreciation refers to two aspects of the same concept:•the decrease in value of assets (fair value depreciation), and•the allocation of the cost of assets to periods in which the assets are used (depreciation with the matching principle).
	The former affects the balance sheet of a business or entity, and the latter affects the net income that they report. Generally the cost is allocated, as depreciation expense, among the periods in which the asset is expected to be used. This expense is recognized by businesses for financial reporting and tax purposes.
Economic growth	Economic growth is the increase in the market value of the goods and services produced by an economy over time. It is conventionally measured as the percent rate of increase in real gross domestic product, or real GDP. Of more importance is the growth of the ratio of GDP to population (GDP per capita), which is also called per capita income. An increase in per capita income is referred to as intensive growth.
Fixed capital	Fixed capital is a concept in economics and accounting, first theoretically analysed in some depth by the economist David Ricardo. It refers to any kind of real or physical capital (fixed asset) that is not used up in the production of a product and is contrasted with circulating capital such as raw materials, operating expenses and the like.
	Fixed capital is that portion of the total capital that is invested in fixed assets (such as land, buildings, vehicles, plant and equipment) that stay in the business almost permanently, or at the very least, for more than one accounting period.
Dividend	A dividend is a payment made by a corporation to its shareholders, usually as a distribution of profits. When a corporation earns a profit or surplus, it can either re-invest it in the business (called retained earnings), or it can distribute it to shareholders. A corporation may retain a portion of its earnings and pay the remainder as a dividend.
Laffer curve	In economics, the Laffer curve is a representation of the relationship between possible rates of taxation and the resulting levels of government revenue. It illustrates the concept of taxable income elasticity--i.e., taxable income will change in response to changes in the rate of taxation. It postulates that no tax revenue will be raised at the extreme tax rates of 0% and 100% and that there must be at least one rate where tax revenue would be a non-zero maximum.
Corporate tax	Many countries impose corporate tax, also called corporation tax or company tax, on the income or capital of some types of legal entities. A similar tax may be imposed at state or lower levels. The taxes may also be referred to as income tax or capital tax.
Production	Production is a process of combining various material inputs and immaterial inputs in order to make something for consumption (the output). It is the act of creating output, a good or service which has value and contributes to the utility of individuals.

25. Measuring Domestic Output and National Income

Consumption	Consumption is a major concept in economics and is also studied by many other social sciences. Economists are particularly interested in the relationship between consumption and income, and therefore in economics the consumption function plays a major role. Different schools of economists define production and consumption differently.
Consumption of fixed capital	Consumption of fixed capital is a term used in business accounts, tax assessments and national accounts for depreciation of fixed assets. CFC is used in preference to 'depreciation' to emphasize that fixed capital is used up in the process of generating new output, and because unlike depreciation it is not valued at historic cost but at current market value (so-called 'economic depreciation'); CFC may also include other expenses incurred in using or installing fixed assets beyond actual depreciation charges. Normally the term applies only to producing enterprises, but sometimes it applies also to real estate assets.
Net domestic product	The net domestic product equals the gross domestic product (GDP) minus depreciation on a country's capital goods. Net domestic product accounts for capital that has been consumed over the year in the form of housing, vehicle, or machinery deterioration. The depreciation accounted for is often referred to as 'capital consumption allowance' and represents the amount of capital that would be needed to replace those depreciated assets.
Personal income	In economics, personal income refers to an individual's total earnings from wages, investment enterprises, and other ventures. It is the sum of all the incomes actually received by all the individuals or household during a given period. Personal income is that income which is actually received by the individuals or households in a country during the year from all sources.
Price index	A price index is a normalized average of price relatives for a given class of goods or services in a given region, during a given interval of time. It is a statistic designed to help to compare how these price relatives, taken as a whole, differ between time periods or geographical locations. Price indexes have several potential uses.
Lehman Brothers	Lehman Brothers Holdings Inc. (former NYSE ticker symbol LEH) was a global financial services firm. Before declaring bankruptcy in 2008, Lehman was the fourth-largest investment bank in the US (behind Goldman Sachs, Morgan Stanley, and Merrill Lynch), doing business in investment banking, equity and fixed-income sales and trading (especially U.S. Treasury securities), research, investment management, private equity, and private banking.
OPEC	OPEC is an international organization whose mission is to coordinate the policies of the oil-producing countries. The goal is to secure a steady income to the member states and to secure supply of oil to consumers.

25. Measuring Domestic Output and National Income

Well-being	Well-being or welfare is a general term for the condition of an individual or group, for example their social, economic, psychological, spiritual or medical state; high well-being means that, in some sense, the individual or group's experience is positive, while low well-being is associated with negative happenings.
	In economics, the term is used for one or more Quantitative measures intended to assess the quality of life of a group, for example, in the capabilities approach and the economics of happiness. Like the related cognate terms 'wealth' and 'welfare', economics sources may contrast the state with its opposite.
Quality	Quality in business, engineering and manufacturing has a pragmatic interpretation as the non-inferiority or superiority of something; it is also defined as fitness for purpose. Quality is a perceptual, conditional, and somewhat subjective attribute and may be understood differently by different people. Consumers may focus on the specification quality of a product/service, or how it compares to competitors in the marketplace.

1. _____ is a term used in business accounts, tax assessments and national accounts for depreciation of fixed assets. CFC is used in preference to 'depreciation' to emphasize that fixed capital is used up in the process of generating new output, and because unlike depreciation it is not valued at historic cost but at current market value (so-called 'economic depreciation'); CFC may also include other expenses incurred in using or installing fixed assets beyond actual depreciation charges. Normally the term applies only to producing enterprises, but sometimes it applies also to real estate assets.

   a. Base and superstructure
   b. Budapest School
   c. Capital accumulation
   d. Consumption of fixed capital

2. _____ is the exchange of capital, goods, and services across international borders or territories. In most countries, such trade represents a significant share of gross domestic product (GDP). While _____ has been present throughout much of history, its economic, social, and political importance has been on the rise in recent centuries.

   a. 2008 G-20 Washington summit
   b. Backsourcing
   c. Bimetallism
   d. International trade

3. . _____ is the consumption and savings opportunity gained by an entity within a specified timeframe, which is generally expressed in monetary terms.

However, for households and individuals, '_____ is the sum of all the wages, salaries, profits, interests payments, rents and other forms of earnings received... in a given period of time.'

In the field of public economics, the term may refer to the accumulation of both monetary and non-monetary consumption ability, with the former (monetary) being used as a proxy for total _____.

a. Income
b. Battle of Annaberg
c. Freikorps Lichtschlag
d. Freikorps Oberland

4. A _____ is an agreement, communication, or movement carried out between a buyer and a seller to exchange an asset for payment. It involves a change in the status of the finances of two or more businesses or individuals. The buyer and seller are separate entities or objects, often involving the exchange of items of value, such as information, goods, services, and money.

a. Balloon payment mortgage
b. Financial transaction
c. Collateral
d. Compound annual growth rate

5. In economics, a _____ or a hard good is a good that does not quickly wear out, or more specifically, one that yields utility over time rather than being completely consumed in one use. Items like bricks could be considered perfectly _____s, because they should theoretically never wear out. Highly _____s such as refrigerators, cars, or mobile phones usually continue to be useful for three or more years of use, so _____s are typically characterized by long periods between successive purchases.

a. Bad
b. Case
c. Common good
d. Durable good

1. d
2. d
3. a
4. b
5. d

26. Economic Growth

CHAPTER OUTLINE: KEY TERMS, PEOPLE, PLACES, CONCEPTS

	Economic growth
	Lehman Brothers
	Industrial Revolution
	Product
	Income
	Commercial bank
	Human capital
	International trade
	Free trade
	Intellectual property
	Production
	Growth accounting
	Productivity
	Council of Economic Advisers
	Accounting
	Great Recession
	Infrastructure
	Opportunity cost
	Quantitative easing
	Recession
	Capital

26. Economic Growth

CHAPTER OUTLINE: KEY TERMS, PEOPLE, PLACES, CONCEPTS

	Labor force
	OPEC
	Economies of scale
	PayPal
	National income
	Network effect
	North American Free Trade Agreement
	World Trade Organization
	Total cost
	Baby Boomers
	Social security

CHAPTER HIGHLIGHTS & NOTES: KEY TERMS, PEOPLE, PLACES, CONCEPTS

Economic growth	Economic growth is the increase in the market value of the goods and services produced by an economy over time. It is conventionally measured as the percent rate of increase in real gross domestic product, or real GDP. Of more importance is the growth of the ratio of GDP to population (GDP per capita), which is also called per capita income. An increase in per capita income is referred to as intensive growth.
Lehman Brothers	Lehman Brothers Holdings Inc. (former NYSE ticker symbol LEH) was a global financial services firm. Before declaring bankruptcy in 2008, Lehman was the fourth-largest investment bank in the US (behind Goldman Sachs, Morgan Stanley, and Merrill Lynch), doing business in investment banking, equity and fixed-income sales and trading (especially U.S. Treasury securities), research, investment management, private equity, and private banking.

26. Economic Growth

Industrial Revolution	The Industrial Revolution was the transition to new manufacturing processes in the period from about 1760 to sometime between 1820 and 1840. This transition included going from hand production methods to machines, new chemical manufacturing and iron production processes, improved efficiency of water power, the increasing use of steam power and the development of machine tools. It also included the change from wood and other bio-fuels to coal. Textiles were the dominant industry of the Industrial Revolution in terms of employment, value of output and capital invested.
Product	In marketing, a product is anything that can be offered to a market that might satisfy a want or need. In retailing, products are called merchandise. In manufacturing, products are bought as raw materials and sold as finished goods.
Income	Income is the consumption and savings opportunity gained by an entity within a specified timeframe, which is generally expressed in monetary terms. However, for households and individuals, 'income is the sum of all the wages, salaries, profits, interests payments, rents and other forms of earnings received... in a given period of time.' In the field of public economics, the term may refer to the accumulation of both monetary and non-monetary consumption ability, with the former (monetary) being used as a proxy for total income.
Commercial bank	A commercial bank is a type of bank that provides services such as accepting deposits, making business loans, and offering basic investment products. Commercial bank can also refer to a bank or a division of a bank that mostly deals with deposits and loans from corporations or large businesses, as opposed to individual members of the public. In the US the term commercial bank was often used to distinguish it from an investment bank due to differences in bank regulation.
Human capital	Human capital is the stock of competencies, knowledge, habits, social and personality attributes, including creativity, cognitive abilities, embodied in the ability to perform labor so as to produce economic value. It is an aggregate economic view of the human being acting within economies, which is an attempt to capture the social, biological, cultural and psychological complexity as they interact in explicit and/or economic transactions. Many theories explicitly connect investment in human capital development to education, and the role of human capital in economic development, productivity growth, and innovation has frequently been cited as a justification for government subsidies for education and job skills training.
International trade	International trade is the exchange of capital, goods, and services across international borders or territories. In most countries, such trade represents a significant share of gross domestic product (GDP).

26. Economic Growth

Free trade	Free trade is a policy in international markets in which governments do not restrict imports or exports. Free trade is exemplified by the European Union / European Economic Area and the North American Free Trade Agreement, which have established open markets. Most nations are today members of the World Trade Organization (WTO) multilateral trade agreements.
Intellectual property	Intellectual property rights are the legally recognized exclusive rights to creations of the mind. Under intellectual property law, owners are granted certain exclusive rights to a variety of intangible assets, such as musical, literary, and artistic works; discoveries and inventions; and words, phrases, symbols, and designs. Common types of intellectual property rights include copyright, trademarks, patents, industrial design rights, trade dress, and in some jurisdictions trade secrets.
Production	Production is a process of combining various material inputs and immaterial inputs in order to make something for consumption (the output). It is the act of creating output, a good or service which has value and contributes to the utility of individuals. Economic well-being is created in a production process, meaning all economic activities that aim directly or indirectly to satisfy human needs.
Growth accounting	Growth accounting is a procedure used in economics to measure the contribution of different factors to economic growth and to indirectly compute the rate of technological progress, measured as a residual, in an economy. This methodology was introduced by Robert Solow in 1957. Growth accounting decomposes the growth rate of economy's total output into that which is due to increases in the amount of factors used--usually the increase in the amount of capital and labor--and that which cannot be accounted for by observable changes in factor utilization.
Productivity	Productivity is the ratio of output to inputs in production; it is an average measure of the efficiency of production. Efficiency of production means production's capability to create incomes which is measured by the formula real output value minus real input value. Increasing national productivity can raise living standards because more real income improves people's ability to purchase goods and services, enjoy leisure, improve housing and education and contribute to social and environmental programs.
Council of Economic Advisers	The Council of Economic Advisers is a group of economists and captains of industry who advise the Scottish Government. It was established in 2007, meeting for the first time on 21 September. Minutes of its quarterly meetings will be published a fortnight after each meeting.
Accounting	Accounting, or accountancy, is the measurement, processing and communication of financial information about economic entities. Accounting, which has been called the 'language of business', measures the results of an organization's economic activities and conveys this information to a variety of users including investors, creditors, management, and regulators.

26. Economic Growth

Great Recession	The Great Recession was a global economic decline in the late 2000s. According to aggregated national data, a worldwide recession began in Q3-2008 and ended in Q1-2009.
	It is related to a liquidity crisis, commonly being dated to have started when several central banks had to step in with liquidity lending to the interbank lending market on 9 August 2007. This was a response to a situation where BNP Paribas temporarily had to block money withdrawals from three hedge funds--citing a 'complete evaporation of liquidity'.
Infrastructure	Infrastructure is basic physical and organizational structures needed for the operation of a society or enterprise, or the services and facilities necessary for an economy to function. It can be generally defined as the set of interconnected structural elements that provide framework supporting an entire structure of development. It is an important term for judging a country or region's development.
Opportunity cost	In microeconomic theory, the opportunity cost of a choice is the value of the best alternative forgone, in a situation in which a choice needs to be made between several mutually exclusive alternatives given limited resources. Assuming the best choice is made, it is the 'cost' incurred by not enjoying the benefit that would be had by taking the second best choice available. The New Oxford American Dictionary defines it as 'the loss of potential gain from other alternatives when one alternative is chosen'.
Quantitative easing	Quantitative easing is an unconventional monetary policy used by central banks to stimulate the economy when standard monetary policy has become ineffective. A central bank implements quantitative easing by buying specified amounts of financial assets from commercial banks and other private institutions, thus raising the prices of those financial assets and lowering their yield, while simultaneously increasing the monetary base. This is distinguished from the more usual policy of buying or selling short term government bonds in order to keep interbank interest rates at a specified target value.
Recession	In economics, a recession is a business cycle contraction. It is a general slowdown in economic activity. Macroeconomic indicators such as GDP (gross domestic product), investment spending, capacity utilization, household income, business profits, and inflation fall, while bankruptcies and the unemployment rate rise.
Capital	In economics, capital goods, real capital, or capital assets are already-produced durable goods or any non-financial asset that is used in production of goods or services.
	Capital goods are not significantly consumed in the production process though they may depreciate. How a capital good or is maintained or returned to its pre-production state varies with the type of capital involved.
Labor force	The labor force is the actual number of people available for work.

26. Economic Growth

	The labor force of a country includes both the employed and the unemployed. The labor force participation rate, LFPR (or economic activity rate, EAR), is the ratio between the labor force and the overall size of their cohort (national population of the same age range).
OPEC	OPEC is an international organization whose mission is to coordinate the policies of the oil-producing countries. The goal is to secure a steady income to the member states and to secure supply of oil to consumers. OPEC is an intergovernmental organization that was created at the Baghdad Conference on 10-14 September 1960, by Iraq, Kuwait, Iran, Saudi Arabia and Venezuela.
Economies of scale	In microeconomics, economies of scale are the cost advantages that enterprises obtain due to size, output, or scale of operation, with cost per unit of output generally decreasing with increasing scale as fixed costs are spread out over more units of output. Often operational efficiency is also greater with increasing scale, leading to lower variable cost as well. Economies of scale apply to a variety of organizational and business situations and at various levels, such as a business or manufacturing unit, plant or an entire enterprise.
PayPal	PayPal is an international e-commerce business allowing payments and money transfers to be made through the Internet. Online money transfers serve as electronic alternatives to paying with traditional paper methods, such as checks and money orders. It is subject to the US economic sanction list, and subject to other rules and interventions required by US laws or government.
National income	A variety of measures of national income and output are used in economics to estimate total economic activity in a country or region, including gross domestic product, gross national product (GNP), net national income and adjusted national income. All are specially concerned with counting the total amount of goods and services produced within some 'boundary'. The boundary is usually defined by geography or citizenship, and may also restrict the goods and services that are counted.
Network effect	In economics and business, a network effect is the effect that one user of a good or service has on the value of that product to other people. When network effect is present, the value of a product or service is dependent on the number of others using it. The classic example is the telephone.
North American Free Trade Agreement	The North American Free Trade Agreement is an agreement signed by Canada, Mexico, and the United States, creating a trilateral rules-based trade bloc in North America. The agreement came into force on January 1, 1994. It superseded the Canada-United States Free Trade Agreement between the U.S. and Canada.

North American Free Trade Agreement has two supplements: the North American Agreement on Environmental Cooperation (NAAEC) and the North American Agreement on Labor Cooperation (NAALC).

In terms of combined purchasing power parity GDP of its members, as of 2007 the trade bloc is the largest in the world and second largest by nominal GDP comparison.

World Trade Organization	The World Trade Organization is an organization that intends to supervise and liberalize international trade. The organization officially commenced on 1 January 1995 under the Marrakech Agreement, replacing the General Agreement on Tariffs and Trade (GATT), which commenced in 1948. The organization deals with regulation of trade between participating countries; it provides a framework for negotiating and formalizing trade agreements, and a dispute resolution process aimed at enforcing participant's adherence to World Trade Organization agreements, which are signed by representatives of member governments and ratified by their parliaments. Most of the issues that the World Trade Organization focuses on derive from previous trade negotiations, especially from the Uruguay Round (1986-1994).
Total cost	In economics, and cost accounting, total cost describes the total economic cost of production and is made up of variable costs, which vary according to the quantity of a good produced and include inputs such as labor and raw materials, plus fixed costs, which are independent of the quantity of a good produced and include inputs (capital) that cannot be varied in the short term, such as buildings and machinery. Total cost in economics includes the total opportunity cost of each factor of production as part of its fixed or variable costs. The rate at which total cost changes as the amount produced changes is called marginal cost.
Baby Boomers	Baby boomers are people born during the demographic Post-World War II baby boom between the years 1946 and 1964. According to the U.S. Census Bureau, the term 'baby boomer' is also used in a cultural context. Therefore, it is impossible to achieve broad consensus of a precise date definition, even within a given territory. Different groups, organizations, individuals, and scholars may have widely varying opinions on what constitutes a baby boomer, both technically and culturally.
Social security	Social security is a concept enshrined in Article 22 of the Universal Declaration of Human Rights which states, Everyone, as a member of society, has the right to social security and is entitled to realization, through national effort and international co-operation and in accordance with the organization and resources of each State, of the economic, social and cultural rights indispensable for his dignity and the free development of his personality. In simple terms, the signatories agree that society in which a person lives should help them to develop and to make the most of all the advantages (culture, work, social welfare) which are offered to them in the country.

26. Economic Growth

1. In economics, a _____ is a business cycle contraction. It is a general slowdown in economic activity. Macroeconomic indicators such as GDP (gross domestic product), investment spending, capacity utilization, household income, business profits, and inflation fall, while bankruptcies and the unemployment rate rise.

    a. Depression
    b. General glut
    c. Recession
    d. Great Recession in South America

2. _____ is the increase in the market value of the goods and services produced by an economy over time. It is conventionally measured as the percent rate of increase in real gross domestic product, or real GDP. Of more importance is the growth of the ratio of GDP to population (GDP per capita), which is also called per capita income. An increase in per capita income is referred to as intensive growth.

    a. Baker cube
    b. Bereavement benefit
    c. Biological standard of living
    d. Economic growth

3. A variety of measures of _____ and output are used in economics to estimate total economic activity in a country or region, including gross domestic product, gross national product (GNP), net _____ and adjusted _____. All are specially concerned with counting the total amount of goods and services produced within some 'boundary'. The boundary is usually defined by geography or citizenship, and may also restrict the goods and services that are counted.

    a. Fuel protests in the United Kingdom
    b. 3V
    c. National income
    d. Bankgiro

4. _____ rights are the legally recognized exclusive rights to creations of the mind. Under _____ law, owners are granted certain exclusive rights to a variety of intangible assets, such as musical, literary, and artistic works; discoveries and inventions; and words, phrases, symbols, and designs. Common types of _____ rights include copyright, trademarks, patents, industrial design rights, trade dress, and in some jurisdictions trade secrets.

    a. Centre for Innovation and Structural Change
    b. Cognitive-cultural economy
    c. Communities of innovation
    d. Intellectual property

5. . The _____ was the transition to new manufacturing processes in the period from about 1760 to sometime between 1820 and 1840. This transition included going from hand production methods to machines, new chemical manufacturing and iron production processes, improved efficiency of water power, the increasing use of steam power and the development of machine tools. It also included the change from wood and other bio-fuels to coal.

Textiles were the dominant industry of the _____ in terms of employment, value of output and capital invested.

a. Bendigo Petition

b. Bacon

c. Industrial Revolution

d. Commercial Revolution

1. c
2. d
3. c
4. d
5. c

27. Business Cycles, Unemployment, and Inflation

CHAPTER OUTLINE: KEY TERMS, PEOPLE, PLACES, CONCEPTS

_____ | Business cycle

_____ | Great Depression

_____ | Great Recession

_____ | Recession

_____ | Trough

_____ | Derivative

_____ | Capital

_____ | Capital good

_____ | Durable good

_____ | Labor force

_____ | Production

_____ | Discouraged worker

_____ | Structural unemployment

_____ | Actual GDP

_____ | Economic cost

_____ | Full employment

_____ | Natural rate of unemployment

_____ | Social security

_____ | Demographics

_____ | Wage ratio

_____ | Consumer price index

Inflation

International trade

Laffer curve

OPEC

Deflation

Taylor rule

Cost-push inflation

Demand-pull inflation

Economic freedom

Federal Reserve System

Supply shock

Core inflation

Feudalism

Real income

Baby Boomers

Fixed income

Income

Pricing

Purchasing power

Transfer payment

Creditor

	Federal funds
	Real interest rate
	Interest rate
	Cartel
	Economic growth
	Hyperinflation
	Minimum wage
	Republic

CHAPTER HIGHLIGHTS & NOTES: KEY TERMS, PEOPLE, PLACES, CONCEPTS

Business cycle	The term business cycle refers fluctuations in aggregate production, trade and activity over several months or years in a market economy.
	The business cycle is the upward and downward movements of levels of gross domestic product (GDP) and refers to the period of expansions and contractions in the level of economic activities (business fluctuations) around its long-term growth trend.
	These fluctuations occur around a long-term growth trend, and typically involve shifts over time between periods of relatively rapid economic growth (an expansion or boom), and periods of relative stagnation or decline (a contraction or recession).
Great Depression	The Great Depression was a severe worldwide economic depression in the decade preceding World War II. The timing of the Great Depression varied across nations, but in most countries it started in 1930 and lasted until the late 1930s or middle 1940s. It was the longest, deepest, and most widespread depression of the 20th century.
	In the 21st century, the Great Depression is commonly used as an example of how far the world's economy can decline.

27. Business Cycles, Unemployment, and Inflation

Great Recession	The Great Recession was a global economic decline in the late 2000s. According to aggregated national data, a worldwide recession began in Q3-2008 and ended in Q1-2009. It is related to a liquidity crisis, commonly being dated to have started when several central banks had to step in with liquidity lending to the interbank lending market on 9 August 2007. This was a response to a situation where BNP Paribas temporarily had to block money withdrawals from three hedge funds--citing a 'complete evaporation of liquidity'.
Recession	In economics, a recession is a business cycle contraction. It is a general slowdown in economic activity. Macroeconomic indicators such as GDP (gross domestic product), investment spending, capacity utilization, household income, business profits, and inflation fall, while bankruptcies and the unemployment rate rise.
Trough	In economics, a trough is a low turning point or a local minimum of a business cycle. The time evolution of many variables of economics exhibit a wave like behavior with local maxima (peaks) followed by local minima (troughs). A business cycle may be defined as the period between two consecutive peaks.
Derivative	A derivative is a financial contract which derives its value from the performance of another entity such as an asset, index, or interest rate, called the 'underlying'. Derivatives are one of the three main categories of financial instruments, the other two being equities (i.e. stocks) and debt (i.e. bonds and mortgages). Derivatives include a variety of financial contracts, including futures, forwards, swaps, options, and variations of these such as caps, floors, collars, and credit default swaps.
Capital	In economics, capital goods, real capital, or capital assets are already-produced durable goods or any non-financial asset that is used in production of goods or services. Capital goods are not significantly consumed in the production process though they may depreciate. How a capital good or is maintained or returned to its pre-production state varies with the type of capital involved.
Capital good	A capital good is a durable good that is used in the production of goods or services. Capital goods are one of the three types of producer goods, the other two being land and labor, which are also known collectively as primary factors of production. This classification originated during the classical economic period and has remained the dominant method for classification.
Durable good	In economics, a durable good or a hard good is a good that does not quickly wear out, or more specifically, one that yields utility over time rather than being completely consumed in one use. Items like bricks could be considered perfectly durable goods, because they should theoretically never wear out.

Labor force	The labor force is the actual number of people available for work. The labor force of a country includes both the employed and the unemployed. The labor force participation rate, LFPR (or economic activity rate, EAR), is the ratio between the labor force and the overall size of their cohort (national population of the same age range).
Production	Production is a process of combining various material inputs and immaterial inputs in order to make something for consumption (the output). It is the act of creating output, a good or service which has value and contributes to the utility of individuals. Economic well-being is created in a production process, meaning all economic activities that aim directly or indirectly to satisfy human needs.
Discouraged worker	Not to be confused with Disgruntled worker. In economics, a discouraged worker is a person of legal employment age who is not actively seeking employment or who does not find employment after long-term unemployment. This is usually because an individual has given up looking or has had no success in finding a job, hence the term 'discouraged'.
Structural unemployment	Structural unemployment is a form of unemployment where, at a given wage, the quantity of labor supplied exceeds the quantity of labor demanded, because there is a fundamental mismatch between the number of people who want to work and the number of jobs that are available. The unemployed workers may lack the skills needed for the jobs, or they may not live in the part of the country or world where the jobs are available. Structural unemployment is one of the five major categories of unemployment distinguished by economists.
Actual GDP	In economics, potential output refers to the highest level of real Gross Domestic Product output that can be sustained over the long term. The existence of a limit is due to natural and institutional constraints. If actual GDP rises and stays above potential output, then (in the absence of wage and price controls) inflation tends to increase as demand for factors of production exceeds supply.
Economic cost	The economic cost of a decision depends on both the cost of the alternative chosen and the benefit that the best alternative would have provided if chosen. Economic cost differs from accounting cost because it includes opportunity cost. As an example, consider the economic cost of attending college.
Full employment	Full employment, in macroeconomics, is the level of employment rates where there is no cyclical or deficient-demand unemployment. It is defined by the majority of mainstream economists as being an acceptable level of unemployment somewhere above 0%. The discrepancy from 0% arises due to non-cyclical types of unemployment.
Natural rate of unemployment	The natural rate of unemployment is a concept of economic activity developed in particular by Milton Friedman and Edmund Phelps in the 1960s, both recipients of the Nobel prize in economics.

27. Business Cycles, Unemployment, and Inflation

	In both cases, the development of the concept is cited as a main motivation behind the prize. It represents the hypothetical unemployment rate consistent with aggregate production being at the 'long-run' level.
Social security	Social security is a concept enshrined in Article 22 of the Universal Declaration of Human Rights which states, Everyone, as a member of society, has the right to social security and is entitled to realization, through national effort and international co-operation and in accordance with the organization and resources of each State, of the economic, social and cultural rights indispensable for his dignity and the free development of his personality. In simple terms, the signatories agree that society in which a person lives should help them to develop and to make the most of all the advantages (culture, work, social welfare) which are offered to them in the country.
	Social security may also refer to the action programs of government intended to promote the welfare of the population through assistance measures guaranteeing access to sufficient resources for food and shelter and to promote health and well-being for the population at large and potentially vulnerable segments such as children, the elderly, the sick and the unemployed.
Demographics	Demographics are the quantifiable statistics of a given population. Demographics are also used to identify the study of quantifiable subsets within a given population which characterize that population at a specific point in time.
	Demographic data is used widely in public opinion polling and marketing.
Wage ratio	In economics, the wage ratio refers to the ratio of the top salaries in a group to the bottom salaries. It is a measure of wage dispersion.
Consumer price index	The Belgian Consumer Price Index is a list of prices of goods and services, kept by the Belgian Federal Government Service Economy. The Index is updated on a monthly basis, and reflects the evolution in the cost of living.
	The Belgian system tracks two indices: the general Consumer Price Index and the Health Index.
Inflation	In economics, inflation is a sustained increase in the general price level of goods and services in an economy over a period of time. When the general price level rises, each unit of currency buys fewer goods and services. Consequently, inflation reflects a reduction in the purchasing power per unit of money - a loss of real value in the medium of exchange and unit of account within the economy.
International trade	International trade is the exchange of capital, goods, and services across international borders or territories. In most countries, such trade represents a significant share of gross domestic product (GDP).

Laffer curve	In economics, the Laffer curve is a representation of the relationship between possible rates of taxation and the resulting levels of government revenue. It illustrates the concept of taxable income elasticity--i.e., taxable income will change in response to changes in the rate of taxation. It postulates that no tax revenue will be raised at the extreme tax rates of 0% and 100% and that there must be at least one rate where tax revenue would be a non-zero maximum.
OPEC	OPEC is an international organization whose mission is to coordinate the policies of the oil-producing countries. The goal is to secure a steady income to the member states and to secure supply of oil to consumers. OPEC is an intergovernmental organization that was created at the Baghdad Conference on 10-14 September 1960, by Iraq, Kuwait, Iran, Saudi Arabia and Venezuela.
Deflation	In economics, deflation is a decrease in the general price level of goods and services. Deflation occurs when the inflation rate falls below 0% (a negative inflation rate). This should not be confused with disinflation, a slow-down in the inflation rate (i.e., when inflation declines to lower levels).
Taylor rule	In economics, a Taylor rule is a monetary-policy rule that stipulates how much the central bank should change the nominal interest rate in response to changes in inflation, output, or other economic conditions. In particular, the rule stipulates that for each one-percent increase in inflation, the central bank should raise the nominal interest rate by more than one percentage point. This aspect of the rule is often called the Taylor principle.
Cost-push inflation	Cost-push inflation is an alleged type of inflation caused by substantial increases in the cost of important goods or services where no suitable alternative is available. A situation that has been often cited of this was the oil crisis of the 1970s, which some economists see as a major cause of the inflation experienced in the Western world in that decade. It is argued that this inflation resulted from increases in the cost of petroleum imposed by the member states of OPEC. Since petroleum is so important to industrialised economies, a large increase in its price can lead to the increase in the price of most products, raising the inflation rate.
Demand-pull inflation	Demand-pull inflation is asserted to arise when aggregate demand in an economy outpaces aggregate supply. It involves inflation rising as real gross domestic product rises and unemployment falls, as the economy moves along the Phillips curve. This is commonly described as 'too much money chasing too few goods'.
Economic freedom	Economic freedom or economic liberty or right to economic liberty denotes the ability of members of a society to undertake economic direction and actions. This is a term used in economic and policy debates as well as a politicoeconomic philosophy. As with freedom generally, there are various definitions, but no universally accepted concept of economic freedom.

27. Business Cycles, Unemployment, and Inflation

Federal Reserve System	The Federal Reserve System is the central banking system of the United States. It was created on December 23, 1913, with the enactment of the Federal Reserve Act, largely in response to a series of financial panics, particularly a severe panic in 1907. Over time, the roles and responsibilities of the Federal Reserve System have expanded, and its structure has evolved. Events such as the Great Depression were major factors leading to changes in the system.
Supply shock	A supply shock is an event that suddenly changes the price of a commodity or service. It may be caused by a sudden increase or decrease in the supply of a particular good. This sudden change affects the equilibrium price.
Core inflation	Core inflation represents the long run trend in the price level. In measuring long run inflation, transitory price changes should be excluded. One way of accomplishing this is by excluding items frequently subject to volatile prices, like food and energy.
Feudalism	Feudalism was a set of legal and military customs in medieval Europe that flourished between the 9th and 15th centuries. Broadly defined, it was a system for structuring society around relationships derived from the holding of land in exchange for service or labour. Although derived from the Latin word feodum or feudum (fief), then in use, the term feudalism and the system it describes were not conceived of as a formal political system by the people living in the medieval period.
Real income	Real income is the income of individuals or nations after adjusting for inflation. It is calculated by subtracting inflation from the nominal income. Real variables, such as real income, real GDP, and real interest rate are variables that are measured in physical units, while nominal variables such as nominal income, nominal GDP, and nominal interest rate are measured in monetary units.
Baby Boomers	Baby boomers are people born during the demographic Post-World War II baby boom between the years 1946 and 1964. According to the U.S. Census Bureau, the term 'baby boomer' is also used in a cultural context. Therefore, it is impossible to achieve broad consensus of a precise date definition, even within a given territory. Different groups, organizations, individuals, and scholars may have widely varying opinions on what constitutes a baby boomer, both technically and culturally.
Fixed income	Fixed income refers to any type of investment under which the borrower/issuer is obliged to make payments of a fixed amount on a fixed schedule: for example, if the borrower has to pay interest at a fixed rate once a year, and to repay the principal amount on maturity. Fixed-income securities can be contrasted with equity securities, often referred to as stocks and shares, that create no obligation to pay dividends or any other form of income.

Income	Income is the consumption and savings opportunity gained by an entity within a specified timeframe, which is generally expressed in monetary terms. However, for households and individuals, 'income is the sum of all the wages, salaries, profits, interests payments, rents and other forms of earnings received... in a given period of time.'
	In the field of public economics, the term may refer to the accumulation of both monetary and non-monetary consumption ability, with the former (monetary) being used as a proxy for total income.
Pricing	Pricing is the process of determining what a company will receive in exchange for its product. Pricing factors are manufacturing cost, market place, competition, market condition, brand, and quality of product. Pricing is also a key variable in microeconomic price allocation theory.
Purchasing power	Purchasing power is the number of goods or services that can be purchased with a unit of currency. For example, if one had taken one unit of currency to a store in the 1950s, it is probable that it would have been possible to buy a greater number of items than would today, indicating that one would have had a greater purchasing power in the 1950s. Currency can be either a commodity money, like gold or silver, or fiat currency, or free-floating market-valued currency like US dollars.
Transfer payment	In economics, a transfer payment is a redistribution of income in the market system. These payments are considered to be non-exhaustive because they do not directly absorb resources or create output. In other words, the transfer is made without any exchange of goods or services.
Creditor	A creditor is a party that has a claim on the services of a second party. It is a person or institution to whom money is owed. The first party, in general, has provided some property or service to the second party under the assumption (usually enforced by contract) that the second party will return an equivalent property and service.
Federal funds	In the United States, federal funds are overnight borrowings between banks and other entities to maintain their bank reserves at the Federal Reserve. Banks keep reserves at Federal Reserve Banks to meet their reserve requirements and to clear financial transactions. Transactions in the federal funds market enable depository institutions with reserve balances in excess of reserve requirements to lend reserves to institutions with reserve deficiencies.
Real interest rate	The real interest rate is the rate of interest an investor expects to receive after allowing for inflation. It can be described more formally by the Fisher equation, which states that the real interest rate is approximately the nominal interest rate minus the inflation rate. If, for example, an investor were able to lock in a 5% interest rate for the coming year and anticipated a 2% rise in prices, they would expect to earn a real interest rate of 3%.
Interest rate	An interest rate is the rate at which interest is paid by a borrower for the use of money that they borrow from a lender (creditor). Specifically, the interest rate is a percent of principal (P) paid a certain amount of times (m) per period (usually quoted per annum).

27. Business Cycles, Unemployment, and Inflation

Cartel	A cartel is a formal 'agreement' among competing firms. It is a formal organization of producers and manufacturers that agree to fix prices, marketing, and production. Cartels usually occur in an oligopolistic industry, where the number of sellers is small (usually because barriers to entry, most notably startup costs, are high) and the products being traded are usually commodities.
Economic growth	Economic growth is the increase in the market value of the goods and services produced by an economy over time. It is conventionally measured as the percent rate of increase in real gross domestic product, or real GDP. Of more importance is the growth of the ratio of GDP to population (GDP per capita), which is also called per capita income. An increase in per capita income is referred to as intensive growth.
Hyperinflation	In economics, hyperinflation occurs when a country experiences very high and usually accelerating rates of monetary and price inflation, causing the population to minimize their holdings of money. Under such conditions, the general price level within an economy increases rapidly as the official currency quickly loses real value. Meanwhile, the real value of economic items generally stay the same with respect to one another, and remain relatively stable in terms of foreign currencies.
Minimum wage	A minimum wage is the lowest hourly, daily or monthly remuneration that employers may legally pay to workers. Equivalently, it is the lowest wage at which workers may sell their labor. Although minimum wage laws are in effect in many jurisdictions, differences of opinion exist about the benefits and drawbacks of a minimum wage.
Republic	Republic is a left-wing political party in the Faroe Islands committed to Faroese independence. It was founded in 1948 as a reaction to independence not being proclaimed after a public vote on the matter showed a significant plurality (almost a majority) for it in 1946. In 1998 Høgni Hoydal succeeded Heini O. Heinesen as party leader.

1. _____, in macroeconomics, is the level of employment rates where there is no cyclical or deficient-demand unemployment. It is defined by the majority of mainstream economists as being an acceptable level of unemployment somewhere above 0%. The discrepancy from 0% arises due to non-cyclical types of unemployment.

    a. Fuel protests in the United Kingdom
    b. Battle of Annaberg
    c. Full employment
    d. Freikorps Oberland

2. _____ is an alleged type of inflation caused by substantial increases in the cost of important goods or services where no suitable alternative is available. A situation that has been often cited of this was the oil crisis of the 1970s, which some economists see as a major cause of the inflation experienced in the Western world in that decade. It is argued that this inflation resulted from increases in the cost of petroleum imposed by the member states of OPEC. Since petroleum is so important to industrialised economies, a large increase in its price can lead to the increase in the price of most products, raising the inflation rate.

    a. Built-in inflation
    b. Core inflation
    c. Cost-push inflation
    d. Battle of Annaberg

3. _____ is a form of unemployment where, at a given wage, the quantity of labor supplied exceeds the quantity of labor demanded, because there is a fundamental mismatch between the number of people who want to work and the number of jobs that are available. The unemployed workers may lack the skills needed for the jobs, or they may not live in the part of the country or world where the jobs are available. _____ is one of the five major categories of unemployment distinguished by economists.

    a. Structural unemployment
    b. Labour Force Survey
    c. Layoff
    d. Male unemployment

4. _____ is asserted to arise when aggregate demand in an economy outpaces aggregate supply. It involves inflation rising as real gross domestic product rises and unemployment falls, as the economy moves along the Phillips curve. This is commonly described as 'too much money chasing too few goods'.

    a. Demand-pull inflation
    b. Core inflation
    c. Cost-push inflation
    d. Countermarked coin

5. . In economics, _____ goods, real _____, or _____ assets are already-produced durable goods or any non-financial asset that is used in production of goods or services.

27. Business Cycles, Unemployment, and Inflation

_____ goods are not significantly consumed in the production process though they may depreciate. How a _____ good or is maintained or returned to its pre-production state varies with the type of _____ involved.

a. James Bonar
b. Capital
c. Shimshon Bichler
d. Fuel protests in the United Kingdom

ANSWER KEY
27. Business Cycles, Unemployment, and Inflation

1. c
2. c
3. a
4. a
5. b

You can take the complete Chapter Practice Test

for 27. Business Cycles, Unemployment, and Inflation
on all key terms, persons, places, and concepts.

Online 99 Cents

http://www.JustTheFacts101.com

Use www.JustTheFacts101.com for all your study needs

including Facts101's online interactive problem solving labs in

chemistry, statistics, mathematics, and more.

28. Basic Macroeconomic Relationships

CHAPTER OUTLINE: KEY TERMS, PEOPLE, PLACES, CONCEPTS

	Fiscal policy
	Macroeconomics
	Ceteris paribus
	Consumption
	Elasticity
	Income
	Price elasticity
	Expression
	Average propensity to consume
	Average propensity to save
	Marginal propensity to consume
	Marginal propensity to save
	National income
	Product
	Wealth effect
	Federal funds
	Interest rate
	Great Recession
	Laffer curve
	Paradox of thrift
	Recession

28. Basic Macroeconomic Relationships

	Real interest rate
	Demand curve
	Operating cost
	Capital
	Capital good
	Corporate tax
	Gross private domestic investment
	Planned change
	Economic freedom
	Instability
	Multiplier

CHAPTER HIGHLIGHTS & NOTES: KEY TERMS, PEOPLE, PLACES, CONCEPTS

Fiscal policy	In economics and political science, fiscal policy is the use of government revenue collection and expenditure (spending) to influence the economy, or else it involves the government changing the levels of taxation and government spending in order to influence Aggregate Demand and the level of economic activity. The two main instruments of fiscal policy are changes in the level and composition of taxation and government spending in various sectors. These changes can affect the following macroeconomic variables in an economy:•Aggregate demand and the level of economic activity;•The distribution of income;•The pattern of resource allocation within the government sector and relative to the private sector. Fiscal policy refers to the use of the government budget to influence economic activity.
Macroeconomics	Macroeconomics is the study of the macroeconomy.

	It is a branch of economics dealing with the performance, structure, behavior, and decision-making of an economy as a whole, rather than individual markets. This includes national, regional, and global economies.
Ceteris paribus	Ceteris paribus or caeteris paribus is a Latin phrase meaning 'with other things the same' or 'all other things being equal or held constant.' As an ablative absolute, it is commonly posed to mean 'all other things being equal.' A prediction or a statement about causal, empirical, or logical relation between two states of affairs is ceteris paribus via acknowledgement that the prediction can fail or the relation can be abolished by intervening factors. A ceteris paribus assumption is often key to scientific inquiry, as scientists seek to screen out factors that perturb a relation of interest. Thus, epidemiologists seek to control independent variables as factors that may influence dependent variables--the outcomes or effects of interest.
Consumption	Consumption is a major concept in economics and is also studied by many other social sciences. Economists are particularly interested in the relationship between consumption and income, and therefore in economics the consumption function plays a major role. Different schools of economists define production and consumption differently.
Elasticity	In economics, elasticity is the measurement of how responsive an economic variable is to a change in another. For example:•'If I lower the price of my product, how much more will I sell?'•'If I raise the price of one good, how will that affect sales of this other good?'•'If we learn that a resource is becoming scarce, will people scramble to acquire it?' An elastic variable (or elasticity value greater than 1) is one which responds more than proportionally to changes in other variables. In contrast, an inelastic variable (or elasticity value less than 1) is one which changes less than proportionally in response to changes in other variables.
Income	Income is the consumption and savings opportunity gained by an entity within a specified timeframe, which is generally expressed in monetary terms. However, for households and individuals, 'income is the sum of all the wages, salaries, profits, interests payments, rents and other forms of earnings received... in a given period of time.' In the field of public economics, the term may refer to the accumulation of both monetary and non-monetary consumption ability, with the former (monetary) being used as a proxy for total income.
Price elasticity	Price elasticity of demand is a measure used in economics to show the responsiveness, or elasticity, of the quantity demanded of a good or service to a change in its price. More precisely, it gives the percentage change in quantity demanded in response to a one percent change in price (ceteris paribus, i.e. holding constant all the other determinants of demand, such as income).

28. Basic Macroeconomic Relationships

Expression	In mathematics, an expression is a finite combination of symbols that is well-formed according to rules that depend on the context. Symbols can designate numbers (constants), variables, operations, functions, and other mathematical symbols, as well as punctuation, symbols of grouping, and other syntactic symbols. The use of expressions can range from the simple: $0 + 0$ to the complex: $$f(a) + \sum_{k=1}^{n} \frac{1}{k!} \frac{d^k}{dt^k}\Big|_{t=0} f(u(t)) + \int_0^1 \frac{(1-t)^n}{n!} \frac{d^{n+1}}{dt^{n+1}} f(u(t))\, dt.$$ We can think of algebraic expressions as generalizations of common arithmetic operations that are formed by combining numbers, variables, and mathematical operations.
Average propensity to consume	Average propensity to consume is the percentage of income spent. To find the percentage of income spent, one needs to divide consumption by income, or $$APC = \frac{C}{Y}.$$ Sometimes, disposable income is used as the denominator instead, so $$APC = \frac{C}{Y - T}$$,where C is the amount spent, Y is pre-tax income, and T is taxes. The inverse is the average propensity to save (APS).
Average propensity to save	The average propensity to save, also known as the savings ratio, is an economics term that refers to the proportion of income which is saved, usually expressed for household savings as a percentage of total household disposable income. The ratio differs considerably over time and between countries. The savings ratio can be affected by (for example): the proportion of older people, as they have less motivation and capability to save; the rate of inflation, as expectations of rising prices can encourage people to spend now rather than later (monetary base/mass depreciation).
Marginal propensity to consume	In economics, the marginal propensity to consume is a metric that quantifies induced consumption, the concept that the increase in personal consumer spending (consumption) occurs with an increase in disposable income (income after taxes and transfers). The proportion of disposable income which individuals spend on consumption is known as propensity to consume. MPC is the proportion of additional income that an individual consumes.
Marginal propensity to save	The marginal propensity to save refers to the increase in saving (non-purchase of current goods and services) that results from an increase in income i.e. The marginal propensity to save might be defined as the proportion of each additional dollar of household income that is used for saving. It is also used as an alternative term for the slope of the saving line.

28. Basic Macroeconomic Relationships

National income	A variety of measures of national income and output are used in economics to estimate total economic activity in a country or region, including gross domestic product, gross national product (GNP), net national income and adjusted national income. All are specially concerned with counting the total amount of goods and services produced within some 'boundary'. The boundary is usually defined by geography or citizenship, and may also restrict the goods and services that are counted.
Product	In marketing, a product is anything that can be offered to a market that might satisfy a want or need. In retailing, products are called merchandise. In manufacturing, products are bought as raw materials and sold as finished goods.
Wealth effect	The wealth effect is an economic term, referring to an increase in spending that accompanies an increase (decrease) in perceived wealth.
Federal funds	In the United States, federal funds are overnight borrowings between banks and other entities to maintain their bank reserves at the Federal Reserve. Banks keep reserves at Federal Reserve Banks to meet their reserve requirements and to clear financial transactions. Transactions in the federal funds market enable depository institutions with reserve balances in excess of reserve requirements to lend reserves to institutions with reserve deficiencies.
Interest rate	An interest rate is the rate at which interest is paid by a borrower for the use of money that they borrow from a lender (creditor). Specifically, the interest rate is a percent of principal (P) paid a certain amount of times (m) per period (usually quoted per annum). For example, a small company borrows capital from a bank to buy new assets for its business, and in return the lender receives interest at a predetermined interest rate for deferring the use of funds and instead lending it to the borrower.
Great Recession	The Great Recession was a global economic decline in the late 2000s. According to aggregated national data, a worldwide recession began in Q3-2008 and ended in Q1-2009. It is related to a liquidity crisis, commonly being dated to have started when several central banks had to step in with liquidity lending to the interbank lending market on 9 August 2007. This was a response to a situation where BNP Paribas temporarily had to block money withdrawals from three hedge funds--citing a 'complete evaporation of liquidity'.
Laffer curve	In economics, the Laffer curve is a representation of the relationship between possible rates of taxation and the resulting levels of government revenue. It illustrates the concept of taxable income elasticity--i.e., taxable income will change in response to changes in the rate of taxation. It postulates that no tax revenue will be raised at the extreme tax rates of 0% and 100% and that there must be at least one rate where tax revenue would be a non-zero maximum.

28. Basic Macroeconomic Relationships

Paradox of thrift	The paradox of thrift is a paradox of economics, popularized by John Maynard Keynes, though it had been stated as early as 1714 in The Fable of the Bees, and similar sentiments date to antiquity. The paradox states that if everyone tries to save more money during times of economic recession, then aggregate demand will fall and will in turn lower total savings in the population because of the decrease in consumption and economic growth. The paradox is, narrowly speaking, that total savings may fall even when individual savings attempt to rise, and, broadly speaking, that increase in savings may be harmful to an economy.
Recession	In economics, a recession is a business cycle contraction. It is a general slowdown in economic activity. Macroeconomic indicators such as GDP (gross domestic product), investment spending, capacity utilization, household income, business profits, and inflation fall, while bankruptcies and the unemployment rate rise.
Real interest rate	The real interest rate is the rate of interest an investor expects to receive after allowing for inflation. It can be described more formally by the Fisher equation, which states that the real interest rate is approximately the nominal interest rate minus the inflation rate. If, for example, an investor were able to lock in a 5% interest rate for the coming year and anticipated a 2% rise in prices, they would expect to earn a real interest rate of 3%.
Demand curve	In economics, the demand curve is the graph depicting the relationship between the price of a certain commodity and the amount of it that consumers are willing and able to purchase at that given price. It is a graphic representation of a demand schedule. The demand curve for all consumers together follows from the demand curve of every individual consumer: the individual demands at each price are added together.
Operating cost	Operating costs are the expenses which are related to the operation of a business, or to the operation of a device, component, piece of equipment or facility. They are the cost of resources used by an organization just to maintain its existence.
Capital	In economics, capital goods, real capital, or capital assets are already-produced durable goods or any non-financial asset that is used in production of goods or services. Capital goods are not significantly consumed in the production process though they may depreciate. How a capital good or is maintained or returned to its pre-production state varies with the type of capital involved.
Capital good	A capital good is a durable good that is used in the production of goods or services. Capital goods are one of the three types of producer goods, the other two being land and labor, which are also known collectively as primary factors of production. This classification originated during the classical economic period and has remained the dominant method for classification.

Corporate tax	Many countries impose corporate tax, also called corporation tax or company tax, on the income or capital of some types of legal entities. A similar tax may be imposed at state or lower levels. The taxes may also be referred to as income tax or capital tax.
Gross private domestic investment	Gross private domestic investment is the measure of investment used to compute GDP in economic measurement of nations. This is an important component of GDP because it provides an indicator of the future productive capacity of the economy. It includes replacement purchases plus net additions to capital assets plus investments in inventories.
Planned change	One of the foundational definitions in the field of organizational development is planned change: "Organization Development is an effort planned, organization-wide, and managed from the top, to increase organization effectiveness and health through planned interventions in the organization's 'processes,' using behavioral-science knowledge." -- Richard Beckhard, "Organization development: Strategies and Models", Reading, MA: Addison-Wesley, 1969, p. 9. To understand the practice of OD, some of the key terms, embedded in Beckhard's formulation, include:•Planned - carefully thought through; based on data; documented•Effectiveness - as measured by actual organizational performance versus desired organizational performance•Health - as measured by the organization's ability to respond, grow and adapt in its environmental context•Intervention - the specific action(s) selected for implementation that are intended to bring about the envisioned change•Processes - how work gets done in an organization; e.g. delivery of service, billing, repair, etc..
Economic freedom	Economic freedom or economic liberty or right to economic liberty denotes the ability of members of a society to undertake economic direction and actions. This is a term used in economic and policy debates as well as a politicoeconomic philosophy. As with freedom generally, there are various definitions, but no universally accepted concept of economic freedom.
Instability	In numerous fields of study, the component of instability within a system is generally characterized by some of the outputs or internal states growing without bounds. Not all systems that are not stable are unstable; systems can also be marginally stable or exhibit limit cycle behavior. In control theory, a system is unstable if any of the roots of its characteristic equation has real part greater than zero (or if zero is a repeated root).
Multiplier	In economics, a multiplier is a factor of proportionality that measures how much an endogenous variable changes in response to a change in some exogenous variable.

28. Basic Macroeconomic Relationships

For example, suppose variable x changes by 1 unit, which causes another variable y to change by M units. Then the multiplier is M.

CHAPTER QUIZ: KEY TERMS, PEOPLE, PLACES, CONCEPTS

1. _____ of demand is a measure used in economics to show the responsiveness, or elasticity, of the quantity demanded of a good or service to a change in its price. More precisely, it gives the percentage change in quantity demanded in response to a one percent change in price (ceteris paribus, i.e. holding constant all the other determinants of demand, such as income).

   _____(ies) are almost always negative, although analysts tend to ignore the sign even though this can lead to ambiguity.

   a. Fuel protests in the United Kingdom
   b. Battle of Annaberg
   c. Price elasticity
   d. Freikorps Oberland

2. In the United States, _____ are overnight borrowings between banks and other entities to maintain their bank reserves at the Federal Reserve. Banks keep reserves at Federal Reserve Banks to meet their reserve requirements and to clear financial transactions. Transactions in the _____ market enable depository institutions with reserve balances in excess of reserve requirements to lend reserves to institutions with reserve deficiencies.

   a. Base period
   b. Federal funds
   c. Blanket order
   d. Bond

3. . In economics, _____ is the measurement of how responsive an economic variable is to a change in another. For example:•'If I lower the price of my product, how much more will I sell?'•'If I raise the price of one good, how will that affect sales of this other good?'•'If we learn that a resource is becoming scarce, will people scramble to acquire it?'

   An elastic variable (or _____ value greater than 1) is one which responds more than proportionally to changes in other variables. In contrast, an inelastic variable (or _____ value less than 1) is one which changes less than proportionally in response to changes in other variables.

   a. Benefit principle
   b. Bliss point
   c. Elasticity

4. The _____ refers to the increase in saving (non-purchase of current goods and services) that results from an increase in income i.e. The _____ might be defined as the proportion of each additional dollar of household income that is used for saving. It is also used as an alternative term for the slope of the saving line. For example, if a household earns one extra dollar, and the _____ is 0.35, then of that dollar, the household will spend 65 cents and save 35 cents.

    a. Marginal propensity to save
    b. Budget constraint
    c. Cost curve
    d. Demand curve

5. The _____ was a global economic decline in the late 2000s. According to aggregated national data, a worldwide recession began in Q3-2008 and ended in Q1-2009.

    It is related to a liquidity crisis, commonly being dated to have started when several central banks had to step in with liquidity lending to the interbank lending market on 9 August 2007. This was a response to a situation where BNP Paribas temporarily had to block money withdrawals from three hedge funds--citing a 'complete evaporation of liquidity'.

    a. Commercial Revolution
    b. Mercantilism
    c. Great Recession
    d. 1 kroon coin

1. c
2. b
3. c
4. a
5. c

You can take the complete Chapter Practice Test

for 28. Basic Macroeconomic Relationships
on all key terms, persons, places, and concepts.

Online 99 Cents

http://www.JustTheFacts101.com

Use www.JustTheFacts101.com for all your study needs

including Facts101's online interactive problem solving labs in

chemistry, statistics, mathematics, and more.

29. The Aggregate Expenditures Model

CHAPTER OUTLINE: KEY TERMS, PEOPLE, PLACES, CONCEPTS

	Aggregate expenditure
	Great Depression
	Expression
	Leakage
	Net export
	Multiplier
	Income
	International trade
	National income
	Open economy
	Product
	Misery index
	International economics
	Devaluation
	Great Recession
	Recession
	Monopoly
	Natural monopoly
	Public sector
	Laffer curve
	Lump-sum tax

CHAPTER OUTLINE: KEY TERMS, PEOPLE, PLACES, CONCEPTS

Full employment

Barter

CHAPTER HIGHLIGHTS & NOTES: KEY TERMS, PEOPLE, PLACES, CONCEPTS

Aggregate expenditure	In economics, Aggregate Expenditure is a measure of national income. Aggregate Expenditure is defined as the current value of all the finished goods and services in the economy. The aggregate expenditure is thus the sum total of all the expenditures undertaken in the economy by the factors during a given time period.
Great Depression	The Great Depression was a severe worldwide economic depression in the decade preceding World War II. The timing of the Great Depression varied across nations, but in most countries it started in 1930 and lasted until the late 1930s or middle 1940s. It was the longest, deepest, and most widespread depression of the 20th century. In the 21st century, the Great Depression is commonly used as an example of how far the world's economy can decline.
Expression	In mathematics, an expression is a finite combination of symbols that is well-formed according to rules that depend on the context. Symbols can designate numbers (constants), variables, operations, functions, and other mathematical symbols, as well as punctuation, symbols of grouping, and other syntactic symbols. The use of expressions can range from the simple: $0 + 0$ to the complex: $f(a) + \sum_{k=1}^{n} \frac{1}{k!} \frac{d^k}{dt^k}\bigg|_{t=0} f(u(t)) + \int_0^1 \frac{(1-t)^n}{n!} \frac{d^{n+1}}{dt^{n+1}} f(u(t))\, dt.$ We can think of algebraic expressions as generalizations of common arithmetic operations that are formed by combining numbers, variables, and mathematical operations.
Leakage	In economics, a leakage is the non-consumption uses of income, including saving, taxes, and imports. In the Keynesian injection-leakage or circular flow model, leakages are combined with injections to identify equilibrium aggregate output. The model is best viewed as a circular flow between national income, output, consumption, and factor payments.

29. The Aggregate Expenditures Model

Net export	The commercial balance or net exports, is the difference between the monetary value of exports and imports of output in an economy over a certain period, measured in the currency of that economy. It is the relationship between a nation's imports and exports. A positive balance is known as a trade surplus if it consists of exporting more than is imported; a negative balance is referred to as a trade deficit or, informally, a trade gap.
Multiplier	In economics, a multiplier is a factor of proportionality that measures how much an endogenous variable changes in response to a change in some exogenous variable. For example, suppose variable x changes by 1 unit, which causes another variable y to change by M units. Then the multiplier is M.
Income	Income is the consumption and savings opportunity gained by an entity within a specified timeframe, which is generally expressed in monetary terms. However, for households and individuals, 'income is the sum of all the wages, salaries, profits, interests payments, rents and other forms of earnings received... in a given period of time.' In the field of public economics, the term may refer to the accumulation of both monetary and non-monetary consumption ability, with the former (monetary) being used as a proxy for total income.
International trade	International trade is the exchange of capital, goods, and services across international borders or territories. In most countries, such trade represents a significant share of gross domestic product (GDP). While international trade has been present throughout much of history, its economic, social, and political importance has been on the rise in recent centuries.
National income	A variety of measures of national income and output are used in economics to estimate total economic activity in a country or region, including gross domestic product, gross national product (GNP), net national income and adjusted national income. All are specially concerned with counting the total amount of goods and services produced within some 'boundary'. The boundary is usually defined by geography or citizenship, and may also restrict the goods and services that are counted.
Open economy	An open economy is an economy in which there are economic activities between domestic community and outside, e.g. people, including businesses, can trade in goods and services with other people and businesses in the international community, and flow of funds as investment across the border. Trade can be in the form of managerial exchange, technology transfers, all kinds of goods and services. Although, there are certain exceptions that cannot be exchanged, like, railway services of a country cannot be traded with another to avail this service, a country has to produce its own.
Product	In marketing, a product is anything that can be offered to a market that might satisfy a want or need. In retailing, products are called merchandise.

Misery index	The misery index is an economic indicator, created by economist Arthur Okun, and found by adding the unemployment rate to the inflation rate. It is assumed that both a higher rate of unemployment and a worsening of inflation create economic and social costs for a country.
International economics	International economics is concerned with the effects upon economic activity of international differences in productive resources and consumer preferences and the international institutions that affect them. It seeks to explain the patterns and consequences of transactions and interactions between the inhabitants of different countries, including trade, investment and migration. •International trade studies goods-and-services flows across international boundaries from supply-and-demand factors, economic integration, international factor movements, and policy variables such as tariff rates and trade quotas.•International finance studies the flow of capital across international financial markets, and the effects of these movements on exchange rates.•International monetary economics and macroeconomics studies money and macro flows across countries.•International political economy from international relations studies issues and impacts from for example international conflicts, international negotiations, and international sanctions; national security and economic nationalism; and international agreements and observance.
Devaluation	Devaluation in modern monetary policy is a reduction in the value of a currency with respect to those goods, services or other monetary units with which that currency can be exchanged. 'Devaluation' means official lowering of the value of a country's currency within a fixed exchange rate system, by which the monetary authority formally sets a new fixed rate with respect to a foreign reference currency. In contrast, depreciation is used to describe a decrease in a currency's value (relative to other major currency benchmarks) due to market forces, not government or central bank policy actions.
Great Recession	The Great Recession was a global economic decline in the late 2000s. According to aggregated national data, a worldwide recession began in Q3-2008 and ended in Q1-2009. It is related to a liquidity crisis, commonly being dated to have started when several central banks had to step in with liquidity lending to the interbank lending market on 9 August 2007. This was a response to a situation where BNP Paribas temporarily had to block money withdrawals from three hedge funds--citing a 'complete evaporation of liquidity'.
Recession	In economics, a recession is a business cycle contraction. It is a general slowdown in economic activity. Macroeconomic indicators such as GDP (gross domestic product), investment spending, capacity utilization, household income, business profits, and inflation fall, while bankruptcies and the unemployment rate rise.

29. The Aggregate Expenditures Model

Monopoly	A monopoly (from Greek monos μ???? + polein p??e?? (to sell)) exists when a specific person or enterprise is the only supplier of a particular commodity (this contrasts with a monopsony which relates to a single entity's control of a market to purchase a good or service, and with oligopoly which consists of a few entities dominating an industry). Monopolies are thus characterized by a lack of economic competition to produce the good or service and a lack of viable substitute goods. The verb 'monopolize' refers to the process by which a company gains the ability to raise prices or exclude competitors.
Natural monopoly	A monopoly is a firm which is the only one producing and selling a particular product. A natural monopoly is a monopoly in an industry in which it is most efficient (involving the lowest long-run average cost) for production to be concentrated in a single firm. This market situation gives the largest supplier in an industry, often the first supplier in a market, an overwhelming cost advantage over other actual and potential competitors, so a natural monopoly situation generally leads to an actual monopoly.
Public sector	The public sector refers to the part of the economy concerned with providing various government services. The composition of the public sector varies by country, but in most countries the public sector includes such services as the military, police, public transit and care of public roads, public education, along with healthcare and those working for the government itself, such as elected officials. The public sector might provide services that a non-payer cannot be excluded from (such as street lighting), services which benefit all of society rather than just the individual who uses the service.
Laffer curve	In economics, the Laffer curve is a representation of the relationship between possible rates of taxation and the resulting levels of government revenue. It illustrates the concept of taxable income elasticity--i.e., taxable income will change in response to changes in the rate of taxation. It postulates that no tax revenue will be raised at the extreme tax rates of 0% and 100% and that there must be at least one rate where tax revenue would be a non-zero maximum.
Lump-sum tax	A lump-sum tax is a tax that is a fixed amount, no matter the change in circumstance of the taxed entity. (A lump-sum subsidy or lump-sum redistribution is defined similarly). It is one of the various modes used for taxation: income, things owned (property taxes), money spent (sales taxes), miscellaneous (excise taxes).
Full employment	Full employment, in macroeconomics, is the level of employment rates where there is no cyclical or deficient-demand unemployment. It is defined by the majority of mainstream economists as being an acceptable level of unemployment somewhere above 0%. The discrepancy from 0% arises due to non-cyclical types of unemployment.
Barter	Barter is a system of exchange by which goods or services are directly exchanged for other goods or services without using a medium of exchange, such as money.

It is distinguishable from gift economies in that the reciprocal exchange is immediate and not delayed in time. It is usually bilateral, but may be multilateral (i.e., mediated through barter organizations) and usually exists parallel to monetary systems in most developed countries, though to a very limited extent.

CHAPTER QUIZ: KEY TERMS, PEOPLE, PLACES, CONCEPTS

1. _____ is concerned with the effects upon economic activity of international differences in productive resources and consumer preferences and the international institutions that affect them. It seeks to explain the patterns and consequences of transactions and interactions between the inhabitants of different countries, including trade, investment and migration. •International trade studies goods-and-services flows across international boundaries from supply-and-demand factors, economic integration, international factor movements, and policy variables such as tariff rates and trade quotas.•International finance studies the flow of capital across international financial markets, and the effects of these movements on exchange rates.•International monetary economics and macroeconomics studies money and macro flows across countries.•International political economy from international relations studies issues and impacts from for example international conflicts, international negotiations, and international sanctions; national security and economic nationalism; and international agreements and observance.

   a. Fuel protests in the United Kingdom
   b. International economics
   c. Freikorps Lichtschlag
   d. Freikorps Oberland

2. In marketing, a _____ is anything that can be offered to a market that might satisfy a want or need. In retailing, _____s are called merchandise. In manufacturing, _____s are bought as raw materials and sold as finished goods.

   a. Product
   b. Balanced scorecard
   c. Bestshoring
   d. Boutique manufacturing

3. . The _____ was a severe worldwide economic depression in the decade preceding World War II. The timing of the _____ varied across nations, but in most countries it started in 1930 and lasted until the late 1930s or middle 1940s. It was the longest, deepest, and most widespread depression of the 20th century.

   In the 21st century, the _____ is commonly used as an example of how far the world's economy can decline.

   a. Great Depression
   b. Charcuterie

c. Bacon

d. Brandenburger Gold Coast

4. In economics, _____ is a measure of national income. _____ is defined as the current value of all the finished goods and services in the economy. The _____ is thus the sum total of all the expenditures undertaken in the economy by the factors during a given time period.

a. Aggregate expenditure

b. Battle of Annaberg

c. Freikorps Lichtschlag

d. Freikorps Oberland

5. In mathematics, an _____ is a finite combination of symbols that is well-formed according to rules that depend on the context. Symbols can designate numbers (constants), variables, operations, functions, and other mathematical symbols, as well as punctuation, symbols of grouping, and other syntactic symbols. The use of _____s can range from the simple: $0 + 0$

to the complex:

$$f(a) + \sum_{k=1}^{n} \frac{1}{k!} \frac{d^k}{dt^k}\bigg|_{t=0} f(u(t)) + \int_0^1 \frac{(1-t)^n}{n!} \frac{d^{n+1}}{dt^{n+1}} f(u(t))\, dt.$$

We can think of algebraic _____s as generalizations of common arithmetic operations that are formed by combining numbers, variables, and mathematical operations.

a. 100 Best Workplaces in Europe

b. Career portfolio

c. CESG Claims Tested Mark

d. Expression

ANSWER KEY
29. The Aggregate Expenditures Model

1. b
2. a
3. a
4. a
5. d

You can take the complete Chapter Practice Test

for 29. The Aggregate Expenditures Model
on all key terms, persons, places, and concepts.

Online 99 Cents

http://www.JustTheFacts101.com

Use www.JustTheFacts101.com for all your study needs

including Facts101's online interactive problem solving labs in

chemistry, statistics, mathematics, and more.

30. Aggregate Demand and Aggregate Supply

CHAPTER OUTLINE: KEY TERMS, PEOPLE, PLACES, CONCEPTS

_____ | Aggregate demand

_____ | Aggregate supply

_____ | Demand curve

_____ | Income

_____ | National income

_____ | Product

_____ | Wealth effect

_____ | Consumer spending

_____ | Federal funds

_____ | Laffer curve

_____ | Net export

_____ | Personal income

_____ | Real interest rate

_____ | Corporate tax

_____ | Government spending

_____ | Gross private domestic investment

_____ | Interest rate

_____ | Monopoly

_____ | Natural monopoly

_____ | Phillips curve

_____ | Production

30. Aggregate Demand and Aggregate Supply
CHAPTER OUTLINE: KEY TERMS, PEOPLE, PLACES, CONCEPTS

_____ | Short run

_____ | Implicit cost

_____ | OPEC

_____ | Productivity

_____ | Cartel

_____ | Price level

_____ | Demand-pull inflation

_____ | Business cycle

_____ | Deflation

_____ | Disinflation

_____ | Menu cost

_____ | Cost-push inflation

_____ | Efficiency wage

_____ | Full employment

_____ | Minimum wage

_____ | Inflation

_____ | Great Moderation

_____ | Great Recession

_____ | New economy

_____ | Recession

_____ | Great Depression

30. Aggregate Demand and Aggregate Supply

CHAPTER OUTLINE: KEY TERMS, PEOPLE, PLACES, CONCEPTS

| Aggregate expenditure |

Aggregate demand	In macroeconomics, aggregate demand is the total demand for final goods and services in the economy at a given time and price level. It specifies the amounts of goods and services that will be purchased at all possible price levels. This is the demand for the gross domestic product of a country.
Aggregate supply	In economics, aggregate supply is the total supply of goods and services that firms in a national economy plan on selling during a specific time period. It is the total amount of goods and services that firms are willing to sell at a given price level in an economy.
Demand curve	In economics, the demand curve is the graph depicting the relationship between the price of a certain commodity and the amount of it that consumers are willing and able to purchase at that given price. It is a graphic representation of a demand schedule. The demand curve for all consumers together follows from the demand curve of every individual consumer: the individual demands at each price are added together.
Income	Income is the consumption and savings opportunity gained by an entity within a specified timeframe, which is generally expressed in monetary terms. However, for households and individuals, 'income is the sum of all the wages, salaries, profits, interests payments, rents and other forms of earnings received... in a given period of time.' In the field of public economics, the term may refer to the accumulation of both monetary and non-monetary consumption ability, with the former (monetary) being used as a proxy for total income.
National income	A variety of measures of national income and output are used in economics to estimate total economic activity in a country or region, including gross domestic product, gross national product (GNP), net national income and adjusted national income. All are specially concerned with counting the total amount of goods and services produced within some 'boundary'. The boundary is usually defined by geography or citizenship, and may also restrict the goods and services that are counted.
Product	In marketing, a product is anything that can be offered to a market that might satisfy a want or need. In retailing, products are called merchandise. In manufacturing, products are bought as raw materials and sold as finished goods.

30. Aggregate Demand and Aggregate Supply

Wealth effect	The wealth effect is an economic term, referring to an increase in spending that accompanies an increase (decrease) in perceived wealth.
Consumer spending	Consumer spending or consumer demand or consumption is also known as personal consumption expenditure. It is the largest part of aggregate demand or effective demand at the macroeconomic level. There are two variants of consumption in the aggregate demand model, including induced consumption and autonomous consumption.
Federal funds	In the United States, federal funds are overnight borrowings between banks and other entities to maintain their bank reserves at the Federal Reserve. Banks keep reserves at Federal Reserve Banks to meet their reserve requirements and to clear financial transactions. Transactions in the federal funds market enable depository institutions with reserve balances in excess of reserve requirements to lend reserves to institutions with reserve deficiencies.
Laffer curve	In economics, the Laffer curve is a representation of the relationship between possible rates of taxation and the resulting levels of government revenue. It illustrates the concept of taxable income elasticity--i.e., taxable income will change in response to changes in the rate of taxation. It postulates that no tax revenue will be raised at the extreme tax rates of 0% and 100% and that there must be at least one rate where tax revenue would be a non-zero maximum.
Net export	The commercial balance or net exports, is the difference between the monetary value of exports and imports of output in an economy over a certain period, measured in the currency of that economy. It is the relationship between a nation's imports and exports. A positive balance is known as a trade surplus if it consists of exporting more than is imported; a negative balance is referred to as a trade deficit or, informally, a trade gap.
Personal income	In economics, personal income refers to an individual's total earnings from wages, investment enterprises, and other ventures. It is the sum of all the incomes actually received by all the individuals or household during a given period. Personal income is that income which is actually received by the individuals or households in a country during the year from all sources.
Real interest rate	The real interest rate is the rate of interest an investor expects to receive after allowing for inflation. It can be described more formally by the Fisher equation, which states that the real interest rate is approximately the nominal interest rate minus the inflation rate. If, for example, an investor were able to lock in a 5% interest rate for the coming year and anticipated a 2% rise in prices, they would expect to earn a real interest rate of 3%.
Corporate tax	Many countries impose corporate tax, also called corporation tax or company tax, on the income or capital of some types of legal entities. A similar tax may be imposed at state or lower levels. The taxes may also be referred to as income tax or capital tax.

Government spending	In National Income Accounting, government spending, government expenditure, or government spending on goods and services includes all government consumption and investment but excludes transfer payments made by a state. Government acquisition of goods and services for current use to directly satisfy individual or collective needs of the members of the community is classed as government final consumption expenditure. Government acquisition of goods and services intended to create future benefits, such as infrastructure investment or research spending, is classed as government investment (government gross fixed capital formation).
Gross private domestic investment	Gross private domestic investment is the measure of investment used to compute GDP in economic measurement of nations. This is an important component of GDP because it provides an indicator of the future productive capacity of the economy. It includes replacement purchases plus net additions to capital assets plus investments in inventories.
Interest rate	An interest rate is the rate at which interest is paid by a borrower for the use of money that they borrow from a lender (creditor). Specifically, the interest rate is a percent of principal (P) paid a certain amount of times (m) per period (usually quoted per annum). For example, a small company borrows capital from a bank to buy new assets for its business, and in return the lender receives interest at a predetermined interest rate for deferring the use of funds and instead lending it to the borrower.
Monopoly	A monopoly (from Greek monos μ???? + polein p??e?? (to sell)) exists when a specific person or enterprise is the only supplier of a particular commodity (this contrasts with a monopsony which relates to a single entity's control of a market to purchase a good or service, and with oligopoly which consists of a few entities dominating an industry). Monopolies are thus characterized by a lack of economic competition to produce the good or service and a lack of viable substitute goods. The verb 'monopolize' refers to the process by which a company gains the ability to raise prices or exclude competitors.
Natural monopoly	A monopoly is a firm which is the only one producing and selling a particular product. A natural monopoly is a monopoly in an industry in which it is most efficient (involving the lowest long-run average cost) for production to be concentrated in a single firm. This market situation gives the largest supplier in an industry, often the first supplier in a market, an overwhelming cost advantage over other actual and potential competitors, so a natural monopoly situation generally leads to an actual monopoly.
Phillips curve	In economics, the Phillips curve is a historical inverse relationship between rates of unemployment and corresponding rates of inflation that result in an economy. Stated simply, decreased unemployment, (i.e., increased levels of employment) in an economy will correlate with higher rates of inflation.

30. Aggregate Demand and Aggregate Supply

CHAPTER HIGHLIGHTS & NOTES: KEY TERMS, PEOPLE, PLACES, CONCEPTS

Production	Production is a process of combining various material inputs and immaterial inputs in order to make something for consumption (the output). It is the act of creating output, a good or service which has value and contributes to the utility of individuals. Economic well-being is created in a production process, meaning all economic activities that aim directly or indirectly to satisfy human needs.
Short run	In microeconomics, the long run is the conceptual time period in which there are no fixed factors of production as to changing the output level by changing the capital stock or by entering or leaving an industry. The long run contrasts with the short run, in which some factors are variable and others are fixed, constraining entry or exit from an industry. In macroeconomics, the long run is the period when the general price level, contractual wage rates, and expectations adjust fully to the state of the economy, in contrast to the short run when these variables may not fully adjust.
Implicit cost	In economics, an implicit cost, also called an imputed cost, implied cost, or notional cost, is the opportunity cost equal to what a firm must give up in order to use factors which it neither purchases nor hires. It is the opposite of an explicit cost, which is borne directly. In other words, an implicit cost is any cost that results from using an asset instead of renting, selling, or lending it.
OPEC	OPEC is an international organization whose mission is to coordinate the policies of the oil-producing countries. The goal is to secure a steady income to the member states and to secure supply of oil to consumers. OPEC is an intergovernmental organization that was created at the Baghdad Conference on 10-14 September 1960, by Iraq, Kuwait, Iran, Saudi Arabia and Venezuela.
Productivity	Productivity is the ratio of output to inputs in production; it is an average measure of the efficiency of production. Efficiency of production means production's capability to create incomes which is measured by the formula real output value minus real input value. Increasing national productivity can raise living standards because more real income improves people's ability to purchase goods and services, enjoy leisure, improve housing and education and contribute to social and environmental programs.
Cartel	A cartel is a formal 'agreement' among competing firms. It is a formal organization of producers and manufacturers that agree to fix prices, marketing, and production. Cartels usually occur in an oligopolistic industry, where the number of sellers is small (usually because barriers to entry, most notably startup costs, are high) and the products being traded are usually commodities.
Price level	The general price level is a hypothetical measure of overall prices for some set of goods and services, in a given region during a given interval, normalized relative to some base set. Typically, a price level is approximated with a price index.

30. Aggregate Demand and Aggregate Supply

Demand-pull inflation	Demand-pull inflation is asserted to arise when aggregate demand in an economy outpaces aggregate supply. It involves inflation rising as real gross domestic product rises and unemployment falls, as the economy moves along the Phillips curve. This is commonly described as 'too much money chasing too few goods'.
Business cycle	The term business cycle refers fluctuations in aggregate production, trade and activity over several months or years in a market economy. The business cycle is the upward and downward movements of levels of gross domestic product (GDP) and refers to the period of expansions and contractions in the level of economic activities (business fluctuations) around its long-term growth trend. These fluctuations occur around a long-term growth trend, and typically involve shifts over time between periods of relatively rapid economic growth (an expansion or boom), and periods of relative stagnation or decline (a contraction or recession).
Deflation	In economics, deflation is a decrease in the general price level of goods and services. Deflation occurs when the inflation rate falls below 0% (a negative inflation rate). This should not be confused with disinflation, a slow-down in the inflation rate (i.e., when inflation declines to lower levels).
Disinflation	Disinflation is a decrease in the rate of inflation - a slowdown in the rate of increase of the general price level of goods and services in a nation's gross domestic product over time. It is the opposite of reflation. Disinflation occurs when the increase in the "consumer price level" slows down from the previous period when the prices were rising.
Menu cost	In economics, a menu cost is the cost to a firm resulting from changing its prices. The name stems from the cost of restaurants literally printing new menus, but economists use it to refer to the costs of changing nominal prices in general. In this broader definition, menu costs might include updating computer systems, re-tagging items, and hiring consultants to develop new pricing strategies as well as the literal costs of printing menus.
Cost-push inflation	Cost-push inflation is an alleged type of inflation caused by substantial increases in the cost of important goods or services where no suitable alternative is available. A situation that has been often cited of this was the oil crisis of the 1970s, which some economists see as a major cause of the inflation experienced in the Western world in that decade. It is argued that this inflation resulted from increases in the cost of petroleum imposed by the member states of OPEC. Since petroleum is so important to industrialised economies, a large increase in its price can lead to the increase in the price of most products, raising the inflation rate.
Efficiency wage	In labor economics, the efficiency wage hypothesis argues that wages, at least in some markets, form in a way that is not market-clearing.

30. Aggregate Demand and Aggregate Supply

	Specifically, it points to the incentive for managers to pay their employees more than the market-clearing wage in order to increase their productivity or efficiency, or reduce costs associated with turnover, in industries where the costs of replacing labor is high. This increased labor productivity and/or decreased costs pay for the higher wages.
Full employment	Full employment, in macroeconomics, is the level of employment rates where there is no cyclical or deficient-demand unemployment. It is defined by the majority of mainstream economists as being an acceptable level of unemployment somewhere above 0%. The discrepancy from 0% arises due to non-cyclical types of unemployment.
Minimum wage	A minimum wage is the lowest hourly, daily or monthly remuneration that employers may legally pay to workers. Equivalently, it is the lowest wage at which workers may sell their labor. Although minimum wage laws are in effect in many jurisdictions, differences of opinion exist about the benefits and drawbacks of a minimum wage.
Inflation	In economics, inflation is a sustained increase in the general price level of goods and services in an economy over a period of time. When the general price level rises, each unit of currency buys fewer goods and services. Consequently, inflation reflects a reduction in the purchasing power per unit of money - a loss of real value in the medium of exchange and unit of account within the economy.
Great Moderation	In economics, the Great Moderation refers to a reduction in the volatility of business cycle fluctuations starting in the mid-1980s, believed to have been caused by institutional and structural changes in developed nations in the later part of the twentieth century. Sometime during the mid-1980s major economic variables such as real gross domestic product growth, industrial production, monthly payroll employment and the unemployment rate began to decline in volatility.
Great Recession	The Great Recession was a global economic decline in the late 2000s. According to aggregated national data, a worldwide recession began in Q3-2008 and ended in Q1-2009. It is related to a liquidity crisis, commonly being dated to have started when several central banks had to step in with liquidity lending to the interbank lending market on 9 August 2007. This was a response to a situation where BNP Paribas temporarily had to block money withdrawals from three hedge funds--citing a 'complete evaporation of liquidity'.
New economy	The new economy is the result of the transition from a manufacturing-based economy to a service-based economy. This particular use of the term was popular during the dot-com bubble of the late 1990s. The high growth, low inflation and high employment of this period led to overly optimistic predictions and many flawed business plans.
Recession	In economics, a recession is a business cycle contraction. It is a general slowdown in economic activity.

30. Aggregate Demand and Aggregate Supply

Great Depression	The Great Depression was a severe worldwide economic depression in the decade preceding World War II. The timing of the Great Depression varied across nations, but in most countries it started in 1930 and lasted until the late 1930s or middle 1940s. It was the longest, deepest, and most widespread depression of the 20th century. In the 21st century, the Great Depression is commonly used as an example of how far the world's economy can decline.
Aggregate expenditure	In economics, Aggregate Expenditure is a measure of national income. Aggregate Expenditure is defined as the current value of all the finished goods and services in the economy. The aggregate expenditure is thus the sum total of all the expenditures undertaken in the economy by the factors during a given time period.

1. _____ is a decrease in the rate of inflation - a slowdown in the rate of increase of the general price level of goods and services in a nation's gross domestic product over time. It is the opposite of reflation. _____ occurs when the increase in the "consumer price level" slows down from the previous period when the prices were rising.

   a. Built-in inflation
   b. Core inflation
   c. Cost-push inflation
   d. Disinflation

2. _____ is the consumption and savings opportunity gained by an entity within a specified timeframe, which is generally expressed in monetary terms. However, for households and individuals, '_____ is the sum of all the wages, salaries, profits, interests payments, rents and other forms of earnings received... in a given period of time.'

   In the field of public economics, the term may refer to the accumulation of both monetary and non-monetary consumption ability, with the former (monetary) being used as a proxy for total _____.

   a. Fuel protests in the United Kingdom
   b. Battle of Annaberg
   c. Income
   d. Freikorps Oberland

3. . _____, in macroeconomics, is the level of employment rates where there is no cyclical or deficient-demand unemployment.

30. Aggregate Demand and Aggregate Supply

It is defined by the majority of mainstream economists as being an acceptable level of unemployment somewhere above 0%. The discrepancy from 0% arises due to non-cyclical types of unemployment.

a. Fuel protests in the United Kingdom
b. Battle of Annaberg
c. Freikorps Lichtschlag
d. Full employment

4. A _____ (from Greek monos μ???? + polein p??e?? (to sell)) exists when a specific person or enterprise is the only supplier of a particular commodity (this contrasts with a monopsony which relates to a single entity's control of a market to purchase a good or service, and with oligopoly which consists of a few entities dominating an industry). _____(ies) are thus characterized by a lack of economic competition to produce the good or service and a lack of viable substitute goods. The verb 'monopolize' refers to the process by which a company gains the ability to raise prices or exclude competitors.

a. Cellophane paradox
b. Competition
c. Monopoly
d. Disequilibrium

5. Many countries impose _____, also called corporation tax or company tax, on the income or capital of some types of legal entities. A similar tax may be imposed at state or lower levels. The taxes may also be referred to as income tax or capital tax.

a. Corporate tax
b. Balanced scorecard
c. Bestshoring
d. Boutique manufacturing

ANSWER KEY
30. Aggregate Demand and Aggregate Supply

1. d
2. c
3. d
4. c
5. a

You can take the complete Chapter Practice Test

for 30. Aggregate Demand and Aggregate Supply
on all key terms, persons, places, and concepts.

Online 99 Cents

http://www.JustTheFacts101.com

Use www.JustTheFacts101.com for all your study needs

including Facts101's online interactive problem solving labs in

chemistry, statistics, mathematics, and more.

31. Fiscal Policy, Deficits, and Debt

CHAPTER OUTLINE: KEY TERMS, PEOPLE, PLACES, CONCEPTS

	Fiscal policy
	Council of Economic Advisers
	Government spending
	Monopoly
	Natural monopoly
	Transfer payment
	Laffer curve
	Great Recession
	Recession
	Stock exchange
	Stock market
	Business cycle
	Consumption smoothing
	Loan guarantee
	State bank
	Corruption
	Great Depression
	Federal Reserve System
	Gross domestic product
	Product
	OPEC

31. Fiscal Policy, Deficits, and Debt

	Health care
	Production
	Incentive
	Income
	Crowding out
	Expression
	Pricing
	Baby Boomers
	Social security

CHAPTER HIGHLIGHTS & NOTES: KEY TERMS, PEOPLE, PLACES, CONCEPTS

Fiscal policy	In economics and political science, fiscal policy is the use of government revenue collection and expenditure (spending) to influence the economy, or else it involves the government changing the levels of taxation and government spending in order to influence Aggregate Demand and the level of economic activity. The two main instruments of fiscal policy are changes in the level and composition of taxation and government spending in various sectors. These changes can affect the following macroeconomic variables in an economy:•Aggregate demand and the level of economic activity;•The distribution of income;•The pattern of resource allocation within the government sector and relative to the private sector. Fiscal policy refers to the use of the government budget to influence economic activity.
Council of Economic Advisers	The Council of Economic Advisers is a group of economists and captains of industry who advise the Scottish Government. It was established in 2007, meeting for the first time on 21 September. Minutes of its quarterly meetings will be published a fortnight after each meeting.

31. Fiscal Policy, Deficits, and Debt

Government spending	In National Income Accounting, government spending, government expenditure, or government spending on goods and services includes all government consumption and investment but excludes transfer payments made by a state. Government acquisition of goods and services for current use to directly satisfy individual or collective needs of the members of the community is classed as government final consumption expenditure. Government acquisition of goods and services intended to create future benefits, such as infrastructure investment or research spending, is classed as government investment (government gross fixed capital formation).
Monopoly	A monopoly (from Greek monos μ???? + polein p??e?? (to sell)) exists when a specific person or enterprise is the only supplier of a particular commodity (this contrasts with a monopsony which relates to a single entity's control of a market to purchase a good or service, and with oligopoly which consists of a few entities dominating an industry). Monopolies are thus characterized by a lack of economic competition to produce the good or service and a lack of viable substitute goods. The verb 'monopolize' refers to the process by which a company gains the ability to raise prices or exclude competitors.
Natural monopoly	A monopoly is a firm which is the only one producing and selling a particular product. A natural monopoly is a monopoly in an industry in which it is most efficient (involving the lowest long-run average cost) for production to be concentrated in a single firm. This market situation gives the largest supplier in an industry, often the first supplier in a market, an overwhelming cost advantage over other actual and potential competitors, so a natural monopoly situation generally leads to an actual monopoly.
Transfer payment	In economics, a transfer payment is a redistribution of income in the market system. These payments are considered to be non-exhaustive because they do not directly absorb resources or create output. In other words, the transfer is made without any exchange of goods or services.
Laffer curve	In economics, the Laffer curve is a representation of the relationship between possible rates of taxation and the resulting levels of government revenue. It illustrates the concept of taxable income elasticity--i.e., taxable income will change in response to changes in the rate of taxation. It postulates that no tax revenue will be raised at the extreme tax rates of 0% and 100% and that there must be at least one rate where tax revenue would be a non-zero maximum.
Great Recession	The Great Recession was a global economic decline in the late 2000s. According to aggregated national data, a worldwide recession began in Q3-2008 and ended in Q1-2009. It is related to a liquidity crisis, commonly being dated to have started when several central banks had to step in with liquidity lending to the interbank lending market on 9 August 2007. This was a response to a situation where BNP Paribas temporarily had to block money withdrawals from three hedge funds--citing a 'complete evaporation of liquidity'.
Recession	In economics, a recession is a business cycle contraction.

31. Fiscal Policy, Deficits, and Debt

	It is a general slowdown in economic activity. Macroeconomic indicators such as GDP (gross domestic product), investment spending, capacity utilization, household income, business profits, and inflation fall, while bankruptcies and the unemployment rate rise.
Stock exchange	A stock exchange is a form of exchange which provides services for stock brokers and traders to trade stocks, bonds, and other securities. Stock exchanges also provide facilities for issue and redemption of securities and other financial instruments, and capital events including the payment of income and dividends. Securities traded on a stock exchange include stock issued by companies, unit trusts, derivatives, pooled investment products and bonds.
Stock market	A stock market or equity market is the aggregation of buyers and sellers of stocks (shares); these are securities listed on a stock exchange as well as those only traded privately.
Business cycle	The term business cycle refers fluctuations in aggregate production, trade and activity over several months or years in a market economy. The business cycle is the upward and downward movements of levels of gross domestic product (GDP) and refers to the period of expansions and contractions in the level of economic activities (business fluctuations) around its long-term growth trend. These fluctuations occur around a long-term growth trend, and typically involve shifts over time between periods of relatively rapid economic growth (an expansion or boom), and periods of relative stagnation or decline (a contraction or recession).
Consumption smoothing	Consumption smoothing is the economic concept used to express the desire of people to have a stable path of consumption. Since Milton Friedman's permanent income theory (1956) and Modigliani and Brumberg (1954) life-cycle model, the idea that agents prefer a stable path of consumption has been widely accepted. This idea came to replace the perception that people had a marginal propensity to consume and therefore current consumption was tied to current income.
Loan guarantee	A loan guarantee, in finance, is a promise by one party to assume the debt obligation of a borrower if that borrower defaults. A guarantee can be limited or unlimited, making the guarantor liable for only a portion or all of the debt. Guarantor mortgages are popular with young borrowers who do not have a large deposit saved and need to borrow 100% of the property value to purchase a property.
State bank	A state bank is generally a financial institution that is chartered by a state. It differs from a reserve bank in that it does not necessarily control monetary policy (indeed, the state in question may have no legal capacity to create monetary policy), but instead usually offers only retail and commercial services.

Corruption	In philosophical, theological, or moral discussions, corruption is spiritual or moral impurity or deviation from an ideal. Corruption may include many activities including bribery and embezzlement. Government, or 'political', corruption occurs when an office-holder or other governmental employee acts in an official capacity for personal gain.
Great Depression	The Great Depression was a severe worldwide economic depression in the decade preceding World War II. The timing of the Great Depression varied across nations, but in most countries it started in 1930 and lasted until the late 1930s or middle 1940s. It was the longest, deepest, and most widespread depression of the 20th century.
	In the 21st century, the Great Depression is commonly used as an example of how far the world's economy can decline.
Federal Reserve System	The Federal Reserve System is the central banking system of the United States. It was created on December 23, 1913, with the enactment of the Federal Reserve Act, largely in response to a series of financial panics, particularly a severe panic in 1907. Over time, the roles and responsibilities of the Federal Reserve System have expanded, and its structure has evolved. Events such as the Great Depression were major factors leading to changes in the system.
Gross domestic product	Gross domestic product is the market value of all officially recognized final goods and services produced within a country in a year, or other given period of time. Gross domestic product per capita is often considered an indicator of a country's standard of living.
	Gross domestic product per capita is not a measure of personal income .
Product	In marketing, a product is anything that can be offered to a market that might satisfy a want or need. In retailing, products are called merchandise. In manufacturing, products are bought as raw materials and sold as finished goods.
OPEC	OPEC is an international organization whose mission is to coordinate the policies of the oil-producing countries. The goal is to secure a steady income to the member states and to secure supply of oil to consumers.
	OPEC is an intergovernmental organization that was created at the Baghdad Conference on 10-14 September 1960, by Iraq, Kuwait, Iran, Saudi Arabia and Venezuela.
Health care	Health care is the diagnosis, treatment, and prevention of disease, illness, injury, and other physical and mental impairments in human beings. Health care is delivered by practitioners in allied health, dentistry, midwifery-obstetrics, medicine, nursing, optometry, pharmacy, psychology and other care providers. It refers to the work done in providing primary care, secondary care, and tertiary care, as well as in public health.

31. Fiscal Policy, Deficits, and Debt

Production	Production is a process of combining various material inputs and immaterial inputs in order to make something for consumption (the output). It is the act of creating output, a good or service which has value and contributes to the utility of individuals. Economic well-being is created in a production process, meaning all economic activities that aim directly or indirectly to satisfy human needs.
Incentive	An incentive is something that motivates an individual to perform an action. The study of incentive structures is central to the study of all economic activities (both in terms of individual decision-making and in terms of co-operation and competition within a larger institutional structure). Economic analysis, then, of the differences between societies (and between different organizations within a society) largely amounts to characterizing the differences in incentive structures faced by individuals involved in these collective efforts.
Income	Income is the consumption and savings opportunity gained by an entity within a specified timeframe, which is generally expressed in monetary terms. However, for households and individuals, 'income is the sum of all the wages, salaries, profits, interests payments, rents and other forms of earnings received... in a given period of time.' In the field of public economics, the term may refer to the accumulation of both monetary and non-monetary consumption ability, with the former (monetary) being used as a proxy for total income.
Crowding out	In economics, crowding out is argued by some economists to occur when increased government borrowing, a kind of expansionary fiscal policy, reduces investment spending. The increased borrowing 'crowds out' private investing. Originally, crowding out was related to an increase in interest rates from the borrowing, but that was broadened to multiple channels that might leave total output little changed or smaller.
Expression	In mathematics, an expression is a finite combination of symbols that is well-formed according to rules that depend on the context. Symbols can designate numbers (constants), variables, operations, functions, and other mathematical symbols, as well as punctuation, symbols of grouping, and other syntactic symbols. The use of expressions can range from the simple: $0 + 0$ to the complex: $$f(a) + \sum_{k=1}^{n} \frac{1}{k!}\frac{d^k}{dt^k}\bigg|_{t=0} f(u(t)) + \int_0^1 \frac{(1-t)^n}{n!}\frac{d^{n+1}}{dt^{n+1}} f(u(t))\, dt.$$ We can think of algebraic expressions as generalizations of common arithmetic operations that are formed by combining numbers, variables, and mathematical operations.
Pricing	Pricing is the process of determining what a company will receive in exchange for its product. Pricing factors are manufacturing cost, market place, competition, market condition, brand, and quality of product.

31. Fiscal Policy, Deficits, and Debt

CHAPTER HIGHLIGHTS & NOTES: KEY TERMS, PEOPLE, PLACES, CONCEPTS

Baby Boomers	Baby boomers are people born during the demographic Post-World War II baby boom between the years 1946 and 1964. According to the U.S. Census Bureau, the term 'baby boomer' is also used in a cultural context. Therefore, it is impossible to achieve broad consensus of a precise date definition, even within a given territory. Different groups, organizations, individuals, and scholars may have widely varying opinions on what constitutes a baby boomer, both technically and culturally.
Social security	Social security is a concept enshrined in Article 22 of the Universal Declaration of Human Rights which states, Everyone, as a member of society, has the right to social security and is entitled to realization, through national effort and international co-operation and in accordance with the organization and resources of each State, of the economic, social and cultural rights indispensable for his dignity and the free development of his personality. In simple terms, the signatories agree that society in which a person lives should help them to develop and to make the most of all the advantages (culture, work, social welfare) which are offered to them in the country. Social security may also refer to the action programs of government intended to promote the welfare of the population through assistance measures guaranteeing access to sufficient resources for food and shelter and to promote health and well-being for the population at large and potentially vulnerable segments such as children, the elderly, the sick and the unemployed.

CHAPTER QUIZ: KEY TERMS, PEOPLE, PLACES, CONCEPTS

1. The _____ is a group of economists and captains of industry who advise the Scottish Government. It was established in 2007, meeting for the first time on 21 September.

   Minutes of its quarterly meetings will be published a fortnight after each meeting.

   a. Capital account convertibility
   b. Centre of Full Employment and Equity
   c. Competitiveness Policy Council
   d. Council of Economic Advisers

2. . A _____, in finance, is a promise by one party to assume the debt obligation of a borrower if that borrower defaults. A guarantee can be limited or unlimited, making the guarantor liable for only a portion or all of the debt.

   Guarantor mortgages are popular with young borrowers who do not have a large deposit saved and need to borrow 100% of the property value to purchase a property.

   a. Black budget

b. Loan guarantee

c. Confidence and supply

d. Federal budget

3. A _____ (from Greek monos μ???? + polein p??e?? (to sell)) exists when a specific person or enterprise is the only supplier of a particular commodity (this contrasts with a monopsony which relates to a single entity's control of a market to purchase a good or service, and with oligopoly which consists of a few entities dominating an industry). _____(ies) are thus characterized by a lack of economic competition to produce the good or service and a lack of viable substitute goods. The verb 'monopolize' refers to the process by which a company gains the ability to raise prices or exclude competitors.

a. Monopoly

b. Competition

c. Deregulation

d. Disequilibrium

4. _____ is the consumption and savings opportunity gained by an entity within a specified timeframe, which is generally expressed in monetary terms. However, for households and individuals, '_____ is the sum of all the wages, salaries, profits, interests payments, rents and other forms of earnings received... in a given period of time.'

In the field of public economics, the term may refer to the accumulation of both monetary and non-monetary consumption ability, with the former (monetary) being used as a proxy for total _____.

a. Income

b. Battle of Annaberg

c. Freikorps Lichtschlag

d. Freikorps Oberland

5. In economics and political science, _____ is the use of government revenue collection and expenditure (spending) to influence the economy, or else it involves the government changing the levels of taxation and government spending in order to influence Aggregate Demand and the level of economic activity. The two main instruments of _____ are changes in the level and composition of taxation and government spending in various sectors. These changes can affect the following macroeconomic variables in an economy:•Aggregate demand and the level of economic activity;•The distribution of income;•The pattern of resource allocation within the government sector and relative to the private sector.

_____ refers to the use of the government budget to influence economic activity.

a. Barnett formula

b. Budget freeze

c. Budgetary policy

d. Fiscal policy

1. d
2. b
3. a
4. a
5. d

32. Money, Banking, and Financial Institutions

CHAPTER OUTLINE: KEY TERMS, PEOPLE, PLACES, CONCEPTS

_____ Cartel

_____ Medium of exchange

_____ Store of value

_____ Unit of account

_____ Money market

_____ Money supply

_____ Commercial bank

_____ Engraving

_____ Federal Reserve Note

_____ Intrinsic value

_____ Savings account

_____ Time deposit

_____ Legal tender

_____ Money as Debt

_____ Laffer curve

_____ National Credit Union Administration

_____ Deposit insurance

_____ Inflation

_____ Purchasing power

_____ Transfer payment

_____ Federal Reserve Act

_____ Federal Reserve System _____

_____ Monetary policy _____

_____ Bank of England _____

_____ Bank of Japan _____

_____ Central bank _____

_____ Federal Reserve Bank _____

_____ Economic freedom _____

_____ Federal Open Market Committee _____

_____ Great Recession _____

_____ Lender of last resort _____

_____ Recession _____

_____ Royal Bank _____

_____ State bank _____

_____ Bank reserves _____

_____ Fiscal agent _____

_____ Reserve requirement _____

_____ Term auction facility _____

_____ Great Depression _____

_____ Financial crisis _____

_____ Interest rate _____

_____ Subprime mortgage crisis _____

CHAPTER OUTLINE: KEY TERMS, PEOPLE, PLACES, CONCEPTS

	Securitization
	Shadow banking system
	Golden West
	Lehman Brothers
	Moral hazard
	Troubled Asset Relief Program
	Commercial paper
	Commercial Paper Funding Facility
	Primary dealer
	Primary Dealer Credit Facility
	Securities lending
	HSBC
	Money laundering
	Pension
	Pension fund
	ROWE

32. Money, Banking, and Financial Institutions

Cartel	A cartel is a formal 'agreement' among competing firms. It is a formal organization of producers and manufacturers that agree to fix prices, marketing, and production. Cartels usually occur in an oligopolistic industry, where the number of sellers is small (usually because barriers to entry, most notably startup costs, are high) and the products being traded are usually commodities.
Medium of exchange	A medium of exchange is an intermediary used in trade to avoid the inconveniences of a pure barter system. By contrast, as William Stanley Jevons argued, in a barter system there must be a coincidence of wants before two people can trade - one must want exactly what the other has to offer, when and where it is offered, so that the exchange can occur. A medium of exchange permits the value of goods to be assessed and rendered in terms of the intermediary, most often, a form of money widely accepted to buy any other good.
Store of value	A store of value is the function of an asset that can be saved, retrieved and exchanged at a later time, and be predictably useful when retrieved. The most common store of value in modern times has been money, currency, or a commodity like gold, or financial capital. The point of any store of value is intrinsic risk management due to an inherent stable demand for the underlying asset.
Unit of account	A unit of account is a standard monetary unit of measurement of value/cost of goods, services, or assets. It is one of three well-known functions of money. It lends meaning to profits, losses, liability, or assets.
Money market	As money became a commodity, the money market became a component of the financial markets for assets involved in short-term borrowing, lending, buying and selling with original maturities of one year or less. Trading in the money markets is done over the counter and is wholesale. Various instruments exist, such as Treasury bills, commercial paper, bankers' acceptances, deposits, certificates of deposit, bills of exchange, repurchase agreements, federal funds, and short-lived mortgage-, and asset-backed securities.
Money supply	In economics, the money supply or money stock, is the total amount of monetary assets available in an economy at a specific time. There are several ways to define 'money,' but standard measures usually include currency in circulation and demand deposits (depositors' easily accessed assets on the books of financial institutions). It is easy to confuse the amount of spending money in the economy with the amount of money in the economy.
Commercial bank	A commercial bank is a type of bank that provides services such as accepting deposits, making business loans, and offering basic investment products. Commercial bank can also refer to a bank or a division of a bank that mostly deals with deposits and loans from corporations or large businesses, as opposed to individual members of the public .

Engraving	Engraving is the practice of incising a design onto a hard, usually flat surface, by cutting grooves into it. The result may be a decorated object in itself, as when silver, gold, steel, or glass are engraved, or may provide an intaglio printing plate, of copper or another metal, for printing images on paper as prints or illustrations; these images are also called engravings. Engraving was a historically important method of producing images on paper in artistic printmaking, in mapmaking, and also for commercial reproductions and illustrations for books and magazines.
Federal Reserve Note	A Federal Reserve Note, also a United States banknote or U.S. banknote, is a type of banknote used in the United States of America. Denominated in United States dollars, Federal Reserve Notes are printed by the United States Bureau of Engraving and Printing on paper made by Crane & Co. of Dalton, Massachusetts. Federal Reserve Notes are the only type of U.S. banknote currently produced. Federal Reserve Notes are authorized by Section 16 of the Federal Reserve Act of 1913 (codified at 12 U.S.C. § 411) and are issued to the Federal Reserve Banks at the discretion of the Board of Governors of the Federal Reserve System.
Intrinsic value	In finance, intrinsic value refers to the value of a company, stock, currency or product determined through fundamental analysis without reference to its market value. It is also frequently called fundamental value. It is ordinarily calculated by summing the discounted future income generated by the asset to obtain the present value.
Savings account	Saving accounts are accounts maintained by retail financial institutions that pay interest but cannot be used directly as money in the narrow sense of a medium of exchange . These accounts let customers set aside a portion of their liquid assets while earning a monetary return. For the bank, money in a savings account may not be callable immediately and in some jurisdictions, does not incur a reserve requirement, freeing up cash from the bank's vault to be lent out with interest.
Time deposit	A time deposit is a money deposit at a banking institution that cannot be withdrawn for a certain 'term' or period of time (unless a penalty is paid). When the term is over it can be withdrawn or it can be held for another term. Generally speaking, the longer the term the better the yield on the money.
Legal tender	Legal tender is a medium of payment allowed by law or recognized by a legal system to be valid for meeting a financial obligation. Paper currency and coins are common forms of legal tender in many countries. The origin of the term 'legal tender' is from Middle English tendren, French tendre (verb form), meaning to offer.
Money as Debt	Money as Debt is a 2006 animated documentary film by Canadian artist and filmmaker Paul Grignon about the monetary systems practised through modern banking.

32. Money, Banking, and Financial Institutions

	The film presents Grignon's view of the process of money creation by banks and its historical background, and warns of his belief in its subsequent unsustainability. Subsequent Money as Debt videos include Money as Debt II (2009) and Money as Debt III: Evolution Beyond Money (2011).
Laffer curve	In economics, the Laffer curve is a representation of the relationship between possible rates of taxation and the resulting levels of government revenue. It illustrates the concept of taxable income elasticity--i.e., taxable income will change in response to changes in the rate of taxation. It postulates that no tax revenue will be raised at the extreme tax rates of 0% and 100% and that there must be at least one rate where tax revenue would be a non-zero maximum.
National Credit Union Administration	The National Credit Union Administration is the independent federal agency created by the U.S. Congress to regulate, charter, and supervise federal credit unions. With the backing of the full faith and credit of the U.S. Government, National Credit Union Administration operates and manages the National Credit Union Share Insurance Fund, insuring the deposits of more than 96 million account holders in all federal credit unions and the overwhelming majority of state-chartered credit unions. As of September 2013, there were 6,620 federally insured credit unions, total assets of more than $1 trillion, and net loans of $631.5 billion.
Deposit insurance	Explicit deposit insurance is a measure implemented in many countries to protect bank depositors, in full or in part, from losses caused by a bank's inability to pay its debts when due. Deposit insurance systems are one component of a financial system safety net that promotes financial stability.
Inflation	In economics, inflation is a sustained increase in the general price level of goods and services in an economy over a period of time. When the general price level rises, each unit of currency buys fewer goods and services. Consequently, inflation reflects a reduction in the purchasing power per unit of money - a loss of real value in the medium of exchange and unit of account within the economy.
Purchasing power	Purchasing power is the number of goods or services that can be purchased with a unit of currency. For example, if one had taken one unit of currency to a store in the 1950s, it is probable that it would have been possible to buy a greater number of items than would today, indicating that one would have had a greater purchasing power in the 1950s. Currency can be either a commodity money, like gold or silver, or fiat currency, or free-floating market-valued currency like US dollars.
Transfer payment	In economics, a transfer payment is a redistribution of income in the market system. These payments are considered to be non-exhaustive because they do not directly absorb resources or create output. In other words, the transfer is made without any exchange of goods or services.
Federal Reserve Act	The Federal Reserve Act is an Act of Congress that created and set up the Federal Reserve System, the central banking system of the United States of America, and granted it the legal authority to issue Federal Reserve Notes, now commonly known as the U.S.

Dollar, and Federal Reserve Bank Notes as legal tender. The Act was signed into law by President Woodrow Wilson.

Federal Reserve System	The Federal Reserve System is the central banking system of the United States. It was created on December 23, 1913, with the enactment of the Federal Reserve Act, largely in response to a series of financial panics, particularly a severe panic in 1907. Over time, the roles and responsibilities of the Federal Reserve System have expanded, and its structure has evolved. Events such as the Great Depression were major factors leading to changes in the system.
Monetary policy	Monetary policy is the process by which the monetary authority of a country controls the supply of money, often targeting a rate of interest for the purpose of promoting economic growth and stability. The official goals usually include relatively stable prices and low unemployment. Monetary economics provides insight into how to craft optimal monetary policy.
Bank of England	The Bank of England, formally the Governor and Company of the Bank of England, is the central bank of the United Kingdom and the model on which most modern central banks have been based. Established in 1694, it is the second oldest central bank in the world, after the Sveriges Riksbank, and the world's 8th oldest bank. It was established to act as the English Government's banker, and is still the banker for the Government of the United Kingdom.
Bank of Japan	The Bank of Japan is the central bank of Japan. The Bank is often called Nichigin for short. It has its headquarters in Chuo, Tokyo.
Central bank	A central bank, reserve bank, or monetary authority is an institution that manages a state's currency, money supply, and interest rates. Central banks also usually oversee the commercial banking system of their respective countries. In contrast to a commercial bank, a central bank possesses a monopoly on increasing the amount of money in the nation, and usually also prints the national currency, which usually serves as the nation's legal tender.
Federal Reserve Bank	A Federal Reserve Bank is a regional bank of the Federal Reserve System, the central banking system of the United States. There are twelve in total, one for each of the twelve Federal Reserve Districts that were created by the Federal Reserve Act of 1913. The banks are jointly responsible for implementing the monetary policy set forth by the Federal Open Market Committee, and are divided as follows: Some banks also possess branches, with the whole system being headquartered at the Eccles Building in Washington, D.C.
Economic freedom	Economic freedom or economic liberty or right to economic liberty denotes the ability of members of a society to undertake economic direction and actions. This is a term used in economic and policy debates as well as a politicoeconomic philosophy. As with freedom generally, there are various definitions, but no universally accepted concept of economic freedom.

32. Money, Banking, and Financial Institutions

Federal Open Market Committee	The Federal Open Market Committee, a committee within the Federal Reserve System (the Fed), is charged under United States law with overseeing the nation's open market operations (i.e., the Fed's buying and selling of United States Treasury securities). It is this Federal Reserve committee which makes key decisions about interest rates and the growth of the United States money supply. It is the principal organ of United States national monetary policy.
Great Recession	The Great Recession was a global economic decline in the late 2000s. According to aggregated national data, a worldwide recession began in Q3-2008 and ended in Q1-2009. It is related to a liquidity crisis, commonly being dated to have started when several central banks had to step in with liquidity lending to the interbank lending market on 9 August 2007. This was a response to a situation where BNP Paribas temporarily had to block money withdrawals from three hedge funds--citing a 'complete evaporation of liquidity'.
Lender of last resort	The term lender of last resort originates from the French expression dernier ressort. While the concept itself had been used previously, the term, 'lender of last resort', was supposedly first used in its current context by Sir Francis Baring in his Observations on the Establishment of the Bank of England which was published in 1797. In 1763 the king was the lender of last resort in Prussia. Different definitions of the lender of last resort exist in the literature.
Recession	In economics, a recession is a business cycle contraction. It is a general slowdown in economic activity. Macroeconomic indicators such as GDP (gross domestic product), investment spending, capacity utilization, household income, business profits, and inflation fall, while bankruptcies and the unemployment rate rise.
Royal Bank	Royal Bank was a private commercial bank established as ÖZ BANK on 2 August 1993. The bank provided financial services for individual customers, small- and mid-size businesses. The last supervisory board took the control over the bank in 2004 and initiated a program on restructuring the financial and control systems. Royal Bank was included into the Baku Stock Exchange in 2006. It had 32 regional branches including the branches in Baku.
State bank	A state bank is generally a financial institution that is chartered by a state. It differs from a reserve bank in that it does not necessarily control monetary policy (indeed, the state in question may have no legal capacity to create monetary policy), but instead usually offers only retail and commercial services. A state bank that has been in operation for five years or less is called a de novo bank.

32. Money, Banking, and Financial Institutions

CHAPTER HIGHLIGHTS & NOTES: KEY TERMS, PEOPLE, PLACES, CONCEPTS

Bank reserves	Bank reserves or central bank reserves are banks' holdings of deposits in accounts with their central bank, plus currency that is physically held in the bank's vault (vault cash). The central banks of some nations set minimum reserve requirements, which require banks to hold deposits at the central bank equivalent to a specified percentage of their liabilities (such as customer deposits). Even when no reserve requirements are set, banks commonly wish to hold some reserves, called desired reserves, against unexpected events such as unusually large net withdrawals by customers or even bank runs.
Fiscal agent	A fiscal agent, fiscal sponsor, or financial agent is a proxy that manages fiscal matters on behalf of another party. A fiscal agent may assist in the redemption of bonds or coupons at maturity, disbursing dividends, and handling tax issues. For example, the United States Federal Reserve is the fiscal agent of the federal government of the United States.
Reserve requirement	The reserve requirement is a central bank regulation employed by most, but not all, of the world's central banks, that sets the minimum fraction of customer deposits and notes that each commercial bank must hold as reserves (rather than lend out). These required reserves are normally in the form of cash stored physically in a bank vault (vault cash) or deposits made with a central bank.
	The required reserve ratio is sometimes used as a tool in monetary policy, influencing the country's borrowing and interest rates by changing the amount of funds available for banks to make loans with.
Term auction facility	The Term Auction Facility is a temporary program managed by the United States Federal Reserve designed to 'address elevated pressures in short-term funding markets.' Under the program the Fed auctions collateralized loans with terms of 28 and 84 days to depository institutions that are 'in generally sound financial condition' and 'are expected to remain so over the terms of Term auction facility loans.' Eligible collateral is the same as that accepted for discount window loans and includes a wide range of financial assets. The program was instituted in December 2007 in response to problems associated with the subprime mortgage crisis and was motivated by a desire to address a widening spread between interest rates on overnight and term (longer than overnight) interbank lending, indicating a retreat from risk-taking by banks. The action was in coordination with simultaneous and similar initiatives undertaken by the Bank of Canada, the Bank of England, the European Central Bank and the Swiss National Bank.
Great Depression	The Great Depression was a severe worldwide economic depression in the decade preceding World War II. The timing of the Great Depression varied across nations, but in most countries it started in 1930 and lasted until the late 1930s or middle 1940s. It was the longest, deepest, and most widespread depression of the 20th century.
	In the 21st century, the Great Depression is commonly used as an example of how far the world's economy can decline.

32. Money, Banking, and Financial Institutions

Financial crisis	The term financial crisis is applied broadly to a variety of situations in which some financial assets suddenly lose a large part of their nominal value. In the 19th and early 20th centuries, many financial crises were associated with banking panics, and many recessions coincided with these panics. Other situations that are often called financial crises include stock market crashes and the bursting of other financial bubbles, currency crises, and sovereign defaults.
Interest rate	An interest rate is the rate at which interest is paid by a borrower for the use of money that they borrow from a lender (creditor). Specifically, the interest rate is a percent of principal (P) paid a certain amount of times (m) per period (usually quoted per annum). For example, a small company borrows capital from a bank to buy new assets for its business, and in return the lender receives interest at a predetermined interest rate for deferring the use of funds and instead lending it to the borrower.
Subprime mortgage crisis	The U.S. subprime mortgage crisis was a set of events and conditions that were significant aspects of a financial crisis and subsequent recession that became manifestly visible in 2008. It was characterized by a rise in subprime mortgage delinquencies and foreclosures, and the resulting decline of securities backed by said mortgages. These mortgage-backed securities (MBS) and collateralized debt obligations (CDO) initially offered attractive rates of return due to the higher interest rates on the mortgages; however, the lower credit quality ultimately caused massive defaults. While elements of the crisis first became more visible during 2007, several major financial institutions collapsed in September 2008, with significant disruption in the flow of credit to businesses and consumers and the onset of a severe global recession.
Securitization	Securitization is the financial practice of pooling various types of contractual debt such as residential mortgages, commercial mortgages, auto loans or credit card debt obligations and selling said consolidated debt as bonds, pass-through securities, or collateralized mortgage obligation, to various investors. The principal and interest on the debt, underlying the security, is paid back to the various investors regularly. Securities backed by mortgage receivables are called mortgage-backed securities (MBS), while those backed by other types of receivables are asset-backed securities (ABS).
Shadow banking system	The shadow banking system is a term for the collection of non-bank financial intermediaries that provide services similar to traditional commercial banks. Former Federal Reserve Chair Ben Bernanke provided a definition in April 2012: 'Shadow banking, as usually defined, comprises a diverse set of institutions and markets that, collectively, carry out traditional banking functions--but do so outside, or in ways only loosely linked to, the traditional system of regulated depository institutions. Examples of important components of the shadow banking system include securitization vehicles, asset-backed commercial paper (ABCP) conduits, money market mutual funds, markets for repurchase agreements (repos), investment banks, and mortgage companies.' Shadow banking has grown in importance to rival traditional depository banking and was a primary factor in the subprime mortgage crisis of 2007-2008 and global recession that followed.

Golden West	The Golden West was an 1852 extreme clipper built by Paul Curtis. The ship had a very active career in the California trade, the guano trade, the coolie trade, the Far East, and Australia. She made a record passage between Japan and San Francisco in 1856.
Lehman Brothers	Lehman Brothers Holdings Inc. (former NYSE ticker symbol LEH) was a global financial services firm. Before declaring bankruptcy in 2008, Lehman was the fourth-largest investment bank in the US (behind Goldman Sachs, Morgan Stanley, and Merrill Lynch), doing business in investment banking, equity and fixed-income sales and trading (especially U.S. Treasury securities), research, investment management, private equity, and private banking.
Moral hazard	In economic theory, a moral hazard is a situation where a party will have a tendency to take risks because the costs that could result will not be felt by the party taking the risk. In other words, it is a tendency to be more willing to take a risk, knowing that the potential costs or burdens of taking such risk will be borne, in whole or in part, by others. A moral hazard may occur where the actions of one party may change to the detriment of another after a financial transaction has taken place.
Troubled Asset Relief Program	The Troubled Asset Relief Program is a program of the United States government to purchase assets and equity from financial institutions to strengthen its financial sector that was signed into law by U.S. President George W. Bush on October 3, 2008. It was a component of the government's measures in 2008 to address the subprime mortgage crisis. The Troubled Asset Relief Program program originally authorized expenditures of $700 billion. The Dodd-Frank Wall Street Reform and Consumer Protection Act reduced the amount authorized to $475 billion.
Commercial paper	Commercial paper, in the global financial market, is an unsecured promissory note with a fixed maturity of no more than 270 days. Commercial paper is a money-market security issued by large corporations to get money to meet short-term debt obligations (for example, payroll), and is backed only by an issuing bank or corporation's promised to pay the face amount on the maturity date specified on the note. Since it is not backed by collateral, only firms with excellent credit ratings from a recognized credit rating agency will be able to sell their commercial paper at a reasonable price.
Commercial Paper Funding Facility	Commercial Paper Funding Facility was a system created by the United States Federal Reserve Board during the Global financial crisis of 2008 to improve liquidity in the short-term funding markets. The Commercial Paper Funding Facility was created on October 27, 2008 and funded a special purpose vehicle (SPV) that purchased three-month unsecured and asset-backed commercial paper (CP) from eligible issuers. This resulted in greater availability of credit for firms doing business.

32. Money, Banking, and Financial Institutions

Primary dealer	A primary dealer is a firm that buys government securities directly from a government, with the intention of reselling them to others, thus acting as a market maker of government securities. The government may regulate the behavior and numbers of its primary dealers and impose conditions of entry. Some governments sell their securities only to primary dealers; some sell them to others as well.
Primary Dealer Credit Facility	On March 17, 2008, in response to the subprime mortgage crisis and the collapse of Bear Stearns, the Federal Reserve announced the creation of a new lending facility, the Primary Dealer Credit Facility . Eligible borrowers include all financial institutions listed as primary dealers, and the term of the loan is a repurchase agreement, or 'repo' loan, whereby the broker dealer sells a security in exchange for funds through the Fed's discount window. The security in question acts as collateral, and the Federal Reserve charges an interest rate equivalent to the Fed's primary credit rate.
Securities lending	In finance, securities lending or stock lending refers to the lending of securities by one party to another. The terms of the loan will be governed by a 'Securities Lending Agreement', which requires that the borrower provides the lender with collateral, in the form of cash, government securities, or a Letter of Credit of value equal to or greater than the loaned securities. The agreement is a contract enforceable under relevant law, which is often specified in the agreement.
HSBC	HSBC Holdings plc is a British multinational banking and financial services company headquartered in London, United Kingdom. It is one of the world's largest banks. It was founded in London in 1991 by the Hongkong and Shanghai Banking Corporation to act as a new group holding company.
Money laundering	Money laundering is the process whereby the proceeds of crime are transformed into ostensibly legitimate money or other assets. However in a number of legal and regulatory system the term money laundering has become conflated with other forms of financial crime, and sometimes used more generally to include misuse of the financial system, including terrorism financing, tax evasion and evading of international sanctions. Most anti-money laundering laws openly conflate money laundering with terrorism financing (which is concerned with destination of funds) when regulating the financial system.
Pension	A pension is a fixed sum to be paid regularly to a person, typically following retirement from service. There are many different types of pensions, including defined benefit plans, defined contribution plans, as well as several others. Pensions should not be confused with severance pay; the former is paid in regular installments, while the latter is paid in one lump sum.
Pension fund	A pension fund is any plan, fund, or scheme which provides retirement income. Pension funds are important to shareholders of listed and private companies. They are especially important to the stock market where large institutional investors dominate.

32. Money, Banking, and Financial Institutions

ROWE	ROWE - ROWE is a human resource management strategy co-created by Jody Thompson and Cali Ressler wherein employees are paid for results rather than the number of hours worked. Cali and Jody, who originally proposed the strategy at Best Buy, have since started a consulting group called CultureRx. The strategy has subsequently been implemented at a second large American retailer, Gap., as well as the Girl Scouts of San Gorgino, J.A. Counter and Associates, the Fairview Health Services I.T. Department.

CHAPTER QUIZ: KEY TERMS, PEOPLE, PLACES, CONCEPTS

1. The _____ is a program of the United States government to purchase assets and equity from financial institutions to strengthen its financial sector that was signed into law by U.S. President George W. Bush on October 3, 2008. It was a component of the government's measures in 2008 to address the subprime mortgage crisis.

   The _____ program originally authorized expenditures of $700 billion. The Dodd-Frank Wall Street Reform and Consumer Protection Act reduced the amount authorized to $475 billion.

   a. Big Four
   b. Cascading failure
   c. Troubled Asset Relief Program
   d. Collective action clause

2. Saving accounts are accounts maintained by retail financial institutions that pay interest but cannot be used directly as money in the narrow sense of a medium of exchange . These accounts let customers set aside a portion of their liquid assets while earning a monetary return. For the bank, money in a _____ may not be callable immediately and in some jurisdictions, does not incur a reserve requirement, freeing up cash from the bank's vault to be lent out with interest.

   a. Bank
   b. Bank account
   c. Bank examiner
   d. Savings account

3. . As money became a commodity, the _____ became a component of the financial markets for assets involved in short-term borrowing, lending, buying and selling with original maturities of one year or less. Trading in the _____s is done over the counter and is wholesale. Various instruments exist, such as Treasury bills, commercial paper, bankers' acceptances, deposits, certificates of deposit, bills of exchange, repurchase agreements, federal funds, and short-lived mortgage-, and asset-backed securities.

   a. Money market
   b. Commercial paper

c. Commercial paper in India

d. Fuel protests in the United Kingdom

4. The _____ is an Act of Congress that created and set up the Federal Reserve System, the central banking system of the United States of America, and granted it the legal authority to issue Federal Reserve Notes, now commonly known as the U.S. Dollar, and Federal Reserve Bank Notes as legal tender. The Act was signed into law by President Woodrow Wilson.

a. Fuel protests in the United Kingdom

b. Federal Reserve Act

c. Freikorps Lichtschlag

d. Freikorps Oberland

5. A _____ is a regional bank of the Federal Reserve System, the central banking system of the United States. There are twelve in total, one for each of the twelve Federal Reserve Districts that were created by the Federal Reserve Act of 1913. The banks are jointly responsible for implementing the monetary policy set forth by the Federal Open Market Committee, and are divided as follows:

Some banks also possess branches, with the whole system being headquartered at the Eccles Building in Washington, D.C.

a. Beige Book

b. Bloomberg L.P. v. Board of Governors of the Federal Reserve System

c. Credit channel

d. Federal Reserve Bank

ANSWER KEY
32. Money, Banking, and Financial Institutions

1. c
2. d
3. a
4. b
5. d

You can take the complete Chapter Practice Test

for 32. Money, Banking, and Financial Institutions
on all key terms, persons, places, and concepts.

Online 99 Cents

http://www.JustTheFacts101.com

Use www.JustTheFacts101.com for all your study needs

including Facts101's online interactive problem solving labs in

chemistry, statistics, mathematics, and more.

33. Money Creation

CHAPTER OUTLINE: KEY TERMS, PEOPLE, PLACES, CONCEPTS

Engraving

Federal Reserve Note

Commercial bank

Balance sheet

Cartel

Net worth

Bank reserves

Reserve requirement

Excess reserves

National Credit Union Administration

Deposit insurance

Fiscal policy

Clearing

Federal funds

Federal funds rate

Leverage

Instability

33. Money Creation

Engraving	Engraving is the practice of incising a design onto a hard, usually flat surface, by cutting grooves into it. The result may be a decorated object in itself, as when silver, gold, steel, or glass are engraved, or may provide an intaglio printing plate, of copper or another metal, for printing images on paper as prints or illustrations; these images are also called engravings. Engraving was a historically important method of producing images on paper in artistic printmaking, in mapmaking, and also for commercial reproductions and illustrations for books and magazines.
Federal Reserve Note	A Federal Reserve Note, also a United States banknote or U.S. banknote, is a type of banknote used in the United States of America. Denominated in United States dollars, Federal Reserve Notes are printed by the United States Bureau of Engraving and Printing on paper made by Crane & Co. of Dalton, Massachusetts. Federal Reserve Notes are the only type of U.S. banknote currently produced. Federal Reserve Notes are authorized by Section 16 of the Federal Reserve Act of 1913 (codified at 12 U.S.C. § 411) and are issued to the Federal Reserve Banks at the discretion of the Board of Governors of the Federal Reserve System.
Commercial bank	A commercial bank is a type of bank that provides services such as accepting deposits, making business loans, and offering basic investment products. Commercial bank can also refer to a bank or a division of a bank that mostly deals with deposits and loans from corporations or large businesses, as opposed to individual members of the public . In the US the term commercial bank was often used to distinguish it from an investment bank due to differences in bank regulation.
Balance sheet	In financial accounting, a balance sheet or statement of financial position is a summary of the financial balances of a sole proprietorship, a business partnership, a corporation or other business organization, such as an LLC or an LLP. Assets, liabilities and ownership equity are listed as of a specific date, such as the end of its financial year. A balance sheet is often described as a 'snapshot of a company's financial condition'. Of the three basic financial statements, the balance sheet is the only statement which applies to a single point in time of a business' calendar year.
Cartel	A cartel is a formal 'agreement' among competing firms. It is a formal organization of producers and manufacturers that agree to fix prices, marketing, and production. Cartels usually occur in an oligopolistic industry, where the number of sellers is small (usually because barriers to entry, most notably startup costs, are high) and the products being traded are usually commodities.
Net worth	In business, net worth is the total assets minus total outside liabilities of an individual or a company. Put another way, net worth is what is owned minus what is owed.

33. Money Creation

Bank reserves	Bank reserves or central bank reserves are banks' holdings of deposits in accounts with their central bank, plus currency that is physically held in the bank's vault (vault cash). The central banks of some nations set minimum reserve requirements, which require banks to hold deposits at the central bank equivalent to a specified percentage of their liabilities (such as customer deposits). Even when no reserve requirements are set, banks commonly wish to hold some reserves, called desired reserves, against unexpected events such as unusually large net withdrawals by customers or even bank runs.
Reserve requirement	The reserve requirement is a central bank regulation employed by most, but not all, of the world's central banks, that sets the minimum fraction of customer deposits and notes that each commercial bank must hold as reserves (rather than lend out). These required reserves are normally in the form of cash stored physically in a bank vault (vault cash) or deposits made with a central bank.
	The required reserve ratio is sometimes used as a tool in monetary policy, influencing the country's borrowing and interest rates by changing the amount of funds available for banks to make loans with.
Excess reserves	In banking, excess reserves are bank reserves in excess of a reserve requirement set by a central bank. They are reserves of cash more than the required amounts.
	In the United States, bank reserves are held as FRB (Federal Reserve Bank) credit in FRB accounts; they are not separated into separate 'minimum reserves' and 'excess reserves' accounts.
National Credit Union Administration	The National Credit Union Administration is the independent federal agency created by the U.S. Congress to regulate, charter, and supervise federal credit unions. With the backing of the full faith and credit of the U.S. Government, National Credit Union Administration operates and manages the National Credit Union Share Insurance Fund, insuring the deposits of more than 96 million account holders in all federal credit unions and the overwhelming majority of state-chartered credit unions. As of September 2013, there were 6,620 federally insured credit unions, total assets of more than $1 trillion, and net loans of $631.5 billion.
Deposit insurance	Explicit deposit insurance is a measure implemented in many countries to protect bank depositors, in full or in part, from losses caused by a bank's inability to pay its debts when due. Deposit insurance systems are one component of a financial system safety net that promotes financial stability.
Fiscal policy	In economics and political science, fiscal policy is the use of government revenue collection and expenditure (spending) to influence the economy, or else it involves the government changing the levels of taxation and government spending in order to influence Aggregate Demand and the level of economic activity. The two main instruments of fiscal policy are changes in the level and composition of taxation and government spending in various sectors.

33. Money Creation

These changes can affect the following macroeconomic variables in an economy:•Aggregate demand and the level of economic activity;•The distribution of income;•The pattern of resource allocation within the government sector and relative to the private sector.

Fiscal policy refers to the use of the government budget to influence economic activity.

Clearing	In banking and finance, clearing denotes all activities from the time a commitment is made for a transaction until it is settled. Clearing of payments is necessary to turn the promise of payment (for example, in the form of a cheque or electronic payment request) into actual movement of money from one bank to another. In trading, clearing is necessary because the speed of trades is much faster than the cycle time for completing the underlying transaction.
Federal funds	In the United States, federal funds are overnight borrowings between banks and other entities to maintain their bank reserves at the Federal Reserve. Banks keep reserves at Federal Reserve Banks to meet their reserve requirements and to clear financial transactions. Transactions in the federal funds market enable depository institutions with reserve balances in excess of reserve requirements to lend reserves to institutions with reserve deficiencies.
Federal funds rate	In the United States, the federal funds rate is the interest rate at which depository institutions actively trade balances held at the Federal Reserve, called federal funds, with each other, usually overnight, on an uncollateralized basis. Institutions with surplus balances in their accounts lend those balances to institutions in need of larger balances. The federal funds rate is an important benchmark in financial markets.
Leverage	In finance, leverage is a general term for any technique to multiply gains and losses. Most often this involves buying more of an asset by using borrowed funds. The belief is that the income from the asset will be more than the pay for the cost of borrowing.
Instability	In numerous fields of study, the component of instability within a system is generally characterized by some of the outputs or internal states growing without bounds. Not all systems that are not stable are unstable; systems can also be marginally stable or exhibit limit cycle behavior. In control theory, a system is unstable if any of the roots of its characteristic equation has real part greater than zero (or if zero is a repeated root).

1. In banking and finance, _____ denotes all activities from the time a commitment is made for a transaction until it is settled. _____ of payments is necessary to turn the promise of payment (for example, in the form of a cheque or electronic payment request) into actual movement of money from one bank to another.

   In trading, _____ is necessary because the speed of trades is much faster than the cycle time for completing the underlying transaction.

   a. Basket
   b. Clearing
   c. Beneficial ownership
   d. Big boy letter

2. _____ or central _____ are banks' holdings of deposits in accounts with their central bank, plus currency that is physically held in the bank's vault (vault cash). The central banks of some nations set minimum reserve requirements, which require banks to hold deposits at the central bank equivalent to a specified percentage of their liabilities (such as customer deposits). Even when no reserve requirements are set, banks commonly wish to hold some reserves, called desired reserves, against unexpected events such as unusually large net withdrawals by customers or even bank runs.

   a. Fuel protests in the United Kingdom
   b. Bank reserves
   c. Freikorps Lichtschlag
   d. Freikorps Oberland

3. _____ is the practice of incising a design onto a hard, usually flat surface, by cutting grooves into it. The result may be a decorated object in itself, as when silver, gold, steel, or glass are engraved, or may provide an intaglio printing plate, of copper or another metal, for printing images on paper as prints or illustrations; these images are also called _____s.

   _____ was a historically important method of producing images on paper in artistic printmaking, in mapmaking, and also for commercial reproductions and illustrations for books and magazines.

   a. Ball
   b. Engraving
   c. Capacitor discharge sintering
   d. Cast iron

4. . In numerous fields of study, the component of _____ within a system is generally characterized by some of the outputs or internal states growing without bounds. Not all systems that are not stable are unstable; systems can also be marginally stable or exhibit limit cycle behavior.

   In control theory, a system is unstable if any of the roots of its characteristic equation has real part greater than zero (or if zero is a repeated root).

   a. Energy Task Force

b. Instability

c. Cessio bonorum

d. Charge-off

5. Explicit _____ is a measure implemented in many countries to protect bank depositors, in full or in part, from losses caused by a bank's inability to pay its debts when due. _____ systems are one component of a financial system safety net that promotes financial stability.

a. Deposit insurance

b. Bank condition

c. Bank regulation

d. Basel Committee on Banking Supervision

1. b
2. b
3. b
4. b
5. a

You can take the complete Chapter Practice Test

for 33. Money Creation
on all key terms, persons, places, and concepts.

Online 99 Cents

http://www.JustTheFacts101.com

Use www.JustTheFacts101.com for all your study needs

including Facts101's online interactive problem solving labs in

chemistry, statistics, mathematics, and more.

34. Interest Rates and Monetary Policy

CHAPTER OUTLINE: KEY TERMS, PEOPLE, PLACES, CONCEPTS

Interest rate

Monetary policy

Balance sheet

Bank reserves

Central bank

Commercial bank

Federal Reserve Bank

Leverage

Asset

Federal Reserve Note

Federal funds

Lender of last resort

Federal funds rate

Federal Open Market Committee

Laffer curve

Taylor rule

Money market

Gross private domestic investment

Product

Great Recession

Recession

34. Interest Rates and Monetary Policy

	Zero lower bound problem
	Subprime mortgage crisis
	Quantitative easing
	Cyclical asymmetry
	Liquidity trap

CHAPTER HIGHLIGHTS & NOTES: KEY TERMS, PEOPLE, PLACES, CONCEPTS

Interest rate	An interest rate is the rate at which interest is paid by a borrower for the use of money that they borrow from a lender (creditor). Specifically, the interest rate is a percent of principal (P) paid a certain amount of times (m) per period (usually quoted per annum). For example, a small company borrows capital from a bank to buy new assets for its business, and in return the lender receives interest at a predetermined interest rate for deferring the use of funds and instead lending it to the borrower.
Monetary policy	Monetary policy is the process by which the monetary authority of a country controls the supply of money, often targeting a rate of interest for the purpose of promoting economic growth and stability. The official goals usually include relatively stable prices and low unemployment. Monetary economics provides insight into how to craft optimal monetary policy.
Balance sheet	In financial accounting, a balance sheet or statement of financial position is a summary of the financial balances of a sole proprietorship, a business partnership, a corporation or other business organization, such as an LLC or an LLP. Assets, liabilities and ownership equity are listed as of a specific date, such as the end of its financial year. A balance sheet is often described as a 'snapshot of a company's financial condition'. Of the three basic financial statements, the balance sheet is the only statement which applies to a single point in time of a business' calendar year.
Bank reserves	Bank reserves or central bank reserves are banks' holdings of deposits in accounts with their central bank, plus currency that is physically held in the bank's vault (vault cash). The central banks of some nations set minimum reserve requirements, which require banks to hold deposits at the central bank equivalent to a specified percentage of their liabilities (such as customer deposits).

34. Interest Rates and Monetary Policy

Central bank	A central bank, reserve bank, or monetary authority is an institution that manages a state's currency, money supply, and interest rates. Central banks also usually oversee the commercial banking system of their respective countries. In contrast to a commercial bank, a central bank possesses a monopoly on increasing the amount of money in the nation, and usually also prints the national currency, which usually serves as the nation's legal tender.
Commercial bank	A commercial bank is a type of bank that provides services such as accepting deposits, making business loans, and offering basic investment products.
	Commercial bank can also refer to a bank or a division of a bank that mostly deals with deposits and loans from corporations or large businesses, as opposed to individual members of the public .
	In the US the term commercial bank was often used to distinguish it from an investment bank due to differences in bank regulation.
Federal Reserve Bank	A Federal Reserve Bank is a regional bank of the Federal Reserve System, the central banking system of the United States. There are twelve in total, one for each of the twelve Federal Reserve Districts that were created by the Federal Reserve Act of 1913. The banks are jointly responsible for implementing the monetary policy set forth by the Federal Open Market Committee, and are divided as follows:
	Some banks also possess branches, with the whole system being headquartered at the Eccles Building in Washington, D.C.
Leverage	In finance, leverage is a general term for any technique to multiply gains and losses. Most often this involves buying more of an asset by using borrowed funds. The belief is that the income from the asset will be more than the pay for the cost of borrowing.
Asset	An 'asset' in economic theory is an output good which can only be partially consumed or input as a factor of production (like a cement mixer) which can only be partially used up in production. The necessary quality for an asset is that value remains after the period of analysis so it can be used as a store of value. As such, financial instruments like corporate bonds and common stocks are assets because they store value for the next period.
Federal Reserve Note	A Federal Reserve Note, also a United States banknote or U.S. banknote, is a type of banknote used in the United States of America. Denominated in United States dollars, Federal Reserve Notes are printed by the United States Bureau of Engraving and Printing on paper made by Crane & Co. of Dalton, Massachusetts. Federal Reserve Notes are the only type of U.S. banknote currently produced.
	Federal Reserve Notes are authorized by Section 16 of the Federal Reserve Act of 1913 (codified at 12 U.S.C.

34. Interest Rates and Monetary Policy

Federal funds	In the United States, federal funds are overnight borrowings between banks and other entities to maintain their bank reserves at the Federal Reserve. Banks keep reserves at Federal Reserve Banks to meet their reserve requirements and to clear financial transactions. Transactions in the federal funds market enable depository institutions with reserve balances in excess of reserve requirements to lend reserves to institutions with reserve deficiencies.
Lender of last resort	The term lender of last resort originates from the French expression dernier ressort. While the concept itself had been used previously, the term, 'lender of last resort', was supposedly first used in its current context by Sir Francis Baring in his Observations on the Establishment of the Bank of England which was published in 1797. In 1763 the king was the lender of last resort in Prussia. Different definitions of the lender of last resort exist in the literature.
Federal funds rate	In the United States, the federal funds rate is the interest rate at which depository institutions actively trade balances held at the Federal Reserve, called federal funds, with each other, usually overnight, on an uncollateralized basis. Institutions with surplus balances in their accounts lend those balances to institutions in need of larger balances. The federal funds rate is an important benchmark in financial markets.
Federal Open Market Committee	The Federal Open Market Committee, a committee within the Federal Reserve System (the Fed), is charged under United States law with overseeing the nation's open market operations (i.e., the Fed's buying and selling of United States Treasury securities). It is this Federal Reserve committee which makes key decisions about interest rates and the growth of the United States money supply. It is the principal organ of United States national monetary policy.
Laffer curve	In economics, the Laffer curve is a representation of the relationship between possible rates of taxation and the resulting levels of government revenue. It illustrates the concept of taxable income elasticity--i.e., taxable income will change in response to changes in the rate of taxation. It postulates that no tax revenue will be raised at the extreme tax rates of 0% and 100% and that there must be at least one rate where tax revenue would be a non-zero maximum.
Taylor rule	In economics, a Taylor rule is a monetary-policy rule that stipulates how much the central bank should change the nominal interest rate in response to changes in inflation, output, or other economic conditions. In particular, the rule stipulates that for each one-percent increase in inflation, the central bank should raise the nominal interest rate by more than one percentage point. This aspect of the rule is often called the Taylor principle.
Money market	As money became a commodity, the money market became a component of the financial markets for assets involved in short-term borrowing, lending, buying and selling with original maturities of one year or less. Trading in the money markets is done over the counter and is wholesale.

34. Interest Rates and Monetary Policy

Gross private domestic investment	Gross private domestic investment is the measure of investment used to compute GDP in economic measurement of nations. This is an important component of GDP because it provides an indicator of the future productive capacity of the economy. It includes replacement purchases plus net additions to capital assets plus investments in inventories.
Product	In marketing, a product is anything that can be offered to a market that might satisfy a want or need. In retailing, products are called merchandise. In manufacturing, products are bought as raw materials and sold as finished goods.
Great Recession	The Great Recession was a global economic decline in the late 2000s. According to aggregated national data, a worldwide recession began in Q3-2008 and ended in Q1-2009. It is related to a liquidity crisis, commonly being dated to have started when several central banks had to step in with liquidity lending to the interbank lending market on 9 August 2007. This was a response to a situation where BNP Paribas temporarily had to block money withdrawals from three hedge funds--citing a 'complete evaporation of liquidity'.
Recession	In economics, a recession is a business cycle contraction. It is a general slowdown in economic activity. Macroeconomic indicators such as GDP (gross domestic product), investment spending, capacity utilization, household income, business profits, and inflation fall, while bankruptcies and the unemployment rate rise.
Zero lower bound problem	The Zero Lower Bound Problem is a macroeconomic situation in which the short-term nominal interest rate is zero, or just above zero, causing a liquidity trap and limiting the capacity that the central bank has to stimulate economic growth. This problem returned to prominence with the Japan's experience during the 90's, and more recently with the subprime crisis. The belief that monetary policy under the ZLB was effective in promoting economy growth has been critiqued by Paul Krugman, Gauti Eggertsson, and Michael Woodford among others.
Subprime mortgage crisis	The U.S. subprime mortgage crisis was a set of events and conditions that were significant aspects of a financial crisis and subsequent recession that became manifestly visible in 2008. It was characterized by a rise in subprime mortgage delinquencies and foreclosures, and the resulting decline of securities backed by said mortgages. These mortgage-backed securities (MBS) and collateralized debt obligations (CDO) initially offered attractive rates of return due to the higher interest rates on the mortgages; however, the lower credit quality ultimately caused massive defaults. While elements of the crisis first became more visible during 2007, several major financial institutions collapsed in September 2008, with significant disruption in the flow of credit to businesses and consumers and the onset of a severe global recession.
Quantitative easing	Quantitative easing is an unconventional monetary policy used by central banks to stimulate the economy when standard monetary policy has become ineffective.

34. Interest Rates and Monetary Policy

	A central bank implements quantitative easing by buying specified amounts of financial assets from commercial banks and other private institutions, thus raising the prices of those financial assets and lowering their yield, while simultaneously increasing the monetary base. This is distinguished from the more usual policy of buying or selling short term government bonds in order to keep interbank interest rates at a specified target value.
Cyclical asymmetry	Cyclical asymmetry is an economic term which describes any large imbalance in economic factors that occur due to purely cyclical reactions by a market or nation. This can include employment rates, debt retention, interest rates, bond strengths, or stock market imbalances.
Liquidity trap	A liquidity trap is a situation described in Keynesian economics in which injections of cash into the private banking system by a central bank fail to lower interest rates and hence make monetary policy ineffective. A liquidity trap is caused when people hoard cash because they expect an adverse event such as deflation, insufficient aggregate demand, or war. Common characteristics of a liquidity trap are interest rates that are close to zero and fluctuations in the money supply that fail to translate into fluctuations in price levels.

1. In economics, a _____ is a monetary-policy rule that stipulates how much the central bank should change the nominal interest rate in response to changes in inflation, output, or other economic conditions. In particular, the rule stipulates that for each one-percent increase in inflation, the central bank should raise the nominal interest rate by more than one percentage point. This aspect of the rule is often called the Taylor principle.

    a. Beige Book
    b. Bloomberg L.P. v. Board of Governors of the Federal Reserve System
    c. Taylor rule
    d. Credit channel

2. In economics, the _____ is a representation of the relationship between possible rates of taxation and the resulting levels of government revenue. It illustrates the concept of taxable income elasticity--i.e., taxable income will change in response to changes in the rate of taxation. It postulates that no tax revenue will be raised at the extreme tax rates of 0% and 100% and that there must be at least one rate where tax revenue would be a non-zero maximum.

    a. Beveridge curve
    b. Laffer curve
    c. Cost curve
    d. Demand curve

3. The _____ was a global economic decline in the late 2000s. According to aggregated national data, a worldwide recession began in Q3-2008 and ended in Q1-2009.

   It is related to a liquidity crisis, commonly being dated to have started when several central banks had to step in with liquidity lending to the interbank lending market on 9 August 2007. This was a response to a situation where BNP Paribas temporarily had to block money withdrawals from three hedge funds--citing a 'complete evaporation of liquidity'.

   a. Commercial Revolution
   b. Mercantilism
   c. Great Recession
   d. 1 kroon coin

4. The _____, a committee within the Federal Reserve System (the Fed), is charged under United States law with overseeing the nation's open market operations (i.e., the Fed's buying and selling of United States Treasury securities). It is this Federal Reserve committee which makes key decisions about interest rates and the growth of the United States money supply.

   It is the principal organ of United States national monetary policy.

   a. Chloroform Committee
   b. Committee
   c. Committee for Finance and Personnel
   d. Federal Open Market Committee

5. An _____ is the rate at which interest is paid by a borrower for the use of money that they borrow from a lender (creditor). Specifically, the _____ is a percent of principal (P) paid a certain amount of times (m) per period (usually quoted per annum). For example, a small company borrows capital from a bank to buy new assets for its business, and in return the lender receives interest at a predetermined _____ for deferring the use of funds and instead lending it to the borrower.

   a. Bernanke doctrine
   b. Discretionary policy
   c. Fuel protests in the United Kingdom
   d. Interest rate

---

1. c

2. b

3. c

4. d

5. d

You can take the complete Chapter Practice Test

for 34. Interest Rates and Monetary Policy
on all key terms, persons, places, and concepts.

Online 99 Cents

http://www.JustTheFacts101.com

Use www.JustTheFacts101.com for all your study needs

including Facts101's online interactive problem solving labs in

chemistry, statistics, mathematics, and more.

35. Financial Economics

_____ Financial economics

_____ Present value

_____ Compound interest

_____ Income

_____ National income

_____ Product

_____ Salary

_____ Salary cap

_____ State bank

_____ Deferred compensation

_____ Lottery

_____ Bankruptcy

_____ Default

_____ Dividend

_____ Limited liability

_____ Index fund

_____ Portfolio

_____ Asset

_____ Diversification

_____ Country risk

_____ Economic freedom

35. Financial Economics

CHAPTER OUTLINE: KEY TERMS, PEOPLE, PLACES, CONCEPTS

	Market portfolio
	Federal funds
	Risk-free interest rate
	Risk premium
	Security market line
	Commercial bank
	Interest rate
	Monetary policy

CHAPTER HIGHLIGHTS & NOTES: KEY TERMS, PEOPLE, PLACES, CONCEPTS

Financial economics	Financial economics is the branch of economics characterized by a 'concentration on monetary activities', in which 'money of one type or another is likely to appear on both sides of a trade'. It is concerned with 'the allocation and deployment of economic resources, both spatially and across time, in an uncertain environment'. It is built on the foundations of microeconomics and decision theory.
Present value	Present value, also known as present discounted value, is a future amount of money that has been discounted to reflect its current value, as if it existed today. The present value is always less than or equal to the future value because money has interest-earning potential, a characteristic referred to as the time value of money. Time value can be described with the simplified phrase, "A dollar today is worth more than a dollar tomorrow".
Compound interest	Compound interest arises when interest is added to the principal of a deposit or loan, so that, from that moment on, the interest that has been added also earns interest. This addition of interest to the principal is called compounding. A bank account, for example, may have its interest compounded every year: in this case, an account with $1000 initial principal and 20% interest per year would have a balance of $1200 at the end of the first year, $1440 at the end of the second year, and so on.

35. Financial Economics

Income	Income is the consumption and savings opportunity gained by an entity within a specified timeframe, which is generally expressed in monetary terms. However, for households and individuals, 'income is the sum of all the wages, salaries, profits, interests payments, rents and other forms of earnings received... in a given period of time.' In the field of public economics, the term may refer to the accumulation of both monetary and non-monetary consumption ability, with the former (monetary) being used as a proxy for total income.
National income	A variety of measures of national income and output are used in economics to estimate total economic activity in a country or region, including gross domestic product, gross national product (GNP), net national income and adjusted national income. All are specially concerned with counting the total amount of goods and services produced within some 'boundary'. The boundary is usually defined by geography or citizenship, and may also restrict the goods and services that are counted.
Product	In marketing, a product is anything that can be offered to a market that might satisfy a want or need. In retailing, products are called merchandise. In manufacturing, products are bought as raw materials and sold as finished goods.
Salary	A salary is a form of periodic payment from an employer to an employee, which may be specified in an employment contract. It is contrasted with piece wages, where each job, hour or other unit is paid separately, rather than on a periodic basis. From the point of a view of running a business, salary can also be viewed as the cost of acquiring and retaining human resources for running operations, and is then termed personnel expense or salary expense.
Salary cap	In professional sports, a salary cap is an agreement or rule that places a limit on the amount of money that a team can spend on player salaries. The limit exists as a per-player limit or a total limit for the team's roster, or both. Several sports leagues have implemented salary caps, both as a method of keeping overall costs down, and to ensure parity between teams so wealthy teams cannot entrench dominance by signing many more top players than their rivals.
State bank	A state bank is generally a financial institution that is chartered by a state. It differs from a reserve bank in that it does not necessarily control monetary policy (indeed, the state in question may have no legal capacity to create monetary policy), but instead usually offers only retail and commercial services. A state bank that has been in operation for five years or less is called a de novo bank.
Deferred compensation	Deferred compensation is an arrangement in which a portion of an employee's income is paid out at a date after which that income is actually earned. Examples of deferred compensation include pensions, retirement plans, and employee stock options.

Lottery	In expected utility theory, a lottery is a discrete distribution of probability on a set of states of nature. The elements of a lottery correspond to the probability that a certain outcome arises from a given state of nature. In economics, individuals are assumed to rank lotteries according to a rational system of preferences, although it is now accepted that people make irrational choices systematically.
Bankruptcy	Bankruptcy is a legal status of a person or other entity that cannot repay the debts it owes to creditors. In most jurisdictions, bankruptcy is imposed by a court order, often initiated by the debtor. Bankruptcy is not the only legal status that an insolvent person or other entity may have, and the term bankruptcy is therefore not a synonym for insolvency.
Default	In finance, default is failure to meet the legal obligations of a loan, for example when a home buyer fails to make a mortgage payment, or when a corporation or government fails to pay a bond which has reached maturity. A national or sovereign default is the failure or refusal of a government to repay its national debt.
Dividend	A dividend is a payment made by a corporation to its shareholders, usually as a distribution of profits. When a corporation earns a profit or surplus, it can either re-invest it in the business (called retained earnings), or it can distribute it to shareholders. A corporation may retain a portion of its earnings and pay the remainder as a dividend.
Limited liability	Limited liability is where a person's financial liability is limited to a fixed sum, most commonly the value of a person's investment in a company or partnership. If a company with limited liability is sued, then the plaintiffs are suing the company, not its owners or investors. A shareholder in a limited company is not personally liable for any of the debts of the company, other than for the value of their investment in that company.
Index fund	An index fund is a collective investment scheme (usually a mutual fund or exchange-traded fund) that aims to replicate the movements of an index of a specific financial market, or a set of rules of ownership that are held constant, regardless of market conditions. As of 2007, index funds made up 11.5% of equity mutual fund assets in the US.
Portfolio	Portfolio is a financial term denoting a collection of investments held by an investment company, hedge fund, financial institution or individual.
Asset	An 'asset' in economic theory is an output good which can only be partially consumed or input as a factor of production (like a cement mixer) which can only be partially used up in production. The necessary quality for an asset is that value remains after the period of analysis so it can be used as a store of value. As such, financial instruments like corporate bonds and common stocks are assets because they store value for the next period.
Diversification	In finance, diversification means reducing non-systematic risk by investing in a variety of assets.

35. Financial Economics

If the asset values do not move up and down in perfect synchrony, a diversified portfolio will have less risk than the weighted average risk of its constituent assets, and often less risk than the least risky of its constituent. Therefore, any risk-averse investor will diversify to at least some extent, with more risk-averse investors diversifying more completely than less risk-averse investors.

Country risk	Country risk refers to the risk of investing in a country, dependent on changes in the business environment that may adversely affect operating profits or the value of assets in a specific country. For example, financial factors such as currency controls, devaluation or regulatory changes, or stability factors such as mass riots, civil war and other potential events contribute to companies' operational risks. This term is also sometimes referred to as political risk; however, country risk is a more general term that generally refers only to risks affecting all companies operating within a particular country.
Economic freedom	Economic freedom or economic liberty or right to economic liberty denotes the ability of members of a society to undertake economic direction and actions. This is a term used in economic and policy debates as well as a politicoeconomic philosophy. As with freedom generally, there are various definitions, but no universally accepted concept of economic freedom.
Market portfolio	Market portfolio is a portfolio consisting of a weighted sum of every asset in the market, with weights in the proportions that they exist in the market, with the necessary assumption that these assets are infinitely divisible.
	Richard Roll's critique states that this is only a theoretical concept, as to create a market portfolio for investment purposes in practice would necessarily include every single possible available asset, including real estate, precious metals, stamp collections, jewelry, and anything with any worth, as the theoretical market being referred to would be the world market. As a result, proxies for the market (such as the FTSE 100 in the UK, DAX in Germany or the S&P 500 in the US) are used in practice by investors.
Federal funds	In the United States, federal funds are overnight borrowings between banks and other entities to maintain their bank reserves at the Federal Reserve. Banks keep reserves at Federal Reserve Banks to meet their reserve requirements and to clear financial transactions. Transactions in the federal funds market enable depository institutions with reserve balances in excess of reserve requirements to lend reserves to institutions with reserve deficiencies.
Risk-free interest rate	Risk-free interest rate is the theoretical rate of return of an investment with no risk of financial loss. One interpretation is that the risk-free rate represents the interest that an investor would expect from an absolutely risk-free investment over a given period of time. Another interpretation is that the risk free rate is the compensation that would be demanded by a representative investor holding a representative market portfolio, comprising all the assets in the economy, (i.e. the risk free rate is the compensation for systematic risk which cannot be eliminated by holding a diversified portfolio).

35. Financial Economics

Risk premium	Risk premium is the minimum amount of money by which the expected return on a risky asset must exceed the known return on a risk-free asset, or the expected return on a less risky asset, in order to induce an individual to hold the risky asset rather than the risk-free asset. (Note that risk premia may be negative). Thus it is the minimum willingness to accept compensation for the risk.
Security market line	Security market line is the representation of the Capital asset pricing model. It displays the expected rate of return of an individual security as a function of systematic, non-diversifiable risk .
Commercial bank	A commercial bank is a type of bank that provides services such as accepting deposits, making business loans, and offering basic investment products. Commercial bank can also refer to a bank or a division of a bank that mostly deals with deposits and loans from corporations or large businesses, as opposed to individual members of the public . In the US the term commercial bank was often used to distinguish it from an investment bank due to differences in bank regulation.
Interest rate	An interest rate is the rate at which interest is paid by a borrower for the use of money that they borrow from a lender (creditor). Specifically, the interest rate is a percent of principal (P) paid a certain amount of times (m) per period (usually quoted per annum). For example, a small company borrows capital from a bank to buy new assets for its business, and in return the lender receives interest at a predetermined interest rate for deferring the use of funds and instead lending it to the borrower.
Monetary policy	Monetary policy is the process by which the monetary authority of a country controls the supply of money, often targeting a rate of interest for the purpose of promoting economic growth and stability. The official goals usually include relatively stable prices and low unemployment. Monetary economics provides insight into how to craft optimal monetary policy.

35. Financial Economics

1. A _____ is a payment made by a corporation to its shareholders, usually as a distribution of profits. When a corporation earns a profit or surplus, it can either re-invest it in the business (called retained earnings), or it can distribute it to shareholders. A corporation may retain a portion of its earnings and pay the remainder as a _____.

   a. Dividend
   b. Battle of Annaberg
   c. Freikorps Lichtschlag
   d. Freikorps Oberland

2. _____, also known as present discounted value, is a future amount of money that has been discounted to reflect its current value, as if it existed today. The _____ is always less than or equal to the future value because money has interest-earning potential, a characteristic referred to as the time value of money. Time value can be described with the simplified phrase, "A dollar today is worth more than a dollar tomorrow".

   a. Balloon payment mortgage
   b. Buydown
   c. Collateral
   d. Present value

3. _____ is the theoretical rate of return of an investment with no risk of financial loss. One interpretation is that the risk-free rate represents the interest that an investor would expect from an absolutely risk-free investment over a given period of time. Another interpretation is that the risk free rate is the compensation that would be demanded by a representative investor holding a representative market portfolio, comprising all the assets in the economy, (i.e. the risk free rate is the compensation for systematic risk which cannot be eliminated by holding a diversified portfolio).

   a. Bailout
   b. Risk-free interest rate
   c. Capital Requirements Directive
   d. Cash flow hedge

4. A _____ is generally a financial institution that is chartered by a state. It differs from a reserve bank in that it does not necessarily control monetary policy (indeed, the state in question may have no legal capacity to create monetary policy), but instead usually offers only retail and commercial services.

   A _____ that has been in operation for five years or less is called a de novo bank.

   a. Bank
   b. State bank
   c. Bank examiner
   d. Bank secrecy

5. . _____ is where a person's financial liability is limited to a fixed sum, most commonly the value of a person's investment in a company or partnership.

35. Financial Economics

If a company with _____ is sued, then the plaintiffs are suing the company, not its owners or investors. A shareholder in a limited company is not personally liable for any of the debts of the company, other than for the value of their investment in that company.

a. Business ecosystem
b. Limited liability
c. Conglomerate merger
d. Consumer economy

1. a
2. d
3. b
4. b
5. b

36. Extending the Analysis of Aggregate Supply

CHAPTER OUTLINE: KEY TERMS, PEOPLE, PLACES, CONCEPTS

	Aggregate supply
	Great Depression
	Long run
	Phillips curve
	Aggregate demand
	Price level
	Demand-pull inflation
	Inflation
	Cost-push inflation
	Economic growth
	Production
	Great Recession
	Recession
	Taylor rule
	Laffer curve
	Macroeconomics
	OPEC
	Stagflation
	Supply shock
	Cartel
	Instability

36. Extending the Analysis of Aggregate Supply

	Misery index
	Disinflation
	Supply-side economics
	Incentive
	Income
	National income
	Product
	Tax rate
	Economic policy
	Federal funds
	Interest rate

CHAPTER HIGHLIGHTS & NOTES: KEY TERMS, PEOPLE, PLACES, CONCEPTS

Aggregate supply	In economics, aggregate supply is the total supply of goods and services that firms in a national economy plan on selling during a specific time period. It is the total amount of goods and services that firms are willing to sell at a given price level in an economy.
Great Depression	The Great Depression was a severe worldwide economic depression in the decade preceding World War II. The timing of the Great Depression varied across nations, but in most countries it started in 1930 and lasted until the late 1930s or middle 1940s. It was the longest, deepest, and most widespread depression of the 20th century. In the 21st century, the Great Depression is commonly used as an example of how far the world's economy can decline.

Long run	In microeconomics, the long run is the conceptual time period in which there are no fixed factors of production as to changing the output level by changing the capital stock or by entering or leaving an industry. The long run contrasts with the short run, in which some factors are variable and others are fixed, constraining entry or exit from an industry. In macroeconomics, the long run is the period when the general price level, contractual wage rates, and expectations adjust fully to the state of the economy, in contrast to the short run when these variables may not fully adjust.
Phillips curve	In economics, the Phillips curve is a historical inverse relationship between rates of unemployment and corresponding rates of inflation that result in an economy. Stated simply, decreased unemployment, (i.e., increased levels of employment) in an economy will correlate with higher rates of inflation. While there is a short run tradeoff between unemployment and inflation, it has not been observed in the long run.
Aggregate demand	In macroeconomics, aggregate demand is the total demand for final goods and services in the economy at a given time and price level. It specifies the amounts of goods and services that will be purchased at all possible price levels. This is the demand for the gross domestic product of a country.
Price level	The general price level is a hypothetical measure of overall prices for some set of goods and services, in a given region during a given interval, normalized relative to some base set. Typically, a price level is approximated with a price index.
Demand-pull inflation	Demand-pull inflation is asserted to arise when aggregate demand in an economy outpaces aggregate supply. It involves inflation rising as real gross domestic product rises and unemployment falls, as the economy moves along the Phillips curve. This is commonly described as 'too much money chasing too few goods'.
Inflation	In economics, inflation is a sustained increase in the general price level of goods and services in an economy over a period of time. When the general price level rises, each unit of currency buys fewer goods and services. Consequently, inflation reflects a reduction in the purchasing power per unit of money - a loss of real value in the medium of exchange and unit of account within the economy.
Cost-push inflation	Cost-push inflation is an alleged type of inflation caused by substantial increases in the cost of important goods or services where no suitable alternative is available. A situation that has been often cited of this was the oil crisis of the 1970s, which some economists see as a major cause of the inflation experienced in the Western world in that decade. It is argued that this inflation resulted from increases in the cost of petroleum imposed by the member states of OPEC.

36. Extending the Analysis of Aggregate Supply

Economic growth	Economic growth is the increase in the market value of the goods and services produced by an economy over time. It is conventionally measured as the percent rate of increase in real gross domestic product, or real GDP. Of more importance is the growth of the ratio of GDP to population (GDP per capita), which is also called per capita income. An increase in per capita income is referred to as intensive growth.
Production	Production is a process of combining various material inputs and immaterial inputs in order to make something for consumption (the output). It is the act of creating output, a good or service which has value and contributes to the utility of individuals. Economic well-being is created in a production process, meaning all economic activities that aim directly or indirectly to satisfy human needs.
Great Recession	The Great Recession was a global economic decline in the late 2000s. According to aggregated national data, a worldwide recession began in Q3-2008 and ended in Q1-2009. It is related to a liquidity crisis, commonly being dated to have started when several central banks had to step in with liquidity lending to the interbank lending market on 9 August 2007. This was a response to a situation where BNP Paribas temporarily had to block money withdrawals from three hedge funds--citing a 'complete evaporation of liquidity'.
Recession	In economics, a recession is a business cycle contraction. It is a general slowdown in economic activity. Macroeconomic indicators such as GDP (gross domestic product), investment spending, capacity utilization, household income, business profits, and inflation fall, while bankruptcies and the unemployment rate rise.
Taylor rule	In economics, a Taylor rule is a monetary-policy rule that stipulates how much the central bank should change the nominal interest rate in response to changes in inflation, output, or other economic conditions. In particular, the rule stipulates that for each one-percent increase in inflation, the central bank should raise the nominal interest rate by more than one percentage point. This aspect of the rule is often called the Taylor principle.
Laffer curve	In economics, the Laffer curve is a representation of the relationship between possible rates of taxation and the resulting levels of government revenue. It illustrates the concept of taxable income elasticity--i.e., taxable income will change in response to changes in the rate of taxation. It postulates that no tax revenue will be raised at the extreme tax rates of 0% and 100% and that there must be at least one rate where tax revenue would be a non-zero maximum.
Macroeconomics	Macroeconomics is the study of the macroeconomy. It is a branch of economics dealing with the performance, structure, behavior, and decision-making of an economy as a whole, rather than individual markets. This includes national, regional, and global economies.
OPEC	OPEC is an international organization whose mission is to coordinate the policies of the oil-producing countries.

The goal is to secure a steady income to the member states and to secure supply of oil to consumers.

OPEC is an intergovernmental organization that was created at the Baghdad Conference on 10-14 September 1960, by Iraq, Kuwait, Iran, Saudi Arabia and Venezuela.

Stagflation	Stagflation, a portmanteau of stagnation and inflation, is a term used in economics to describe a situation where the inflation rate is high, the economic growth rate slows down, and unemployment remains steadily high. It raises a dilemma for economic policy since actions designed to lower inflation may exacerbate unemployment, and vice versa.

The term is generally attributed to a British politician who became chancellor of the exchequer in 1970, Iain Macleod, who coined the phrase in his speech to Parliament in 1965.

In the version of Keynesian macroeconomic theory which was dominant between the end of WWII and the late-1970s, inflation and recession were regarded as mutually exclusive, the relationship between the two being described by the Phillips curve.

Supply shock	A supply shock is an event that suddenly changes the price of a commodity or service. It may be caused by a sudden increase or decrease in the supply of a particular good. This sudden change affects the equilibrium price.
Cartel	A cartel is a formal 'agreement' among competing firms. It is a formal organization of producers and manufacturers that agree to fix prices, marketing, and production. Cartels usually occur in an oligopolistic industry, where the number of sellers is small (usually because barriers to entry, most notably startup costs, are high) and the products being traded are usually commodities.
Instability	In numerous fields of study, the component of instability within a system is generally characterized by some of the outputs or internal states growing without bounds. Not all systems that are not stable are unstable; systems can also be marginally stable or exhibit limit cycle behavior.

In control theory, a system is unstable if any of the roots of its characteristic equation has real part greater than zero (or if zero is a repeated root).

Misery index	The misery index is an economic indicator, created by economist Arthur Okun, and found by adding the unemployment rate to the inflation rate. It is assumed that both a higher rate of unemployment and a worsening of inflation create economic and social costs for a country.
Disinflation	Disinflation is a decrease in the rate of inflation - a slowdown in the rate of increase of the general price level of goods and services in a nation's gross domestic product over time. It is the opposite of reflation.

36. Extending the Analysis of Aggregate Supply

Supply-side economics	Supply-side economics is a school of macroeconomics that argues that economic growth can be most effectively created by lowering barriers for people to produce goods and services as well as invest in capital. According to supply-side economics, consumers will then benefit from a greater supply of goods and services at lower prices; furthermore, the investment and expansion of businesses will increase the demand for employees. Typical policy recommendations of supply-side economists are lower marginal tax rates and less regulation.
Incentive	An incentive is something that motivates an individual to perform an action. The study of incentive structures is central to the study of all economic activities (both in terms of individual decision-making and in terms of co-operation and competition within a larger institutional structure). Economic analysis, then, of the differences between societies (and between different organizations within a society) largely amounts to characterizing the differences in incentive structures faced by individuals involved in these collective efforts.
Income	Income is the consumption and savings opportunity gained by an entity within a specified timeframe, which is generally expressed in monetary terms. However, for households and individuals, 'income is the sum of all the wages, salaries, profits, interests payments, rents and other forms of earnings received... in a given period of time.' In the field of public economics, the term may refer to the accumulation of both monetary and non-monetary consumption ability, with the former (monetary) being used as a proxy for total income.
National income	A variety of measures of national income and output are used in economics to estimate total economic activity in a country or region, including gross domestic product, gross national product (GNP), net national income and adjusted national income. All are specially concerned with counting the total amount of goods and services produced within some 'boundary'. The boundary is usually defined by geography or citizenship, and may also restrict the goods and services that are counted.
Product	In marketing, a product is anything that can be offered to a market that might satisfy a want or need. In retailing, products are called merchandise. In manufacturing, products are bought as raw materials and sold as finished goods.
Tax rate	In a tax system and in economics, the tax rate describes the burden ratio at which a business or person is taxed. There are several methods used to present a tax rate: statutory, average, marginal, and effective. These rates can also be presented using different definitions applied to a tax base: inclusive and exclusive.
Economic policy	Economic policy refers to the actions that governments take in the economic field. It covers the systems for setting interest rates and government budget as well as the labor market, national ownership, and many other areas of government interventions into the economy.

36. Extending the Analysis of Aggregate Supply

Federal funds	In the United States, federal funds are overnight borrowings between banks and other entities to maintain their bank reserves at the Federal Reserve. Banks keep reserves at Federal Reserve Banks to meet their reserve requirements and to clear financial transactions. Transactions in the federal funds market enable depository institutions with reserve balances in excess of reserve requirements to lend reserves to institutions with reserve deficiencies.
Interest rate	An interest rate is the rate at which interest is paid by a borrower for the use of money that they borrow from a lender (creditor). Specifically, the interest rate is a percent of principal (P) paid a certain amount of times (m) per period (usually quoted per annum). For example, a small company borrows capital from a bank to buy new assets for its business, and in return the lender receives interest at a predetermined interest rate for deferring the use of funds and instead lending it to the borrower.

1. In microeconomics, the _____ is the conceptual time period in which there are no fixed factors of production as to changing the output level by changing the capital stock or by entering or leaving an industry. The _____ contrasts with the short run, in which some factors are variable and others are fixed, constraining entry or exit from an industry. In macroeconomics, the _____ is the period when the general price level, contractual wage rates, and expectations adjust fully to the state of the economy, in contrast to the short run when these variables may not fully adjust.

   a. short run
   b. Fuel protests in the United Kingdom
   c. Long run
   d. Brandenburger Gold Coast

2. A _____ is an event that suddenly changes the price of a commodity or service. It may be caused by a sudden increase or decrease in the supply of a particular good. This sudden change affects the equilibrium price.

   a. Boukaseff scale
   b. Business cycle accounting
   c. Supply shock
   d. Consumption function

3. . In economics, a _____ is a business cycle contraction. It is a general slowdown in economic activity. Macroeconomic indicators such as GDP (gross domestic product), investment spending, capacity utilization, household income, business profits, and inflation fall, while bankruptcies and the unemployment rate rise.

   a. Depression

b. General glut

c. Recession

d. Great Recession in South America

4. In macroeconomics, _____ is the total demand for final goods and services in the economy at a given time and price level. It specifies the amounts of goods and services that will be purchased at all possible price levels. This is the demand for the gross domestic product of a country.

a. Fuel protests in the United Kingdom

b. Battle of Annaberg

c. Aggregate demand

d. Freikorps Oberland

5. The general _____ is a hypothetical measure of overall prices for some set of goods and services, in a given region during a given interval, normalized relative to some base set. Typically, a _____ is approximated with a price index.

a. Break-even

b. Price level

c. Cash collection

d. Commercial location development

ANSWER KEY
36. Extending the Analysis of Aggregate Supply

1. c
2. c
3. c
4. c
5. b

You can take the complete Chapter Practice Test

for 36. Extending the Analysis of Aggregate Supply
on all key terms, persons, places, and concepts.

Online 99 Cents

http://www.JustTheFacts101.com

Use www.JustTheFacts101.com for all your study needs

including Facts101's online interactive problem solving labs in

chemistry, statistics, mathematics, and more.

37. Current Issues in Macro Theory and Policy

CHAPTER OUTLINE: KEY TERMS, PEOPLE, PLACES, CONCEPTS

_____ | Aggregate demand

_____ | Aggregate supply

_____ | Equation of exchange

_____ | Fiscal policy

_____ | Great Depression

_____ | Macroeconomics

_____ | Monetarism

_____ | Phillips curve

_____ | Supply shock

_____ | Instability

_____ | Monetary policy

_____ | Business cycle

_____ | Coordination failure

_____ | Great Recession

_____ | Recession

_____ | Demand shock

_____ | Rational expectations

_____ | Classical economics

_____ | Adaptive expectations

_____ | Efficiency wage

_____ | Balanced budget

37. Current Issues in Macro Theory and Policy

_____ | Inflation targeting

_____ | Stabilization policy

_____ | Taylor rule

CHAPTER HIGHLIGHTS & NOTES: KEY TERMS, PEOPLE, PLACES, CONCEPTS

Aggregate demand	In macroeconomics, aggregate demand is the total demand for final goods and services in the economy at a given time and price level. It specifies the amounts of goods and services that will be purchased at all possible price levels. This is the demand for the gross domestic product of a country.
Aggregate supply	In economics, aggregate supply is the total supply of goods and services that firms in a national economy plan on selling during a specific time period. It is the total amount of goods and services that firms are willing to sell at a given price level in an economy.
Equation of exchange	In economics, the equation of exchange is the relation: $M \cdot V = P \cdot Q$ where, for a given period, M is the total nominal amount of money in circulation on average in an economy. V is the velocity of money, that is the average frequency with which a unit of money is spent. P is the price level. Q is an index of real expenditures . Thus PQ is the level of nominal expenditures. This equation is a rearrangement of the definition of velocity: V = PQ / M. As such, without the introduction of any assumptions, it is a tautology. The quantity theory of money adds assumptions about the money supply, the price level, and the effect of interest rates on velocity to create a theory about the causes of inflation and the effects of monetary policy.
Fiscal policy	In economics and political science, fiscal policy is the use of government revenue collection and expenditure (spending) to influence the economy, or else it involves the government changing the levels of taxation and government spending in order to influence Aggregate Demand and the level of economic activity. The two main instruments of fiscal policy are changes in the level and composition of taxation and government spending in various sectors.

These changes can affect the following macroeconomic variables in an economy:•Aggregate demand and the level of economic activity;•The distribution of income;•The pattern of resource allocation within the government sector and relative to the private sector.

Fiscal policy refers to the use of the government budget to influence economic activity.

Great Depression

The Great Depression was a severe worldwide economic depression in the decade preceding World War II. The timing of the Great Depression varied across nations, but in most countries it started in 1930 and lasted until the late 1930s or middle 1940s. It was the longest, deepest, and most widespread depression of the 20th century.

In the 21st century, the Great Depression is commonly used as an example of how far the world's economy can decline.

Macroeconomics

Macroeconomics is the study of the macroeconomy. It is a branch of economics dealing with the performance, structure, behavior, and decision-making of an economy as a whole, rather than individual markets. This includes national, regional, and global economies.

Monetarism

Monetarism is a school of economic thought that emphasizes the role of governments in controlling the amount of money in circulation. It is the view within monetary economics that variation in the money supply has major influences on national output in the short run and the price level over longer periods and that objectives of monetary policy are best met by targeting the growth rate of the money supply.

Monetarism today is mainly associated with the work of Milton Friedman, who was among the generation of economists to accept Keynesian economics and then criticize Keynes' theory of gluts using fiscal policy (government spending).

Phillips curve

In economics, the Phillips curve is a historical inverse relationship between rates of unemployment and corresponding rates of inflation that result in an economy. Stated simply, decreased unemployment, (i.e., increased levels of employment) in an economy will correlate with higher rates of inflation.

While there is a short run tradeoff between unemployment and inflation, it has not been observed in the long run.

Supply shock

A supply shock is an event that suddenly changes the price of a commodity or service. It may be caused by a sudden increase or decrease in the supply of a particular good. This sudden change affects the equilibrium price.

Instability

In numerous fields of study, the component of instability within a system is generally characterized by some of the outputs or internal states growing without bounds.

37. Current Issues in Macro Theory and Policy

	Not all systems that are not stable are unstable; systems can also be marginally stable or exhibit limit cycle behavior.
	In control theory, a system is unstable if any of the roots of its characteristic equation has real part greater than zero (or if zero is a repeated root).
Monetary policy	Monetary policy is the process by which the monetary authority of a country controls the supply of money, often targeting a rate of interest for the purpose of promoting economic growth and stability. The official goals usually include relatively stable prices and low unemployment. Monetary economics provides insight into how to craft optimal monetary policy.
Business cycle	The term business cycle refers fluctuations in aggregate production, trade and activity over several months or years in a market economy.
	The business cycle is the upward and downward movements of levels of gross domestic product (GDP) and refers to the period of expansions and contractions in the level of economic activities (business fluctuations) around its long-term growth trend.
	These fluctuations occur around a long-term growth trend, and typically involve shifts over time between periods of relatively rapid economic growth (an expansion or boom), and periods of relative stagnation or decline (a contraction or recession).
Coordination failure	In economics, coordination failure is a concept that can explain recessions through the failure of firms and other price setters to coordinate. In an economic system with multiple equilibria, coordination failure occurs when a group of firms could achieve a more desirable equilibrium but fail to because they do not coordinate their decision making. Coordination failure can result in a self-fulfilling prophecy.
Great Recession	The Great Recession was a global economic decline in the late 2000s. According to aggregated national data, a worldwide recession began in Q3-2008 and ended in Q1-2009.
	It is related to a liquidity crisis, commonly being dated to have started when several central banks had to step in with liquidity lending to the interbank lending market on 9 August 2007. This was a response to a situation where BNP Paribas temporarily had to block money withdrawals from three hedge funds--citing a 'complete evaporation of liquidity'.
Recession	In economics, a recession is a business cycle contraction. It is a general slowdown in economic activity. Macroeconomic indicators such as GDP (gross domestic product), investment spending, capacity utilization, household income, business profits, and inflation fall, while bankruptcies and the unemployment rate rise.

Rational expectations	Rational expectations is a hypothesis in economics which states that agents' predictions of the future value of economically relevant variables are not systematically wrong in that all errors are random. Equivalently, this is to say that agents' expectations equal true statistical expected values. An alternative formulation is that rational expectations are model-consistent expectations, in that the agents inside the model assume the model's predictions are valid.
Classical economics	Classical economics is widely regarded as the first modern school of economic thought. Its major developers include Adam Smith, Jean-Baptiste Say, David Ricardo, Thomas Malthus and John Stuart Mill. Adam Smith's The Wealth of Nations in 1776 is usually considered to mark the beginning of classical economics.
Adaptive expectations	In economics, adaptive expectations is a hypothesized process by which people form their expectations about what will happen in the future based on what has happened in the past. For example, if inflation has been higher than expected in the past, people would revise expectations for the future. One simple version of adaptive expectations is stated in the following equation, where p^e is the next year's rate of inflation that is currently expected; p^e_{-1} is this year's rate of inflation that was expected last year; and p is this year's actual rate of inflation: $p^e = p^e_{-1} + \lambda(p - p^e_{-1})$ where λ is between 0 and 1. This says that current expectations of future inflation reflect past expectations and an 'error-adjustment' term, in which current expectations are raised (or lowered) according to the gap between actual inflation and previous expectations.
Efficiency wage	In labor economics, the efficiency wage hypothesis argues that wages, at least in some markets, form in a way that is not market-clearing. Specifically, it points to the incentive for managers to pay their employees more than the market-clearing wage in order to increase their productivity or efficiency, or reduce costs associated with turnover, in industries where the costs of replacing labor is high. This increased labor productivity and/or decreased costs pay for the higher wages.
Balanced budget	A balanced budget refers to a budget in which revenues are equal to expenditures. Thus, neither a budget deficit nor a budget surplus exists ('the accounts balance'). More generally, it refers to a budget that has no budget deficit, but could possibly have a budget surplus.
Inflation targeting	Inflation targeting is an economic policy in which a central bank estimates and makes public a projected, or 'target', inflation rate and then attempts to steer actual inflation towards the target through the use of interest rate changes and other monetary tools.

37. Current Issues in Macro Theory and Policy

	Because interest rates and the inflation rate tend to be directly related, the likely moves of the central bank to raise or lower interest rates become more transparent under the policy of inflation targeting. Examples:•if inflation appears to be above the target, the bank is likely to raise interest rates.
Stabilization policy	A stabilization policy is a package or set of measures introduced to stabilize a financial system or economy. The term can refer to policies in two distinct sets of circumstances: business cycle stabilization and crisis stabilization.
Taylor rule	In economics, a Taylor rule is a monetary-policy rule that stipulates how much the central bank should change the nominal interest rate in response to changes in inflation, output, or other economic conditions. In particular, the rule stipulates that for each one-percent increase in inflation, the central bank should raise the nominal interest rate by more than one percentage point. This aspect of the rule is often called the Taylor principle.

1. In macroeconomics, _____ is the total demand for final goods and services in the economy at a given time and price level. It specifies the amounts of goods and services that will be purchased at all possible price levels. This is the demand for the gross domestic product of a country.

    a. Fuel protests in the United Kingdom
    b. Battle of Annaberg
    c. Freikorps Lichtschlag
    d. Aggregate demand

2. In economics, _____ is the total supply of goods and services that firms in a national economy plan on selling during a specific time period. It is the total amount of goods and services that firms are willing to sell at a given price level in an economy.

    a. Fuel protests in the United Kingdom
    b. Battle of Annaberg
    c. Freikorps Lichtschlag
    d. Aggregate supply

3. . In economics and political science, _____ is the use of government revenue collection and expenditure (spending) to influence the economy, or else it involves the government changing the levels of taxation and government spending in order to influence Aggregate Demand and the level of economic activity.

The two main instruments of _____ are changes in the level and composition of taxation and government spending in various sectors. These changes can affect the following macroeconomic variables in an economy:•Aggregate demand and the level of economic activity;•The distribution of income;•The pattern of resource allocation within the government sector and relative to the private sector.

_____ refers to the use of the government budget to influence economic activity.

a. Barnett formula
b. Fiscal policy
c. Budgetary policy
d. California Municipal Treasurers Association

4. A _____ is an event that suddenly changes the price of a commodity or service. It may be caused by a sudden increase or decrease in the supply of a particular good. This sudden change affects the equilibrium price.

a. Boukaseff scale
b. Supply shock
c. Complex multiplier
d. Consumption function

5. In economics, the _____ is the relation: $M \cdot V = P \cdot Q$

where, for a given period, M is the total nominal amount of money in circulation on average in an economy. V is the velocity of money, that is the average frequency with which a unit of money is spent. P is the price level. Q is an index of real expenditures .

Thus PQ is the level of nominal expenditures. This equation is a rearrangement of the definition of velocity: V = PQ / M. As such, without the introduction of any assumptions, it is a tautology. The quantity theory of money adds assumptions about the money supply, the price level, and the effect of interest rates on velocity to create a theory about the causes of inflation and the effects of monetary policy.

a. Equation of exchange
b. Benefit incidence
c. Blanket order
d. Bond

1. d
2. d
3. b
4. b
5. a

38. International Trade

International trade

Great Recession

OPEC

Recession

Cartel

Production

Absolute advantage

Comparative advantage

Open economy

Terms of trade

Gains from trade

Free trade

Explicit cost

Aggregate expenditure

Implicit cost

Trade agreement

Price level

Trade barrier

Export subsidy

Import quota

Protection International

	Infant industry
	Great Depression
	Eurozone
	General Agreement on Tariffs and Trade
	Uruguay Round
	World Trade Organization
	North American Free Trade Agreement
	Offshoring
	Specialization
	Trade Adjustment Assistance
	Protectionism

CHAPTER HIGHLIGHTS & NOTES: KEY TERMS, PEOPLE, PLACES, CONCEPTS

International trade	International trade is the exchange of capital, goods, and services across international borders or territories. In most countries, such trade represents a significant share of gross domestic product (GDP). While international trade has been present throughout much of history, its economic, social, and political importance has been on the rise in recent centuries.
Great Recession	The Great Recession was a global economic decline in the late 2000s. According to aggregated national data, a worldwide recession began in Q3-2008 and ended in Q1-2009. It is related to a liquidity crisis, commonly being dated to have started when several central banks had to step in with liquidity lending to the interbank lending market on 9 August 2007. This was a response to a situation where BNP Paribas temporarily had to block money withdrawals from three hedge funds--citing a 'complete evaporation of liquidity'.

38. International Trade

OPEC	OPEC is an international organization whose mission is to coordinate the policies of the oil-producing countries. The goal is to secure a steady income to the member states and to secure supply of oil to consumers. OPEC is an intergovernmental organization that was created at the Baghdad Conference on 10-14 September 1960, by Iraq, Kuwait, Iran, Saudi Arabia and Venezuela.
Recession	In economics, a recession is a business cycle contraction. It is a general slowdown in economic activity. Macroeconomic indicators such as GDP (gross domestic product), investment spending, capacity utilization, household income, business profits, and inflation fall, while bankruptcies and the unemployment rate rise.
Cartel	A cartel is a formal 'agreement' among competing firms. It is a formal organization of producers and manufacturers that agree to fix prices, marketing, and production. Cartels usually occur in an oligopolistic industry, where the number of sellers is small (usually because barriers to entry, most notably startup costs, are high) and the products being traded are usually commodities.
Production	Production is a process of combining various material inputs and immaterial inputs in order to make something for consumption (the output). It is the act of creating output, a good or service which has value and contributes to the utility of individuals. Economic well-being is created in a production process, meaning all economic activities that aim directly or indirectly to satisfy human needs.
Absolute advantage	In economics, the principle of absolute advantage refers to the ability of a party to produce more of a good or service than competitors, using the same amount of resources. Adam Smith first described the principle of absolute advantage in the context of international trade, using labor as the only input. Since absolute advantage is determined by a simple comparison of labor productivities, it is possible for a party to have no absolute advantage in anything; in that case, according to the theory of absolute advantage, no trade will occur with the other party.
Comparative advantage	In economics, comparative advantage refers to the ability of a party to produce a particular good or service at a lower marginal and opportunity cost over another. Even if one country is more efficient in the production of all goods (absolute advantage in all goods) than the other, both countries will still gain by trading with each other, as long as they have different relative efficiencies. For example, if, using machinery, a worker in one country can produce both shoes and shirts at 6 per hour, and a worker in a country with less machinery can produce either 2 shoes or 4 shirts in an hour, each country can gain from trade because their internal trade-offs between shoes and shirts are different.

38. International Trade

CHAPTER HIGHLIGHTS & NOTES: KEY TERMS, PEOPLE, PLACES, CONCEPTS

Open economy	An open economy is an economy in which there are economic activities between domestic community and outside, e.g. people, including businesses, can trade in goods and services with other people and businesses in the international community, and flow of funds as investment across the border. Trade can be in the form of managerial exchange, technology transfers, all kinds of goods and services. Although, there are certain exceptions that cannot be exchanged, like, railway services of a country cannot be traded with another to avail this service, a country has to produce its own.
Terms of trade	Terms of trade refers to the relative price of exports in terms of imports and is defined as the ratio of export prices to import prices. It can be interpreted as the amount of import goods an economy can purchase per unit of export goods. An improvement of a nation's terms of trade benefits that country in the sense that it can buy more imports for any given level of exports.
Gains from trade	In economics, gains from trade refers to net benefits to agents from allowing an increase in voluntary trading with each other. In technical terms, it is the increase of consumer surplus plus producer surplus from lower tariffs or otherwise liberalizing trade.
Free trade	Free trade is a policy in international markets in which governments do not restrict imports or exports. Free trade is exemplified by the European Union / European Economic Area and the North American Free Trade Agreement, which have established open markets. Most nations are today members of the World Trade Organization (WTO) multilateral trade agreements.
Explicit cost	An explicit cost is a direct payment made to others in the course of running a business, such as wage, rent and materials, as opposed to implicit costs, which are those where no actual payment is made. It is possible still to underestimate these costs, however: for example, pension contributions and other 'perks' must be taken into account when considering the cost of labour. Explicit costs are taken into account along with implicit ones when considering economic profit.
Aggregate expenditure	In economics, Aggregate Expenditure is a measure of national income. Aggregate Expenditure is defined as the current value of all the finished goods and services in the economy. The aggregate expenditure is thus the sum total of all the expenditures undertaken in the economy by the factors during a given time period.
Implicit cost	In economics, an implicit cost, also called an imputed cost, implied cost, or notional cost, is the opportunity cost equal to what a firm must give up in order to use factors which it neither purchases nor hires. It is the opposite of an explicit cost, which is borne directly. In other words, an implicit cost is any cost that results from using an asset instead of renting, selling, or lending it.

38. International Trade

Trade agreement	A trade agreement is a wide ranging tax, tariff and trade treaty that often includes investment guarantees. The most common trade agreements are of the preferential and free trade types are concluded in order to reduce (or eliminate) tariffs, quotas and other trade restrictions on items traded between the signatories.
Price level	The general price level is a hypothetical measure of overall prices for some set of goods and services, in a given region during a given interval, normalized relative to some base set. Typically, a price level is approximated with a price index.
Trade barrier	Trade barriers are government-induced restrictions on international trade. The barriers can take many forms, including the following:•Tariffs•Non-tariff barriers to trade•Import licenses•Export licenses•Import quotas•Subsidies•Voluntary Export Restraints•Local content requirements•Embargo•Currency devaluation•Trade restriction Most trade barriers work on the same principle: the imposition of some sort of cost on trade that raises the price of the traded products. If two or more nations repeatedly use trade barriers against each other, then a trade war results.
Export subsidy	Export subsidy is a government policy to encourage export of goods and discourage sale of goods on the domestic market through direct payments, low-cost loans, tax relief for exporters, or government-financed international advertising. An export subsidy reduces the price paid by foreign importers, which means domestic consumers pay more than foreign consumers. The WTO prohibits most subsidies directly linked to the volume of exports.
Import quota	An import quota is a limit on the quantity of a good that can be produced abroad and sold domestically. It is a type of protectionist trade restriction that sets a physical limit on the quantity of a good that can be imported into a country in a given period of time. If a quota is put on a good, less of it is imported.
Protection International	Protection International is an international non-profit organisation dedicated to the protection of human rights defenders (HRDs). Its stated mission is to enhance the security and the protection of 'threatened civil society actors with non-violent means, especially those who fight for their legitimate rights and for the rights of others as they are guaranteed by the international humanitarian law and the human rights conventions'. Protection International began its activities in 1998 as the former European Office of Peace Brigades International (PBI-BEO) and is headquartered in Brussels.
Infant industry	In economics, an infant industry is a new industry, which in its early stages experiences relative difficulty or is absolutely incapable in competing with established competitors abroad.

Governments are sometimes urged to support the development of infant industries, protecting home industries in their early stages, usually through subsidies or tariffs. Subsidies may be indirect, as in when import duties are imposed or some prohibition against the import of a raw or finished material is imposed.

Great Depression	The Great Depression was a severe worldwide economic depression in the decade preceding World War II. The timing of the Great Depression varied across nations, but in most countries it started in 1930 and lasted until the late 1930s or middle 1940s. It was the longest, deepest, and most widespread depression of the 20th century.
	In the 21st century, the Great Depression is commonly used as an example of how far the world's economy can decline.
Eurozone	The eurozone, officially called the euro area, is an economic and monetary union (EMU) of 18 European Union (EU) member states that have adopted the euro (€) as their common currency and sole legal tender. The eurozone currently consists of Austria, Belgium, Cyprus, Estonia, Finland, France, Germany, Greece, Ireland, Italy, Latvia, Luxembourg, Malta, the Netherlands, Portugal, Slovakia, Slovenia, and Spain. Other EU states (except for the United Kingdom and Denmark) are obliged to join once they meet the criteria to do so.
General Agreement on Tariffs and Trade	The General Agreement on Tariffs and Trade was a multilateral agreement regulating international trade. According to its preamble, its purpose was the 'substantial reduction of tariffs and other trade barriers and the elimination of preferences, on a reciprocal and mutually advantageous basis.' It was negotiated during the United Nations Conference on Trade and Employment and was the outcome of the failure of negotiating governments to create the International Trade Organization (ITO). GATT was signed in 1947 and lasted until 1994, when it was replaced by the World Trade Organization in 1995.
Uruguay Round	The Uruguay Round was the 8th round of multilateral trade negotiations conducted within the framework of the General Agreement on Tariffs and Trade (GATT), spanning from 1986 to 1994 and embracing 123 countries as 'contracting parties'. The Round led to the creation of the World Trade Organization, with GATT remaining as an integral part of the WTO agreements. The broad mandate of the Round had been to extend GATT trade rules to areas previously exempted as too difficult to liberalize (agriculture, textiles) and increasingly important new areas previously not included (trade in services, intellectual property, investment policy trade distortions).
World Trade Organization	The World Trade Organization is an organization that intends to supervise and liberalize international trade. The organization officially commenced on 1 January 1995 under the Marrakech Agreement, replacing the General Agreement on Tariffs and Trade (GATT), which commenced in 1948.

38. International Trade

	The organization deals with regulation of trade between participating countries; it provides a framework for negotiating and formalizing trade agreements, and a dispute resolution process aimed at enforcing participant's adherence to World Trade Organization agreements, which are signed by representatives of member governments and ratified by their parliaments. Most of the issues that the World Trade Organization focuses on derive from previous trade negotiations, especially from the Uruguay Round (1986-1994).
North American Free Trade Agreement	The North American Free Trade Agreement is an agreement signed by Canada, Mexico, and the United States, creating a trilateral rules-based trade bloc in North America. The agreement came into force on January 1, 1994. It superseded the Canada-United States Free Trade Agreement between the U.S. and Canada. North American Free Trade Agreement has two supplements: the North American Agreement on Environmental Cooperation (NAAEC) and the North American Agreement on Labor Cooperation (NAALC). In terms of combined purchasing power parity GDP of its members, as of 2007 the trade bloc is the largest in the world and second largest by nominal GDP comparison.
Offshoring	Offshoring is the relocation by a company of a business process from one country to another-- typically an operational process, such as manufacturing, or supporting processes, such as accounting. Even state governments employ offshoring. More recently, offshoring has been associated primarily with the outsourcing of technical and administrative services supporting domestic and global operations from outside the home country, by means of internal (captive) or external (outsourcing) delivery models.
Specialization	Specialization is the separation of tasks within a system. In a multicellular creature, cells are specialized for functions such as bone construction or oxygen transport. In capitalist societies, individual workers specialize for functions such as building construction or gasoline transport.
Trade Adjustment Assistance	Trade Adjustment Assistance is a federal program of the United States government to act as a way to reduce the damaging impact of imports felt by certain sectors of the U.S. economy. The current structure features four components of Trade Adjustment Assistance: for Workers, Firms, Farmers, and Communities. Each Cabinet level Department was tasked with a different sector of the overall Trade Adjustment Assistance program.
Protectionism	Protectionism is the economic policy of restraining trade between states through methods such as tariffs on imported goods, restrictive quotas, and a variety of other government regulations designed to allow (according to proponents) fair competition between imports and goods and service produced domestically. This policy contrasts with free trade, where government barriers to trade are kept to a minimum.

1. In economics, an _____, also called an imputed cost, implied cost, or notional cost, is the opportunity cost equal to what a firm must give up in order to use factors which it neither purchases nor hires. It is the opposite of an explicit cost, which is borne directly. In other words, an _____ is any cost that results from using an asset instead of renting, selling, or lending it.

   a. Base period
   b. Benefit incidence
   c. Blanket order
   d. Implicit cost

2. _____ is the separation of tasks within a system. In a multicellular creature, cells are specialized for functions such as bone construction or oxygen transport. In capitalist societies, individual workers specialize for functions such as building construction or gasoline transport.

   a. Capacity utilization
   b. Constant elasticity of transformation
   c. Cost driver
   d. Specialization

3. An _____ is a direct payment made to others in the course of running a business, such as wage, rent and materials, as opposed to implicit costs, which are those where no actual payment is made. It is possible still to underestimate these costs, however: for example, pension contributions and other 'perks' must be taken into account when considering the cost of labour.

   _____s are taken into account along with implicit ones when considering economic profit.

   a. Explicit cost
   b. Benefit incidence
   c. Blanket order
   d. Bond

4. The _____ was a global economic decline in the late 2000s. According to aggregated national data, a worldwide recession began in Q3-2008 and ended in Q1-2009.

   It is related to a liquidity crisis, commonly being dated to have started when several central banks had to step in with liquidity lending to the interbank lending market on 9 August 2007. This was a response to a situation where BNP Paribas temporarily had to block money withdrawals from three hedge funds--citing a 'complete evaporation of liquidity'.

   a. Commercial Revolution
   b. Mercantilism
   c. Via Argentaria
   d. Great Recession

5. _____s are government-induced restrictions on international trade. The barriers can take many forms, including the following:•Tariffs•Non-tariff barriers to trade•Import licenses•Export licenses•Import quotas•Subsidies•Voluntary Export Restraints•Local content requirements•Embargo•Currency devaluation•Trade restriction

Most _____s work on the same principle: the imposition of some sort of cost on trade that raises the price of the traded products. If two or more nations repeatedly use _____s against each other, then a trade war results.

a. Trade barrier
b. Backsourcing
c. Bimetallism
d. Bureau de change

ANSWER KEY
38. International Trade

1. d
2. d
3. a
4. d
5. a

You can take the complete Chapter Practice Test

for 38. International Trade
on all key terms, persons, places, and concepts.

Online 99 Cents

http://www.JustTheFacts101.com

Use www.JustTheFacts101.com for all your study needs

including Facts101's online interactive problem solving labs in

chemistry, statistics, mathematics, and more.

CHAPTER OUTLINE: KEY TERMS, PEOPLE, PLACES, CONCEPTS

	Balance of payments
	International trade
	Financial transaction
	Capital
	Current account
	Net investment
	Fixed exchange rate
	Depreciation
	Interest rate
	Production
	Corn exchange
	Currency intervention
	Bretton Woods system
	Future value
	Gold standard
	Great Recession
	International Monetary Fund
	Recession
	Explicit cost
	Speculation
	Income

39. The Balance of Payments, Exchange Rates, and Trade Deficits

Balance of payments	Balance of Payment of a country is defined as, 'Systematic record of all economic transactions between the residents of a foreign country' Thus balance of payments includes all visible and non-visible transactions of a country during a given period, usually a year. It represents a summation of country's current demand and supply of the claims on foreign currencies and of foreign claims on its currency. Balance of payments accounts are an accounting record of all monetary transactions between a country and the rest of the world.
International trade	International trade is the exchange of capital, goods, and services across international borders or territories. In most countries, such trade represents a significant share of gross domestic product (GDP). While international trade has been present throughout much of history, its economic, social, and political importance has been on the rise in recent centuries.
Financial transaction	A financial transaction is an agreement, communication, or movement carried out between a buyer and a seller to exchange an asset for payment. It involves a change in the status of the finances of two or more businesses or individuals. The buyer and seller are separate entities or objects, often involving the exchange of items of value, such as information, goods, services, and money.
Capital	In economics, capital goods, real capital, or capital assets are already-produced durable goods or any non-financial asset that is used in production of goods or services. Capital goods are not significantly consumed in the production process though they may depreciate. How a capital good or is maintained or returned to its pre-production state varies with the type of capital involved.
Current account	In economics, a country's current account is one of the two components of its balance of payments, the other being the capital account. The current account consists of the balance of trade, net factor income (earnings on foreign investments minus payments made to foreign investors) and net cash transfers. The current account balance is one of two major measures of a country's foreign trade (the other being the net capital outflow).
Net investment	In economics, net investment refers to an activity of spending which increases the availability of fixed capital goods or means of production. It is the total spending on new fixed investment minus replacement investment, which simply replaces depreciated capital goods. Net Investment is equal to the Gross investment minus depreciation

39. The Balance of Payments, Exchange Rates, and Trade Deficits

CHAPTER HIGHLIGHTS & NOTES: KEY TERMS, PEOPLE, PLACES, CONCEPTS

Fixed exchange rate	A fixed exchange rate, sometimes called a pegged exchange rate, is also referred to as the Tag of particular Rate, which is a type of exchange rate regime where a currency's value is fixed against the value of another single currency, to a basket of other currencies, or to another measure of value, such as gold. A fixed exchange rate is usually used to stabilize the value of a currency against the currency it is pegged to. This makes trade and investments between the two countries easier and more predictable and is especially useful for small economies in which external trade forms a large part of their GDP. It can also be used as a means to control inflation.
Depreciation	In accountancy, depreciation refers to two aspects of the same concept:•the decrease in value of assets (fair value depreciation), and•the allocation of the cost of assets to periods in which the assets are used (depreciation with the matching principle). The former affects the balance sheet of a business or entity, and the latter affects the net income that they report. Generally the cost is allocated, as depreciation expense, among the periods in which the asset is expected to be used. This expense is recognized by businesses for financial reporting and tax purposes.
Interest rate	An interest rate is the rate at which interest is paid by a borrower for the use of money that they borrow from a lender (creditor). Specifically, the interest rate is a percent of principal (P) paid a certain amount of times (m) per period (usually quoted per annum). For example, a small company borrows capital from a bank to buy new assets for its business, and in return the lender receives interest at a predetermined interest rate for deferring the use of funds and instead lending it to the borrower.
Production	Production is a process of combining various material inputs and immaterial inputs in order to make something for consumption (the output). It is the act of creating output, a good or service which has value and contributes to the utility of individuals. Economic well-being is created in a production process, meaning all economic activities that aim directly or indirectly to satisfy human needs.
Corn exchange	A corn exchange or grain exchange (North American English) was a building where farmers and merchants traded cereal grains. Such trade was common in towns and cities across Great Britain and Ireland until the 19th century, but as the trade became centralised in the 20th century many such buildings were used for other purposes. Several have since become heritage sites.
Currency intervention	Currency intervention, also known as exchange rate intervention or foreign exchange market intervention, is the purchase or the sale of the currency on the exchange market by the fiscal authority or the monetary authority, in order to influence the value of the domestic currency.

39. The Balance of Payments, Exchange Rates, and Trade Deficits

Bretton Woods system	The Bretton Woods system of monetary management established the rules for commercial and financial relations among the world's major industrial states in the mid-20th century. The Bretton Woods system was the first example of a fully negotiated monetary order intended to govern monetary relations among independent nation-states.
	Preparing to rebuild the international economic system while World War II was still raging, 730 delegates from all 44 Allied nations gathered at the Mount Washington Hotel in Bretton Woods, New Hampshire, United States, for the United Nations Monetary and Financial Conference, also known as the Bretton Woods Conference.
Future value	Future value is the value of an asset at a specific date. It measures the nominal future sum of money that a given sum of money is 'worth' at a specified time in the future assuming a certain interest rate, or more generally, rate of return; it is the present value multiplied by the accumulation function. The value does not include corrections for inflation or other factors that affect the true value of money in the future.
Gold standard	Gold points was a term which referred to the rates of foreign exchange likely to cause movements of gold between countries adhering to the gold standard.
Great Recession	The Great Recession was a global economic decline in the late 2000s. According to aggregated national data, a worldwide recession began in Q3-2008 and ended in Q1-2009.
	It is related to a liquidity crisis, commonly being dated to have started when several central banks had to step in with liquidity lending to the interbank lending market on 9 August 2007. This was a response to a situation where BNP Paribas temporarily had to block money withdrawals from three hedge funds--citing a 'complete evaporation of liquidity'.
International Monetary Fund	The International Monetary Fund is an international organization that was initiated in 1944 at the Bretton Woods Conference and formally created in 1945 by 29 member countries. The International Monetary Fund's stated goal was to assist in the reconstruction of the world's international payment system post-World War II. Countries contribute funds to a pool through a quota system from which countries with payment imbalances temporarily can borrow money and other resources. As of the 14th General Review of Quotas in late 2010 the fund stood at SDR476.8bn, or about US$755.7bn at then-current exchange rates.
Recession	In economics, a recession is a business cycle contraction. It is a general slowdown in economic activity. Macroeconomic indicators such as GDP (gross domestic product), investment spending, capacity utilization, household income, business profits, and inflation fall, while bankruptcies and the unemployment rate rise.

39. The Balance of Payments, Exchange Rates, and Trade Deficits

Explicit cost	An explicit cost is a direct payment made to others in the course of running a business, such as wage, rent and materials, as opposed to implicit costs, which are those where no actual payment is made. It is possible still to underestimate these costs, however: for example, pension contributions and other 'perks' must be taken into account when considering the cost of labour.
	Explicit costs are taken into account along with implicit ones when considering economic profit.
Speculation	Speculation is the practice of engaging in risky financial transactions in an attempt to profit from short or medium term fluctuations in the market value of a tradable good such as a financial instrument, rather than attempting to profit from the underlying financial attributes embodied in the instrument such as capital gains, interest, or dividends. Many speculators pay little attention to the fundamental value of a security and instead focus purely on price movements. Speculation can in principle involve any tradable good or financial instrument.
Income	Income is the consumption and savings opportunity gained by an entity within a specified timeframe, which is generally expressed in monetary terms. However, for households and individuals, 'income is the sum of all the wages, salaries, profits, interests payments, rents and other forms of earnings received... in a given period of time.'
	In the field of public economics, the term may refer to the accumulation of both monetary and non-monetary consumption ability, with the former (monetary) being used as a proxy for total income.

CHAPTER QUIZ: KEY TERMS, PEOPLE, PLACES, CONCEPTS

1. Gold points was a term which referred to the rates of foreign exchange likely to cause movements of gold between countries adhering to the _____.

   a. Bank van Lening, Haarlem
   b. History of banking
   c. Gold standard
   d. Bacon

2. . _____(s) of a country is defined as, 'Systematic record of all economic transactions between the residents of a foreign country' Thus _____ includes all visible and non-visible transactions of a country during a given period, usually a year. It represents a summation of country's current demand and supply of the claims on foreign currencies and of foreign claims on its currency.

   _____ accounts are an accounting record of all monetary transactions between a country and the rest of the world.

a. Back-to-back loan
b. Fuel protests in the United Kingdom
c. Balance of payments
d. Freikorps Lichtschlag

3. In accountancy, _____ refers to two aspects of the same concept:•the decrease in value of assets (fair value _____), and•the allocation of the cost of assets to periods in which the assets are used (_____ with the matching principle).

    The former affects the balance sheet of a business or entity, and the latter affects the net income that they report. Generally the cost is allocated, as _____ expense, among the periods in which the asset is expected to be used. This expense is recognized by businesses for financial reporting and tax purposes.

    a. Business ecosystem
    b. Center for Business and Economic Research
    c. Conglomerate merger
    d. Depreciation

4. A _____ or grain exchange (North American English) was a building where farmers and merchants traded cereal grains. Such trade was common in towns and cities across Great Britain and Ireland until the 19th century, but as the trade became centralised in the 20th century many such buildings were used for other purposes. Several have since become heritage sites.

    a. Brent Crude
    b. Corn exchange
    c. Commodity broker
    d. Commodity pool

5. _____ is the exchange of capital, goods, and services across international borders or territories. In most countries, such trade represents a significant share of gross domestic product (GDP). While _____ has been present throughout much of history, its economic, social, and political importance has been on the rise in recent centuries.

    a. 2008 G-20 Washington summit
    b. Backsourcing
    c. International trade
    d. Bureau de change

You can take the complete Chapter Practice Test

for 39. The Balance of Payments, Exchange Rates, and Trade Deficits
on all key terms, persons, places, and concepts.

Online 99 Cents

http://www.JustTheFacts101.com

Use www.JustTheFacts101.com for all your study needs

including Facts101's online interactive problem solving labs in

chemistry, statistics, mathematics, and more.

Other Facts101 e-Books and Tests

Want More?
JustTheFacts101.com...

Jtf101.com provides the outlines and highlights of your textbooks, just like this e-StudyGuide, but also gives you the **PRACTICE TESTS**, and other exclusive study tools for all of your textbooks.

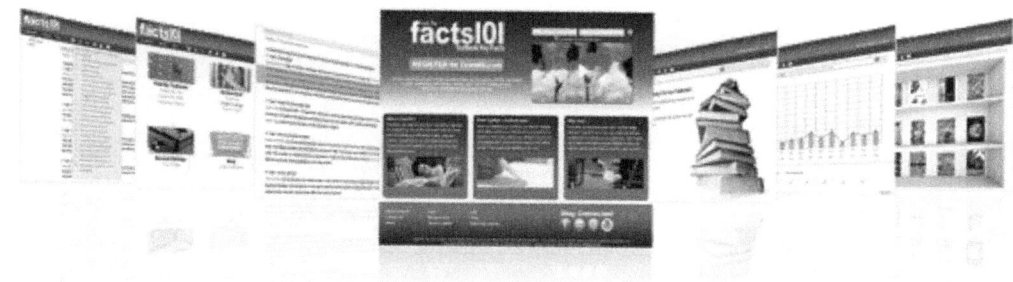

Learn More. *Just click*
http://www.JustTheFacts101.com/